SCREEN WRITERS INC.

Mihir Chitre has written two books of poetry, *Hyphenated* (Sahitya Akademi, 2014) and *School of Age* (Dhauli Books, 2019).

As an advertising creative, Mihir has won over forty national and international awards including two Cannes Lions and a Clio Grand Prix. He has been '30 under 30', 'Rising Star' and 'WPP Young Star' in his advertising career.

Mihir has written and directed the short film *Hello Brick Road* and has written many unmade feature films. Poetry and cinema are two of his biggest passions.

SCREEN WRITERS INC.

33 MASTERS ON THE ART AND CRAFT OF SCREENWRITING

MIHIR CHITRE

Om Books International

First published in 2025 by

Om Books International

Corporate & Editorial Office
A-12, Sector 64, Noida 201 301
Uttar Pradesh, India
Phone: +91 120 477 4100
Email: editorial@ombooks.com
Website: www.ombooksinternational.com

Sales Office
107, Ansari Road, Darya Ganj,
New Delhi 110 002, India
Phone: +91 11 4000 9000
Email: sales@ombooks.com
Website: www.ombooks.com

ISBN: 978-93-6395-503-5

Printed in India

10 9 8 7 6 5 4 3 2 1

Contents

Introduction

Writing for the screen is one of the most challenging and easily the most thankless part of film-making. Steven Spielberg said, 'If it's not on the page, it won't be on the stage.' The first step of any film is to improve the blank page. Casting, direction, acting, lights, sets, production – all happen only after the script is in place. If there is any process of pure creation in film, it is writing. Yet, how many screenwriters in India are known outside of the film industry? You know the stars, of course, and you may even know the actors. Over the last two or three decades, you have begun to know the directors as well. But do you know who wrote the screenplay of your favourite films? In the case that it was the director himself or herself who wrote it, my guess is you haven't bothered much about the writing part of their work. You associate your favourite dialogue with the actor who performed it, you may have even uttered it in dramatic ways at parties or memed it. But do you know the dialogue writer who wrote it? Songs are an essential part of most of our films and you know the singers, of course, and you know the music directors as well. But do you know the lyricist who wrote it?

The problem usually starts with our not knowing the person with the pen or in today's case, with the keyboard. However, in this project, I attempt to go beyond the 'who' and delve into the 'what' and the 'how' of it. What made Sai Paranjpye take to writing and film-making at a time when a female screenwriter and film-maker was unheard of? Or, what made Saurabh Shukla get involved with writing *Satya*? What was the story behind the cult comedy scene from *Daud* – '*Mere pitaji bahut bade shikari the*' (My father was a great huntsman) – written by Sanjay Chhel? What makes Chaitanya Tamhane hold on to his own in a world that approaches cinema differently? How did Swanand Kirkire end up writing '*Bawra Mann Dekhne Chala Yeh Sapna*', and how did Imtiaz Ali arrive at the idea of *Jab We Met* or how did Nitesh Tiwari think of the idea of *Dangal* before writing and making it into one of the highest-grossing films ever in Hindi cinema?

The answers to these and many other questions including, but not limited to, trivia will unravel themselves in this book. These writers reveal their ideas of cinema, their success stories as well as failures, what they would have rather done differently, their utopia, their fears, and how easy or difficult it is to exist and navigate as a writer in the otherwise glamorous world of cinema.

When I took on this project, I had no idea it would reach this far. It started with a couple of interviews and then I grew increasingly interested in knowing more from more people. I pitched the idea of this series to Manjula Narayan, the editor of the books page at *Hindustan Times*, who lapped it up and supported me through this journey that spans over three years. Cinema, along with poetry, is the biggest love of my life. Being a writer myself – though nowhere near as accomplished as any of the people I have interviewed in this book – I have always been curious to find out what a writer must deal with in cinema, and on every occasion, I came back with more than what I thought I would.

Together, these are the writers of over a hundred films and shows. I met them across Malad, Vile Parle, Santacruz, Juhu, Khar, and Bandra, on Zoom calls and Google Meets. One thing I was sure of was that I wanted to have variety in my series and no judgements or reservations that may come from my taste in film. I was interested in journeys. Here are writers who have worked in the mainstream and writers who have worked in abstract and arthouse and then some have been somewhere in between; here are writers who have been to film school and writers who are self-taught; writers who did a large chunk of their work in the 1980s, '90s, the noughties, and 2010s, and writers who began recently; writers who have written for films, those who have written for Over The Top or OTT platforms, those who have written for TV and also those who have written advertisements; those who have written screenplays, those who have written dialogues, those who have written songs and those who have written more than one of the above. The youngest writer here by age is Chandan Kumar and the oldest is Sai Paranjpye. Some come from Delhi, some from Bihar, some from Madhya Pradesh, some from Kerala, some from Pune and Jamshedpur, and many other cities and towns in the vast expanse of this glorious country, while some were born and raised in Bombay. However, all of them found their expression in film in Bombay and all were outsiders to the industry when they started. Each one of these writers is self-made.

I invite you to delve into the minds of the real creators, as I call them, of the films and shows you have liked, disliked, loved, lived, and obsessed over.

ONE

Abhishek Chaubey

The first thing I noticed about Abhishek is how understated, soft-spoken, and to-the-point he was on that afternoon at his office in Versova. He is the director and co-writer of films such as *Udta Punjab*, *Sonchiriya*, *Ishqiya*, and others.

He came across as an extremely well-read person – not many people from the film industry have referred to James Joyce's *Dubliners* to me in a conversation – and someone who knows exactly what he has set out to do as an artist. He has a vision and an opinion on art, which is wonderful.

What made you start with screenwriting?

Well, I grew up in various small cities of Jharkhand and Bihar. My family is from UP – I was born in Ayodhya. My mother's family is primarily from Lucknow. I spent a lot of time in UP during my childhood, but I lived in what was then Bihar, and is now Jharkhand, as my father was posted there. My family is primarily a service-oriented one, but there was always a lot of talk of film in the family, and we would often go to the theatre to watch films. Those were of course hardcore Bollywood films – they were not watching parallel cinema and all that but there was a lot of excitement and talk around films. Watching films remained a big thing for me even when I went to boarding school.

As I was growing up, it had started going beyond where my family was with films, which is to say that I had started looking beyond just thinking about the hero or a few songs. I had started deconstructing stories without any knowledge of course. Most of the films that we make in India follow a formula so whenever there was a film that broke the formula even slightly, I remember getting very excited and thinking about how and what they exactly did. In school, I was more inclined towards the humanities.

I remember we used to have an option to either write an essay or write a story, and I always used to choose to write stories. I used to write stories because I enjoyed writing them. They were, of course, very silly, childhood stories. I think when I went to my boarding school in Hyderabad, my world started opening up because till then I had been a UP boy, living in Bihar, but in Hyderabad, there was suddenly a new language called Telugu, there were people from different communities and backgrounds and stuff like that. And in that environment, the excitement of watching films only grew. I spent most of my weekends watching films. Although Hyderabad in the mid-1990s had single screens, it being a big city, also had a couple of places that showed English films. So, for the first time, I watched some English films. Now, I write in English, but at that time, I couldn't make head or tail of the American accent, and couldn't follow anything the characters were speaking. Yet, I remember watching *Fugitive* and it blew my mind away. I was like, 'What is this!'

After Hyderabad, I went to Delhi to study further, and I got admitted to Hindu College. That's when this pipedream of doing something related to films started shaping up. That was the first time when I started seeing a way to do this. I became a member of the film society in college, and I started doing theatre in Delhi. I also chose my friends carefully. I made friends with people who were interested in world cinema. Till that point in time, for me, there was no concept of a film which is not in English or Hindi, because I used to think, 'How can one watch a film in a language one doesn't understand?' But then I got the opportunity to watch some very good international films. And, as I told you earlier, I was already interested in the grammar of a film at a subconscious level, and after watching those films I started getting aware of the grammar in a conscious way.

Then in the late 1990s, mass communication was becoming a subject of study which was not the case even seven to eight years ago. So now you could tell your parents that you are doing a legitimate course, and the plan is not just to go to Bombay, and sleep on the footpath. So, I came to Bombay and joined Xavier's – XIC. To be honest, it wasn't much of a course back then. It was rather sketchy. More than learning about film, the course offered me a place to stay and a chance to get acquainted with the city. So, till today I haven't done a formal course on screenwriting or film-making. I am largely taught by watching films, and then, of course, by learning on the job. So, after the course, I tried to find my way into the industry, and the first couple of years were a struggle, and of being largely without work. And the thing is I came here to be a director, and the importance of screenwriting wasn't so clear to me back then. It was only after working for a few years that I realized that screenwriting is vital in my journey towards what I wanted to do.

Was there an internal conflict or a certain rebellion in you that made you see the world the way you do?

Well, I am generally not a very loud person. So, I'd say, there was a quiet rebellion in me. I – and I think all of us – come from a very conservative society. And it is conservative to a fault. I always had a problem with that. I found our customs and our prejudices quite hilarious, and I was profoundly disturbed by some of them. I come from an orthodox, upper-caste family, and to see those prejudices being played out in the real world, by people who are your loved ones, was frankly quite disturbing. I think, as an Indian, I don't know how anyone can miss it. If you are a good person, you are at the receiving end of it, and if you're a north Indian, male, and upper-caste, damn you if you can't stop it, and if you don't feel disgusted by it. I think some of my films do unconsciously reflect that.

However, at the same time, I am also an aesthete. I don't think of film just as a means to express my dissatisfaction towards the world. I look at film as an art, I am drawn towards the aesthetics of it, and I am not an activist. Of course, I am conscious and worried about certain things around me, and my films might reveal some of those things, but in equal parts, I make films because I am obsessed with the art and craft of cinema. The importance of the film is in its beauty more than its commentary about the world. That beauty itself reflects a stance and a worldview. And in beauty, prejudices don't exist. That's why we need art. I don't think we need art to create commentaries, we need it to create beauty so that people can absorb it.

Now, you are more known as a director than a screenwriter. In India, success is equated with directors but rarely with screenwriters. And some people remove themselves from the act of screenwriting once they make it big as directors. Where do you stand on that?

So far, that hasn't happened to me. But never say never. You don't know where life takes you. But I don't see how it's possible for me not to be involved with the writing of a film that I direct. I think it's very hard to see where screenwriting ends, and direction starts. I have heard a lot of people say in interviews, 'I had to stop thinking as a screenwriter, I had to think like a director.' Frankly, I don't know how that works. Leave aside the format of screenwriting for a second, but essentially, what you're doing as a screenwriter is putting down a story with audio-visual cues.

So, you know, when you are in the initial stages of a film, where you are thrashing out a story, it is kind of stupid for you to think if a shot should be taken from the top angle or not. I think that's foolish. You need to think about the theme of the story, the plot, and what is happening to the characters. Because that's the DNA of the film, and you can't play around with the DNA. But what happens is that as the screenplay gets more and more solidified, when you have got your beats in place, and all of that happens, you might get some visual ideas about how to shoot a particular scene. At a later stage like that, it's fine. But to be honest, you are still screenwriting it. So, I think screenwriting and direction are very closely linked.

You have collaborated with other screenwriters. Particularly, Sudip Sharma and Vishal Bhardwaj. I would like to know how the process of collaboration with other writers, who in some cases are directors, works for you.

I think screenwriting is something that can be done completely alone, but it also works beautifully in collaboration. It's not just a feature of India, but even in the West, it happens often. I mean, Paul Schrader is one of the greatest writers, but a Martin Scorsese film is a Martin Scorsese film whether it's Schrader writing it or anybody else. But having said that, a lot of times in Bombay, directors take screenwriting credit because they have hung out with the screenwriter while he was developing the script. That doesn't happen so much in the West. The contracts are not like that.

I think collaborative writing is also a feature of the form that you are dealing with. In poetry, for instance, it is impossible. With novels, some writers owe their debt to their editor – there are some legendary editors like that. So, when it comes to structure, theme, and characters, there are a lot of discussions that you could have with others when it comes to screenwriting. One thing I know for sure is that there is no one right way to go about it. I can tell you how I work, but it may not work for you.

The way I work is I spend a lot of time with my writers, thrashing out the nuts and bolts of a story, and I try to arrive at a point when we have a story that works for us, the essentials, the building blocks are in place, we have a sense of flow, a sense of theme and a sense of mood as well. It's important to know what kind of film you are making. Structure is very important to me. I think the mystery of a story lies in its structure. So, I spend a lot of time doing the structure. Once we are done with that, we go our ways, and they send the material to me, and I keep making corrections. In all of this, 60-70 per cent of the time is gone. I delay the actual writing process to the nth hour. By this time, you don't have much room to play with and things are kind of airtight. Now, all that remains to be done is writing the scene.

However, this is how I operate with some of the younger writers. With every person the process is different. With Sudip, I had a lot more to contribute to *Udta Punjab* because that was the first time we were working with each other and were still finding each other. On *Sonchiriya*, I did not take the screenplay credit because, by that time, we had achieved such a great rapport that I did not do anything more than some minor changes to the screenplay, and he wrote it entirely.

With Vishal, I had to do the beat sheets and everything. Also, he writes by hand, and he used to write dialogue. So, I had to write the scenes and everything. It was his script most of the time that we were writing. With *Ishqiya* and *Dedh Ishqiya*, I could take a lot of liberty because I was also directing the films. But on his scripts, if I had to make a change, I had to address it to him before changing anything.

Most of your films are such that I can imagine, at a script level, they would have been extremely difficult to sell in Bollywood. And yet, not only did you manage to make them but also found mainstream success with some of them. How did you achieve this rare and stellar feat?

Yes, people had walked out of the narration of *Udta Punjab*, and all those things happened. But I think what you call an achievement is not much to take credit for because we do what we can. This is what I came here to do, this is what I know, and this is what I like to do. In a way, it is a conscious call, but it's not born out of the fact that I desperately want to do something different. It's more to do with the fact that if I don't do it this way, I won't be able to sleep at night. Look, film-making is very hard. You have to sometimes work seventeen-eighteen hours a day. It takes a toll on your body. And if you are not happy with what you are doing, it's a terrible place to be. If you just want to make money, film-making is not a thing.

Now, about getting these films made, which I fortunately could, entails some historical factors. Anybody trying to get such things made in or before the 1990s would have found it very hard. Going against the grain at that time would make it difficult to attract funding. You know, till the 1950s, and a part of the 1960s, there was a genuine cinema movement in this country. There was Guru Dutt, there was Bimal Roy, and other directors as well who were making middle-of-the-road cinema. People think it was the era of social consciousness, but social consciousness is there in commercial films as well. Every run-off-the-mill dacoit film would tell you, '*Ladkiyon ki izzat karo*.' (Respect women.) So, now, it's not social consciousness that was special about these films – it was the aesthetic.

Then in the 1970s and 1980s, you had a beautiful place for some of these smaller films. They even had their own set of stars such as Naseer, Shabana, Smita, Om, and those guys. So, if I lived in that era, those were the films I would have made or gravitated towards because the other option was too mainstream. If you are a Manmohan Desai, it would be silly for you to make this kind of cinema, but for those of us who were or are not, that was the place to be. Because I can't do the Manmohan Desai kind naturally.

By the time, it came to my era, maybe because of what had happened in the industry over the past few decades that niche was available … it may not have been easy or readily available … but it was there. And fortunately, I could get in. I think, in my work, some features of mainstream cinema are present. For instance, I have always had a problem with song and dance, but I do use music. I do use humour as well because everyone can identify with it. A laugh is a laugh. I know that people from a younger generation detest the concept of narration, but I don't mind narrating my films. These are some adjustments that I have made to make my films happen. And I think it's a happy alliance because these are things I enjoy as well. For instance, I really enjoy a great set of visuals cut to a great piece of music. I mean, who doesn't? So, I can do that, and therefore I can excite the imagination of a particular actor or a producer.

Is working with stars a compromise of your vision of storytelling?

The way it works is that when a big star is attached to your film, there are much higher budgets to play with. And it's not just their fees, but a star enhances the overall production budget of a film, which is very helpful. I am a visual director, and I like to design things, so the extra budget that a star brings with them is useful. And it's not that I have twenty pieces of additional equipment lying on the set. I like to direct within the budget. But yes, I have shot according to light. I like to believe there is at least some sense of visual design to my films, and that costs money.

Now, to answer your question about a creative compromise, let's be honest, there is some compromise. Because I think it's impossible for any star, and I mean any star, to completely leave aside their image. That can't happen. So, it is not possible to make a film in India without any compromise. But you need to try and minimize the compromise and also know what to compromise on.

Can you walk me through the journey of conceptualizing, writing, and making *Udta Punjab*?

It was a time when I was still editing *Dedh Ishqiya*. I wanted to do something with drugs. At that time, I had some idea of different people across the country using and abusing drugs. I had a notion that the war on drugs cannot be fought. It's a losing war. Only an individual can win a war like that by overcoming the addiction, but you can't fight the system. And that's what I wanted to make a film on. That's why the drug users in *Udta Punjab* win but people who are fighting the menace lose. So, I had this vague idea.

I had only recently met Sudip (Sharma) and I had taken to his writing. I had read the script of *Nh10* – it was not even shot at the time – and I had quite liked it. Plus, Sudip and I had met some six to eight months before this, and we used to get along really well, we used to hang out together. So, I told him my idea and it was Sudip who came up with the idea to do it in Punjab. And it kind of made sense to me immediately. This was just the initial idea. After this, we took another six months. It involved a lot of research, and Sudip spent truckloads of time on it. He is terrific with research.

Now, I have professional research people involved in my projects, but with Sudip, I never felt the need to. So, from there, my characters took shape, and the story kept evolving for the next many, many months. For about one year, we were only posting index cards on the board. But by the time we finished with this process, we were through with the story, we were absolutely clear about what was happening in the film. From then onwards we did not take much time.

Sudip is very fast, and he started writing the screenplay. Both of us had a feeling that we had a problem in the third act, but we just told ourselves that it would take care of itself. By the time we reached the third act, we realized there was a genuine problem and if we didn't do something about it, this was going to become a four-and-a-half-hour film. So, we got back to the drawing board and changed a lot of things. Initially, the character that Kareena played was a man, but that's when we changed it into a woman and gave her and the cop some sort of an equation. Similarly, we changed many other things as well. Once we were done with the script, getting funding for it was very, very difficult. I went to a lot of places, some people were genuinely interested. But unlike *Ishqiya* and *Dedh Ishqiya*, *Udta Punjab* is very bleak. So, some people told me if I wanted to make this film, I would have to make it in the bare minimum budget with, say, five crore rupees, a very small unit, and stuff like that. So, I started thinking of the film from that angle. Had it happened that way, it may have been a grittier and much more intense film. But then I met Vikram (Motwane) and once it went to Phantom, everything changed, and we had it made with much better budgets and a star cast as well.

In writing *Omkara*, you and Vishal set out to adapt none other than Shakespeare. How daunting was the task?

Look, I read Shakespeare in college because I am a literature student. So, I was acquainted with his work. When I read the first half of the script of *Omkara*, I was very impressed with it. Because Vishal had not studied Shakespeare in college, and by the time he started adapting

Shakespeare, he was never daunted by the idea of Shakespeare. He was very impressed with the basic conflict of the story. And, before *Omkara*, he had only done one other adaptation of his which was *Maqbool* which he wrote with Abbas (Tyrewala). Vishal wanted to do another adaptation and the two of us kept discussing it. In his first draft of *Omkara*, a lot of the mood of *Othello* was already there.

Now, at that point Vishal had a film with Aamir Khan called *Mr. & Mrs. Mehta*, which imploded in production. Suddenly, he didn't have a film lined up and had the time to get to this. Around the same time, he met Ajay Devgn, who offered to work with Vishal if he did another Shakespeare. So, it was a nice coincidence of sorts. Now, Ajay only had dates in January, and we were in November. So, I was worried that Vishal had a chance to make a really big film and he hadn't written anything, and it could all be a mess. So, we had two choices to set the story in. Either DU politics or a western UP gangster film. We decided on the latter, which was closer to what I had in mind.

Omkara had a unique journey, and I have never been able to work like that before and after. We spent a week in Meerut, meeting a few gangsters, and made a note of some wonderful lines, characters, and behaviours. From there, we immediately went to Mussoorie, and with all the data and the world that we had imagined, we wrote the film in eighteen days! That is nuts. It's insane. But finishing a script like *Omkara* in eighteen days is exceptional. Our backs were against the wall, and it just happened. If we try it again, I am not sure it will happen. So, this cannot be used as a reference.

How did the journey of *Kaminey* start? Also, do you agree that *Kaminey* is one of the weaker films that you have written?

Vishal had once conducted a workshop in Africa and someone had got his script to the workshop, which Vishal had really liked. It was set in the slums of Nairobi. So, when it came to *Kaminey*, Vishal called up that guy and asked him if his film was made. It wasn't and Vishal officially bought the rights from him, and we adapted it. That guy is also credited in the film.

Well, I wouldn't say I am too unhappy with the film. I think the last third of the film has a problem. But I am a writer on the film, and Vishal's vision for *Kaminey* was different from what he had had for *Maqbool* and *Omkara* and those films. With *Kaminey*, he wanted to have fun. It was never supposed to have the seriousness of those films. Also, he wanted to explore the technical side of film-making. It is so sharp, the way it looks, the way it moves. Even the writing is like that – witty, punchy. So, it was meant to thrill on the surface instead of shaking you from within.

I don't have a problem with that. If that's what we want to do, that's what we want to do. And we wrote it to the brief. Also, I was there only on the first draft of the film because I was getting into the prep of *Ishqiya*. So, Sabrina Dhawan came on board to help Vishal with the later drafts. And Supratik (Sen) was the other writer on it.

I think if there is anything that can be called 'Indian zany', it is *Ishqiya*. Can you take me through its journey?

I was looking for a film to direct myself because I had worked with Vishal and written with him for several years. I was a little tired of the process and Vishal was tired of me too. So, he told me it was time I made something of my own. I was looking for a subject and I had a story I had written long back. I wanted to do something like a comedy noir. So, I wrote down the basic idea as a three-pager and pitched it to Vishal. He immediately loved it. But then the writing process went crazy because Vishal and I were so much in love with our craft, writing crazy scenes and dialogues, that somewhere we lost sight of the plot. We had some hilarious scenes, but it was really not going anywhere. It would have at the best been a zany art film, which I wouldn't mind, but it would have bombed at the box office for sure. So, it came to a point when we thought of moving on to some other project, but I had belief in the characters.

That's when Vishal got Sabrina on board, and I worked with her for a month, when she cracked the idea of Krishna's (the character played by Vidya Balan) past and her husband's backstory. The fact that her husband is alive and not dead was Sabrina's idea. And that sort of completed the film and got it back on track. Then I rewrote almost the entire script which went on for about a year and a half. For that year and a half, I did not make a single rupee, and that was surely a painful time. But then fortunately the film was made and it became what it did.

What is success for a screenwriter?

Easy availability of funds for the next film. Maybe even a raise. Money is definitely a factor. Also, general appreciation. Your peers, your colleagues, your friends, if they genuinely appreciate your work that means something to you.

What is a failure for a screenwriter?

I think I experienced some of it with *Matru Ki Bijlee Ka Mandola* though I don't think it is as badly written as it is made out to be.

Name a few films and film-makers who have influenced you.

There are various kinds of influences. When it comes to film grammar and aesthetics, it's the masters. French masters like Truffaut or Godard or other European masters such as Bergman.

For me, the mood and the tone of the film are very important. Sometimes, they are the most important things for me. Sometimes, themes are not as important to me. So, when it comes to those, Kubrick and the Coen brothers are huge influences. *Fargo* is my all-time favourite.

I also really admire a lot of Indian film-makers who have managed to do 'alternatives'. Because I think India is a very difficult country to do it, especially Hindi cinema is notoriously difficult to do it in. So, I respect a lot of people from the 1950s and 1980s parallel cinema. Especially Shyam Benegal. I think *Bhumika* is one of my all-time favourite films.

TWO

Anjum Rajabali

I met Anjum Rajabali at his house in Juhu at around noon. During the conversation, we joked that he has been a screenwriter for nearly as long as I have been alive. Such is the range of his experience in the industry that he has seen at least three different eras of Bollywood first-hand. He is the writer of several films including *Droh Kaal*, *Ghulam*, *The Legend of Bhagat Singh*, and *Rajneeti*.

Along with practising screenwriting, he also teaches it and holds an important position at the SWA (Screenwriters Association), while constantly fighting for the rights of the screenwriter. Talking to Anjum Rajabali was like sitting in a classroom, trying to absorb all the wisdom I could.

How did you decide to become a screenwriter at a time when it wasn't even considered a job? What was the industry like in the late 1980s and early 1990s for a writer?

Frankly speaking, it was a pure accident. Complete coincidence. I never wrote anything as a child, I never thought of myself as a creative person. My association with films was only as a viewer. I used to enjoy watching films, and that's about it. I was in a boarding school in Belgaum for seven years after which I went to Pune for my graduation. And I came to Bombay to be a psychoanalyst. I wanted to become a professional practising therapist in the framework of psychoanalysis. Though I did train for a few years, that pursuit did not work out. Then I worked as an information research person, but I was empty from within. I was competent and I was getting a good salary but I knew that wasn't something I wanted to do.

Then, one day, as a matter of pure chance, through a dog, I met Baba (Azmi) and Tanvi (Azmi), who lived close by in Janki Kutir in Juhu. My wife met Tanvi in a laundry and she liked our dog very much. Then a time came when, since both my wife and I were working, it was getting difficult for us to look after the dog. Baba loved dogs. So we approached Baba and Tanvi. Baba made an offer that throughout the day, the dog could stay with them, and in the evening when we came back from work, we could collect it. That arrangement worked perfectly for us. This was in 1988. Eventually, because of the dog, we came very close. The four of us became like a family. Baba, being a cinematographer, would get us to watch films on the big screen and a lot of discussions would take place. Baba wanted to become a director. So, one day, he asked me if I would write a script for him. I told him he was insane because I had nothing to do with writing till that point in my life. You won't believe, till that point, I had never written a single story in my life. I told him I had no idea what a script even was or how it was written. But Baba insisted and told me that anybody could write.

That was the impression in the film industry at that time. Writing wasn't considered a specialized craft. Anybody would write anything and then the director would take over. So, in February 1992, purely to get him off my back, I thought let me see what this creature of screenwriting looks like, and put something down. Since I didn't know anything about screenwriting, I started imagining how the story would play out on the screen, and I decided I would just describe what I saw in my mind's eye. So, I wrote a portion about a young boy who goes to boarding school in a village, and how the happiest day of his life turns into the worst day of his life.

The character was close to my personal experiences, and I wrote about thirteen-fourteen pages. I wrote it like a novel because I wasn't aware of the format.

When I read it out to Baba and Tanvi, they were very taken up. They told me it was very dramatic, tight, and very visual. Somewhere I had stumbled upon the secret of screenwriting that you have to see it play on the screen. So, that is where it began. He told me that regardless of whether he makes a film or not, I should pursue this. Because I had enjoyed writing it, and because his reaction was so ecstatic, I thought maybe I should push it and I decided to make a hobby out of it. So, I started pursuing this while I still worked my job.

A couple of months down the line, another coincidence happened. Somewhere in April 1992, through a common friend, I bumped into Govind Nihalani. We got talking and we realized that we had common interests. When he asked me what I did in life, I told him that I was trying to write a script. He was curious. So I described to him what I was writing. I realized that the themes that would appeal to me were the same that he was thinking about at that time. How to make difficult moral choices and whether any redemption was possible. It's a universal question that happened to be gripping both of us at that time.

So, he asked me to share what I had written and after reading it, he asked me if I would read something that he had written. And what he had written was the one-liner and the beat sheet of what eventually became *Droh Kaal*. It was called *Drohi* at that time. I put all my intellect to work, which was a bit of a mistake because you don't just want to read a film intellectually, you should also read it experientially. But for whatever it was worth, I told him that there was a major problem with what the main character was doing. He told me he agreed with me and asked me for a solution. I told him that the character was too complete and there had to be some vulnerability, some crack, some flaw of his that would get exposed, and then he would buckle. So, then I changed the relationship of the character with his wife and introduced another character as well.

Govind thought it was very interesting, and it could just be what he was looking for. And then he asked me to write it for him. I told him he was taking a huge chance and I had never written a full script till that time. Besides, he was Govind Nihalani! Would I welcome the chance to work with him? Of course. But it would be a huge risk for him. And I told him all this honestly. He said, 'You leave that to me. I have a good feeling about this.' I agreed and I went fully into it. The eight-ten pages that he had given me, I turned those into a first draft of about 120-130 pages. I had never written a screenplay in my life and at that time there was no screenwriting software so I wrote the whole thing like a play. Govind liked what I had written and some feedback followed. So, I did four drafts. And that was the time I was beginning to get a sense of what dramatization and screenwriting were. And Govind is Govind. His understanding of drama is A-grade. He accepted my last draft and asked me if I could work on more ideas with him. Then there was a short story we were trying to adapt, then there was another one.

While all this was going on, another thing happened. Baba had shot *Dil* with Indu (Indra Kumar), which had Aamir (Khan). So, they had become good friends. And Baba told Aamir about me and told him I wrote quite appealingly. So I met Aamir. The dog, at this time, gave birth to six pups, one of which Aamir took. And that's how we became close. So the dog got me Baba; Baba got me Aamir; Govind, I got on my own, but the dog has played a pivotal role in my life. In fact, a lot of credit goes to Baba because he really encouraged me a lot. He is one of my closest friends.

One day, out of the blue, Aamir called and asked me if I would go and see him at (Mahesh) Bhatt's office. They wanted me to adapt *On the Waterfront*. I was a bit squeamish about that initially because it was already a made film. At that time, Mahesh Bhatt was to direct the film they had called me for and he told me I'd be able to do my own thing, but *On the Waterfront* was the way they wanted to go. I went and saw the film and was very impressed. I transcribed *On the Waterfront* and tried to study it. I learnt a lot from that transcription. In this Hindi adaptation, the story had to be relocated to India and all that, so I just took the nucleus of *On the Waterfront*, the story of an ambivalent character who lives under the shadow of his elder brother but at some point, a moral crisis hits and he has to make a choice. But then it was done very differently, the first half was entirely different.

They liked what I had done and they also liked the original elements that I had brought in. I brought an Indian sensibility to the story and I began to own the character of Siddharth Marathe by adding a lot of personal touches to him, and I was no longer thinking of *On the Waterfront*. The film that this eventually became is, of course, *Ghulam*, which was originally called *Zakhmi*.

Ghulam was offered to me in 1993, so while all this was going on, *Droh Kaal* was yet to be released. And I kid you not, I had thirty-six offers to write films. Imagine, at this point, I didn't have a single release! It happened because the word spread in the industry that I was working with the Bhatts and Govind Nihalani and everyone began calling me. Subhash Ghai called me because he heard about me. Shekhar Kapur called me because he heard about me. Yash Chopra called me after he saw the preview of *Droh Kaal*. Sunny Deol, some south people, and even Manoj Kumar called me. Someone even sent me a bag full of money to sign me on because, in those days, it all used to be cash transactions. So I was getting overwhelmed and I kept saying no to everyone. Subhash Ghai, of course, I said yes to. But for everyone else, I refused.

Some people advised me that most films don't get made, and I should just take the signing amount and say yes to everyone. But I didn't want to work like that. It was just a mad place at that time. Newspapers wrote about me, I had full-page writers running about me, and all this was happening without a release and after just one release (*Droh Kaal*). You won't believe it … it was such a crazy place that someone told me, 'I believe you actually write.' I said, 'I am a writer. Of course, I write. Don't other writers write?' That person said, 'No, they don't write. They just discuss, some notes are made and that's how we go onto the floors.' Someone else had offered me a film that was 60 per cent shot and they didn't know what to do after that. So, they approached me to complete the film. I said, 'How can I write a film when more than half of it is already shot?' As soon as they had an idea, or the 'subject' as it was called then, they would start casting, they would start production design, without any script in place. The film industry was an absolutely mad place at that time.

Certain films that I took up did not happen. The Subhash Ghai film, for instance, did not happen because he and I disagreed on some things. *Ghulam* took a long time to be made, but after it was released, a flurry of films came my way. And it was then, in 1997, that I finally quit my job and decided to pursue this full-time. While I was still holding onto my job, I happened to write five films that eventually got made: *Droh Kaal*, *Kachche Dhaage*, *Pukar*, *China Gate*, and *Ghulam*. Then, there was *The Legend of Bhagat Singh* in 2002. From 2002 to 2010, there was a lull. Some films fell away, some did not work. And then again, after 2010 four films came out one after the other and then there was again a gap. That's how life has been as a screenwriter.

Barring relatively short phases like Salim-Javed, why has the screenwriter never assumed much importance in the history of Hindi cinema whereas they have always been a well-established entity in the West?

If you really look at the history of Indian screenwriting, in the beginning, there were visionary directors such as Dadasaheb Phalke and Fateh Lal. Then came Mehboob Khan, Bimal Roy, Guru Dutt, and the like. They understood narrative and oftentimes, even if a full script wasn't in place, they knew where to take the film and only the dialogue would be filled in later. They had an intuitive sense of the rhythm of a screenplay. Many of these would have a writer working with them but the script wasn't essentially driven by the director. The writer would be on a salary at the director's office and would write whatever he was asked to.

There were some writers like Pandit Mukhram Sharma who were capable of independently developing a script and taking it to the directors and also disagreeing with them on occasions. But then, there were very few of them. The idea that the writer is the first film-maker and could have a vision that is independent of the director never really existed in Hindi cinema unlike in the West. Our early film-makers were highly influenced by our epics, myths, folktales, etc., and they tried to tell the same stories on film whereas in Hollywood, that did not exist. So, they took an industrial approach to film-making by treating it as a new product and creating formats and definite roles and responsibilities. I'm sorry to say this but if you look at a film like *Mother India*, it is a classic with a strong story, superb direction, and all that. But if you look at it, it's a very tedious screenplay. It would be fair to say it's a boring screenplay. Same with *Gunga Jumna*.

People focussed on dialogue but never on the screenplay. Farsi theatre had a huge influence on Hindi cinema of the old. The loud storytelling, song and dance, all come from there. Even some classical theatre people looked down upon Farsi theatre but it was popular so Hindi cinema took narratives from there.

Until Salim-Javed, we rarely had anyone successfully writing a script on their own and pitching it to a director. Salim Sahib would write very tight screenplays and Javed Sahib would write superb dialogue. They became superstars but unfortunately, it never became a tradition that other writers would also receive the same treatment. Salim-Javed became a unique thing when they worked and after their phase was over, we were back to where we were. Salim-Javed did not leave a trail. Salim-Javed separated in 1979. Some of their unmade films came out later but that was over. And then came the 1980s with video piracy, black money, criminal empires got involved and the whole thing became a mess. The quality of films seriously deteriorated. And then in the 1990s, it started picking up again.

When I joined the industry in the early 1990s, a little bit of hangover from the earlier decades remained. Someone once asked me to write a full screenplay in one week after showing me the mahurat shot that they had already taken. Even with Mr Ghai, I had to tell him that writing is a solitary activity and I need one month just to myself to produce the first draft. He expected that we meet every week, maybe even every day, and discuss things. Even with Raj (Kumar Santoshi) – whom I was introduced to by Aamir (Khan) – it used to be like a darbar in the director's office. I had seen Raj's work and I really admired it – *Damini*, *Ghayal*, and *Andaz Apna Apna* were all fabulous pieces of work. Even *Ghatak* was a tight script. So, when I met him, he asked me, 'Why am I hearing your name everywhere?' This was around 1994-95. I said, 'Perhaps because of the sheer ignorance that your industry treats screenwriting with. Maybe because I know some terminology and I can use words like structure and all that, people take me seriously.'

The first time we worked together was on a film that never got made. When I went to his office, six-seven people were sitting around him. One of them was a distributor, one was what was called a 'money agent', and one, you won't believe, was a driver. Upon my asking, Raj said that the driver was there because he was in the audience. I told him that the audience comes in after the work is done – not in the process of creation! That day, I told him that I'd never work with him if this happened one more time. I was clear that construction is a specialized skill and it can't happen with so many people in the room. I told him I had to do it alone, and only when I felt the need to, I will reach out to him. And I made it clear that I couldn't have any of those people involved in the process. But Raj took this very gracefully and from the next time, there was no one else involved in our discussions.

Is it true that you are the first person who started asking for legal writer contracts?

Yes, that's true. Writing contracts were unheard of back in the day, and it made a lot of people furious. One day a producer asked me sarcastically if I didn't trust him. I said, 'I don't trust my own memory. What if tomorrow I come to you and tell you that the amount we orally agreed on was higher than what was decided? What happens then?' I said contracts are essential in protecting both parties. Then I started asking for stamp-paper agreements. That further infuriated producers. They told me it's a family oriented business that works on trust. But I said, 'This is how I work. If you were buying my house, wouldn't you sign an agreement with me? Why should it be any different when you are buying my script?' A lot of people thought I was arrogant. But for me, it was just a simple logical thing that had to be done.

Now, I am involved with the SWA. Back in the 1990s, the fight was to have a writer's contract in place; now it is about having a fair contract in place. The thing is they will only give you a small amount of your total agreed amount upfront. It is called the signing amount. After that, the writer has to finish the whole screenplay – very often, write many drafts. But the big money comes in only after the stars are finalized and it gets to the next stage. I think it's very unfair because the writer has already done all his work and he is only getting a very small signing amount upfront. So, if a film gets cancelled from there, the writer only gets the signing amount despite having finished all his work. How's that fair?

A lot of times, after the writer has done the many drafts, the producers would involve a senior writer to do a 'polish' or the final draft. Or then the director takes over and does that himself. In this case, that person gets the top billing as well as the lead credit. And the young writer who has done so much work gets neither. I don't see how that is at all fair. At SWA we believe that there should be a clear formula and we are working on a clear formula. Money and credit cannot be given on a person's biodata or stature. They should be given on the work. The person who has done the work should get the maximum share of the money and the credit. And there should be a system of fair arbitration between the writer and the producer. So, these are the kinds of things we are working towards in a united way.

Tell me about writing *Rajneeti*, which is one of your biggest hits, and working on other political films such as *Aarakshan* with Prakash Jha.

Prakash is a film-maker who is interested in political subjects. Although I did not write it, I did help Prakash on *Gangajal* and even *Apaharan* to a certain extent. *Rajneeti* was about electoral politics. And I told him that I was not interested. I am interested in politics as a citizen, but as a writer, it doesn't interest me much. But he insisted, and unlike in his previous films, he told me that he didn't just want my help as a script consultant but he wanted me to take the lead and write the film myself.

I wanted to have a story that would interest me. So, for a week, Prakash would come to my house every day between 7.30 p.m. and 10 p.m., and we would have a couple of vodkas, and discuss what kind of story could emerge. So, cousins and some other elements came up but I was still searching for the story that would thematically appeal to me. And then, while working on it, I realized that it was veering towards the Mahabharata. And I am a lover of the Mahabharata. It's not that it was an adaptation of the Mahabharata, but some elements from the epic came up and got sucked into the story. I think the political element came because I relooked at Arjun's character from the Mahabharata, who became the protagonist of the film and was eventually played by Ranbir (Kapoor). Initially, he wants to be away from the mess. He lives in America. But then the moment comes when his father is shot, and he decides to get involved and take things into his own hands. It's like a pre-Bhagavadgita to a post-Bhagavadgita graph. And I thought, what if I took a dark view of Arjun? Because there were several things he did that were questionable. So, the central theme is when you get into politics, you have to get your hands dirty. And Samar, the protagonist who is modelled on Arjun, becomes even worse than the others. I had envisaged that kind of a dystopian end.

Aarakshan was more political but I think it never went the distance. Prakash brought me a story written by Kamlesh Pandey, which Firoz Nadiadwala had brought him. It was a story about an idealistic principal who gets persecuted and then fights back. It didn't interest me because I thought it was a standard story about an honest man fighting the system and all that. I told Prakash that if it is the principal's story, it has to be about education and we must look at an issue that is bothering the education system. And what would be bigger than reservation – an issue that had divided this country? So, after a lot of debate, Prakash accepted this suggestion and registered the title *Aarakshan*. It wasn't called *Aarakshan* before that. The film could have gone the distance but it didn't.

Tell me about writing *China Gate* for Raj Kumar Santoshi. It was quite an unusual film for its time.

One day, Raj and I were chatting on the roadside and the thought came from him. He said, 'Who are our superstars? Who are our

Amitabh Bachchan and Dharam-ji?' Without hesitation, I said, 'Om Puri and Naseeruddin Shah.' And then he said, 'Why don't we make a film with these people?' Then he added, 'What if we make something like a *Seven Samurai*?'

I thought since these people are aging, we have to account for the fact that they have to take something on, which is almost impossible for them to achieve. And then the thoughts started coming in: What if there is a shadow of ignominy on them and they have to redeem themselves? What if they were kicked out of the army after being accused of cowardice? That's a huge disgrace. So, that's how the story shaped up right there where we were standing.

It was a very exciting project for me because of the chance to see people like Om and Naseer working. I spent a long, long time on the set of that film.

What are the films and film-makers that have influenced you?

Of course, Salim-Javed. In my early days, I was influenced by *Deewaar* and some of their other work. Though I have a nuanced view of their work, I count them as an influence. Then I would say, Mehboob Khan and Bimal Roy. Also, Mani Ratnam. At least, his earlier work.

From abroad, it would be the Italian film-maker Michelangelo Antonioni. And for writing, I'd say, William Goldman and Robert Towne were two people whose work I really liked. Especially Towne's *Chinatown* and Goldman's *All the President's Men, Butch Cassidy and the Sundance Kid, Misery*.

Then there are films I would name. *Deewaar, Gunga Jumna. Mughal-e-Azam* is a primary influence. Then *Groundhog Day, Casablanca*. Antonioni's *Il Grido* is a film that I was very shaken by. Then some of the very old works like *Grand Hotel, Ninotchka* have influenced me as well.

THREE

Ashim Ahluwalia

Ashim Ahluwalia's work has always been offbeat. My hunch is it's because he has always found himself somewhere between the mainstream and the arthouse. There is nothing predictable about either the subjects of his films or the choices he makes as to which films and shows he would take up at a point in time.

I did this piece with him over email as he was not in the country when this happened. *Class*, his show which is a Hindi adaptation of the super-hit Spanish show *Elite*, had just been released before we did this exercise. Ashim's work includes the critically acclaimed film *Miss Lovely* and the Arjun Rampal-starrer biopic of Arun Gawli, *Daddy*.

You get the credit as well as the blame for being somewhere between mainstream and arthouse and, sometimes, for being too experimental with your work. What's your stance on that?

I personally thrive on the tension between these two worlds. I think if I worked either in purely mainstream film or remained limited only to arthouse cinema, I would be bored. It's the friction that I love. I try to capture the multiplicity of experiences, complex characters, and dense stories, and for that mainstream film-making can sometimes be too basic. It usually demands childlike plots and a big spectacle and doesn't leave me with enough to think about once the film is done.

And yet I want to be able to reach out to wider audiences and try new things, so I guess I need to engage more mainstream distribution at the same time. And those audiences might not always be ready for new forms, so I think that opinion is fair.

What were your childhood and teenage years like and how did they play a role in your development as a writer?

As a kid, I had a pretty vivid imagination. I would make things out of broken stuff around the house. For example, I turned a broken bed into an imaginary plane when I was about six or seven. I totally imagined and inhabited these worlds that I would create, spending hours sitting there, lost in my own head. So, I think film-making for me is just an extension of building worlds for myself during my childhood. When I write, I find it quite easy to become totally immersed and completely lose track of the real world.

You studied film-making in New York. How did that influence your ideas and the themes you went on to handle eventually?

I'm really grateful to have had that opportunity because I was exposed to all kinds of films, so my vision became very wide. I didn't need to always look to Hollywood or Bollywood, I was watching all kinds of Japanese, Iranian, or Russian cinema, across all eras. I think that played a huge impact on how I see my own work now. I also got to watch Satyajit Ray and Ritwik Ghatak for the first time only when I went abroad. This was obviously right before the internet, and there was no way for me to get access to these films in India.

Miss Lovely **is a unique film. Could you take me in detail through the journey of it from the conception of the idea to writing the script and then making it?**

In the first decade of the new millennium, I wanted to make a documentary on the sex-horror cinema that was still being made at the time, so that was the starting point. It was basically illegal pornography masquerading as feature films with the sex scenes being inserted after the censor process. I was mostly fascinated with this industry that nobody talked about. It was hard to get access and I delved into it for over a year, spending time on film sets, drinking, and hanging out with some seriously wild actors, directors, and casting agents. Half of these guys were on the run from the cops and most had fake names.

I saw all kinds of mad stuff being filmed, and I was very excited to dive in and start shooting. But when I wanted people to speak on camera and let me document their lives, they refused. They were worried about being jailed for pornography or other things, I suppose. So, eventually, I turned all those real stories into a fictional script for a film that I set in the mid-1980s. I just disguised the stories a bit so that the people I interviewed wouldn't get busted for telling me all their dirty secrets. That was the first draft of *Miss Lovely*.

Of course, in 2008 when I started making *Miss Lovely*, nobody in India would finance it. One studio I tried to get money from stole the storyline and made a mainstream film 'inspired' by this world which became quite successful. So, it was quite difficult and depressing and took almost four years to finish. I eventually cobbled together French, US, and Japanese money and that's how we made it. I'm just lucky it got into Cannes. Otherwise my film-making career would have been over.

What, in retrospect, would you change about your film *Daddy*, based on Arun Gawli's life? Or, do you think it works just fine?

I like the film, I think it's a really unconventional biopic in the sense Arun Gawli is at the centre, but you never find out much about him. Was he guilty of those crimes? Was he trapped? Was he good or evil? Or somewhere in between? He remains extremely mysterious. Unlike most biopics which claim to be the real story, and you get the inside scoop on Gandhi or Abraham Lincoln or whoever, I think, in reality, you never know anyone very well, and certainly not a historical figure. You barely even know yourself. So, I wanted *Daddy* to be a film where you know about Gawli but only through other people in his life – through his family, the cops, his enemies. You get different perspectives on him and they all don't match. But you never hear from him, so you have to make up your mind, I don't want to tell you what to think. And after spending time with him when he was out on parole, I can tell you that's exactly what he's like.

I think this was a film that was perhaps too experimental for the wide mainstream release it got because it had multiple timelines running together. The same story is sometimes also told from different perspectives. This was attributed to script problems but I think the real issue is that our audiences are not used to this form of storytelling.

It's also not very filmi, with clever dialogue or slow-motion action sequences as people were perhaps expecting. It's grittier and more realistic. But I have to say I'm really proud of the film, and I feel it may have another life in the near future with newer audiences.

How difficult was it for you to sell your kind of script in your early days?

Kind of impossible. I have scripts I wrote over ten years ago that are still considered too risky to finance. I don't give up easily though. I don't think it makes sense to be afraid of rejection, else nothing interesting will ever get made.

What's your process of writing?

I always start with research. I need to immerse myself in the world, read, and get as much real information and detail as possible. Earlier it was through hanging out and talking to people close to my characters, and now it's through having a research team. I just need to know enough that I understand what makes this world tick, what are its logic systems, what it looks and smells like, and what is its language.

Once I have all these in my head, I need to disconnect. Go away somewhere super remote and disappear until I write a first draft. At that point, I don't speak to anyone until the draft is finished.

Class is a remake of the Spanish show _Elite_. What attracted you to take up the project?

I've wanted to make something about teenagers for a while, the strong, conflicted emotions you feel when you're young.

It was just an accident that one day I was offered the Spanish series _Elite_ for a possible adaptation. I had never watched it before. I had also never done a series or even actually considered it. The original show is really different from the films I make, it felt more like a tele-novella, but there was something really unpredictable about the writing – the characters and the class conflict felt very relevant to India. I wanted freedom to make it my way, which Netflix was quite open to.

When it comes to remaking a European show, what are some rules or conditions that you kept in mind? Could you walk me through the exercise of writing a remake?

I wanted the tale to be the same, but the telling to be completely different. I adapted the show through an Indian lens. Here, other than class there is also caste – so that makes the conflicts more complex. The way families work, and their involvement in children's lives are very different from what they are in Spain, so the parents here play a much larger role than in the original. The way the ultra-wealthy work in India is also different, they can buy their way through most difficult situations, which raises the stakes in a drama.

This is, of course, because there is also more corruption here than in a European scenario. So, in the original, the investigation remains only in flashback, but here the cops are actually part of the crime story, in the sense that they are on the payroll of one of the wealthy parents. There are a lot of social and cultural differences like this, which I had to consider. I just used the original series like one uses a source novel, for the bare plot and character arcs. Honestly, once that was down, _Class_ just began to have a life of its own.

How is film writing different from show writing?

Show writing is more dramatic, several arcs are happening – the arc of each episode, the season arc. You need more hooks to keep audiences engaged for such a long period, almost seven hours in the case of *Class*. Also, characters can't change as much as they do in films, they have to stay closer to their 'personas' so that you can milk them for multiple seasons, etc. It's mostly that their relationships with others change.

In total contrast, in a film, characters change so much by the end that they are sometimes transformed beyond recognition.

Series writing tends to be more dialogue- and plot-heavy, more theatrically written compared to film where a lot can be communicated visually without dialogue. Film closes all the doors on the story whereas series keeps them open so they can continue for many more seasons.

Which film-makers and films have influenced you across different stages of your life?

The Japanese New Wave is probably the most important single influence, especially the films of Shohei Imamura like *Intentions of Murder* and *Endless Desire*. In terms of Indian film-makers, the one I find most inspiring – other than Ray and Ghatak – is G. Aravindan. His films are from some other world.

If Ashim Ahluwalia's life were a film, which one would it be?

The Spirit of the Beehive – Victor Erice.

What An... | 99

How's him with all their thoughts about writing.

FOUR

Avinash Das

Imet Avinash Das one evening at his office in Versova, which is brilliantly named: The Slums of Bollywood. Upon introducing myself as a poet, he said, '*Yeh interview wagairah hota rahega, pehle kuchh poetry sunao bhai.*' (We have plenty of time for such interviews, but you must let me hear your poetry).

I didn't recite poetry to him that day but did it the next time we met for another occasion. Avinash Das wears his politics on his sleeve but that doesn't stop him from being extremely friendly, welcoming, and almost too honest as a person for Bollywood.

He is the writer-director of *Anaarkali of Aarah*, which is bestowed with a 100 per cent rating on Rotten Tomatoes as I write this.

Would it be fair to say that you're a journalist who turned into a film-maker?

Yes, and I'd say that it wasn't a well-planned journey or anything like that. As a journalist, one looks for stories and as a film-maker, as well, one looks for stories. I was a journalist from around 1996 to around 2013-14. I encountered a lot of stories in that span but those stories would get lost, they'd slip away from me. In a newspaper, a story lasts for two or three days. And the fact that many stories died would pain me. So, I was searching for a format where the stories I encounter would live on, where they'd have a larger shelf-life. In this quest, I attempted a novel, I wrote poetry but then I realized that the receiving canvas of film writing is quite powerful and wide. There is more praise in it as well. And that's why I took on this journey. Having said that, it's not an easy journey. I think no journey of passion is an easy one, especially in India. If you are chasing a passion, society or the people in your family don't generally support you. If you are doing a certain kind of work and have found some stability in it, which was journalism in my case, it's difficult to leave it all and start something else. You may have a family to run, and bills to pay. It's not easy. Even if one person in your family says that they are with you, it bolsters your courage. And that's what happened to me and now here I am on this journey.

How does your experience of journalistic writing talk to the film writer in you?

The thing is when I used to write stories earlier, just for fun or even poetry for that matter, I used to write whatever came to my mind. But journalism taught me to be factual. I realized how important facts are, and to be to the point as a writer. Journalism has very little space for feelings. Poetry and stories, on the other hand, have a lot of space for them. So, from poetry, I learnt to articulate my feelings and from journalism, I learnt to understand how much is necessary and how much is not. I think all the types of writing I have done have helped me as a screenwriter. I believe that if you have been involved with writing, of any kind at all, it would be easier for you to write screenplays than for those people who have never written anything.

Would you advise an aspiring young screenwriter to go to a film school to learn the craft?

I can speak with examples. In songwriting, for instance, sometimes you write the lyrics and then the tune is made and sometimes it is the other way around. This has been happening for years. Just like that, even in screenwriting, it could work both ways. Since I have never taken formal training, it's easy for me to say that formal training is useless. I usually pour myself onto the paper. If I had studied screenwriting formally, my discipline of writing for the screen might have been different. I am not saying good or bad – but it would be different. And I don't think of myself as a perfect screenwriter or anything like that. But personally, I believe one mustn't get too involved with technicality. Having said that, if you are not just a screenwriter but a director as well, you will automatically learn a thing or two about the craft – when to cut something down, when not. How to transition from one scene to another, time management, and stuff like that.

Do you think a good screenwriter also needs to have a good sense of editing?

Look, as a human being, you keep editing yourself. You set yourself a time to eat, to sleep, etc. There is a format in which you live your life. Even in writing, you have to keep editing everything you write. I tend to think every writer is an editor in his mind. I think it's very important to be an editor. Without editing, forget writing, you can't even live a fruitful life.

Away from the technical stuff now, what was your childhood like in Bihar?

My childhood was ordinary. Nothing special about it. I grew up as any other lower-middle-class kid. There wasn't particularly an atmosphere of reading and writing at my home, I'd say. But the people were educated. My grandfather, in fact, was a Maithili poet. Maithili is my mother tongue. But after him, in my father's generation, no one really got into writing or literature.

After my grandfather passed away, our family had a bit of a tough time. There wasn't much money in the family. We were in the Darbhanga district of Bihar, about 180 km from Patna. We were in a very small village. My father did a good thing that he took me and my sisters to a town nearby, which was around five to six kilometres away, and put us in a good school. Back in our village, most girls would never study after the tenth standard. But my father put my sisters in a good school and educated them. We studied in a government school. And I was somewhat confused about my studies. I failed in the seventh standard. Back in my school days, I had a nostalgia for my grandfather's poetry. I used to think about it a lot.

At that time, I got exposed to some theatre as well and those experiences which I took in at the time contributed a lot to the person I am today. I remember the first thing I ever wrote was a poem about a girl I liked in school. I still remember those lines:

> *Milan ka waqt hai pratak*
> *Harik hai shaam tanhai*
> *Arey woh din bhi kya*
> *Jiss din tumhari yaad na aayi*

> (The time of our union has come
> Without you, every moment is as dark as the evening
> There are no days
> When you are not on my mind

How important is it for an artist in today's time to be politically inclined?

I don't think it's necessary for an artist to be politically inclined. But the question that arises is that without being politically aware, in a country like ours, you cannot truly understand the meaning of anything. You cannot fully fathom all the layers of a story or an event without being politically aware. I think political awareness makes anything more relevant. So, I think an artist needn't be politically aware but should be if they have to do justice to their art.

Where is the freedom of expression in this country today?

I don't think it exists. But I'll tell you something interesting. In countries where there's a glorious democracy and a lot of freedom of expression, art is largely ineffective. Their art does not have too many shades. But history is testimony to the fact that great literature has been created in places and at times when the state has been converted into a gunda (ruffian) state. Now, for instance, if one says that the state is bad or anti-people, there's nothing great or artistic about saying it. But if the state shoots the person who says stuff like this, the person will have to change the format of his expression. He will still say the same thing but in an indirect manner, right under the nose of the state. If you follow many Russian writers of the early times or even Charlie Chaplin in the times of Hitler, they all changed their format.

If you are an artist, you would know more than one way to say what you must. The quest is to say it effectively and to be able to say it for a long time. Yes, I do believe this is a difficult time for our country. I would call it a sort of an undeclared emergency. But one way to look at it as an artist is that this is a huge opportunity. Some people will change sides, some will go silent, and some will try to write something in their screenplay but the censor board will not let it pass. The people who are able to navigate this scene will be true artists. I think this is the era that will show us who the real artists are.

Have you ever had a goal or sort of a communication objective as a writer about a set of things you wanted to say to the world?

I don't think artists can have a fixed goal. Artists are like flowing water. They will find their direction along the way. But the thing is that a cinema writer, as I call it, has it different from say, a storywriter or a poet. You can think of a poem and write it; imagine a painting and draw it on a canvas. But cinema is not something you can realize just by thinking. It requires a lot more effort, and a whole team, it has a lot of boxes and constraints too. Most importantly, it requires a much higher budget than the other arts we spoke about. As an artist of film, I do have a goal. I want to 'say' a film that nobody else can say or is allowed to say. The problem with Bollywood is that everybody gets confined to a genre. Have you ever heard anyone asking Steven Spielberg what his genre is? He has made everything from *Jurassic Park* to *Schindler's List* to *ET*. But here, everybody is typecast as a genre film-maker. I want to make horror too, in my style. Or, even a serial killer film. At the same time, I want to also tell very rooted village tales like the stories of Phanishwar Nath Renu.

How difficult was it in Bollywood to write and make your critically acclaimed film *Anaarkali of Aarah*, which has a rare Rotten Tomatoes rating of 100/100?

Oh, I didn't know about the Rotten Tomatoes rating. Never checked it. And to be honest, I never sold this film in Bollywood. Way back in 2006 when I was working the night shift in my office, I was exploring YouTube, which was rather new at the time. The night shift in journalism is relatively lean in terms of work. I used to spend most of my time at night doing YouTube searches. During that time, I came across a rather cheap video. A singer was singing something erotically and she had no expression on her face. I thought how she could have such a blank face! She must be thirty-five or thirty-six, but she was looking around sixty. I started searching for the singer's story. And I tried doing a story about that woman in the newspaper. But she was an unknown person and no newspaper would carry it.

For the next four to five years, that story stayed with me. Then finally, one day, my friend Manoj Bajpayee was in Delhi to promote *Gangs of Wasseypur*. Whenever he'd come to Delhi, he'd call me to meet him. Manoj introduced me to one of the producers as his younger brother. I narrated the story to the producer. He asked me if I had a screenplay. I said I did though actually I didn't. We fixed an appointment for after a week for the narration. In that week, I wrote the whole screenplay, in whatever form I could. Then I met the producer for the narration, who had come along with eight to ten others and I narrated my screenplay to them over drinks. The guy said that he loved it and he wanted to do it.

This was 2012. But unfortunately, at that time, it did not work out. Then from 2012 to 2015, I tried to sell it a lot in Bombay. A lot of people, including some of my friends, tried to snatch the film away from me saying that they should direct it and I wouldn't be able to pull it off as my first film. But I wanted to direct it myself. Finally, in 2015, the film happened and I got to direct it too.

Your next film was *Raat Baaki Hai*, which did not do too well. How did you happen to start working on that one?

I got the proposal for the film from Zee5. It was not my idea. When I realized that my friend Siddharth Mishra was writing it, I thought, 'Great, let me direct it.' I consider it a film I did for others, not for myself. But if you have to stay afloat in this business, you will have to balance it out with projects that you want to do and those that you have to do.

You have been a poet, and a storywriter and you have focussed mostly on cinema. What is it about cinema that attracts you so much?

I think cinema has many challenges. It also offers more accolades. Also, I think Hindi cinema has a certain mainstream that needs to change. There are very few people like Shoojit Sircar or Nagraj Manjule who are changing it. Sometimes a film like Amit Masurkar's *Newton* comes along and shows us that this can be done here. But there are very few people who want to make cinema like that. I think in poetry and fiction, there already are enough good writers. Cinema needs more people. At least the kind of cinema I love needs people. That's why I chose to focus on cinema. Even if Bollywood offers you a complete pulp story, you can still give it undercurrents and a *tadka* (spicing-up) of your sensibility.

Have you ever thought of making a full-blown mainstream Bollywood film?

Of course, I have. My favourite subject is history. But in Bollywood, there are many risks of working on a film that deals with it. You will be at risk from the state, the narrative, the censorship. The biggest risk is that of the budget. For example, Anusha Rizvi, who made *Peepli Live*, wanted her second film to be something called 'Sea of Poppies' or *Afeem*, based on Amitav Ghosh's novel. She had budgeted it to be around rupees sixty crore. But when she entered the market to make the film, she was told by producers that with that kind of budget, she must have a star in the film. She was convinced that she couldn't make that film with a star. Unfortunately, the film is not made yet. I think these kinds of stories need to come out. Even I like Amitav Ghosh a lot. I like the writer Sunil Gangopadhyay's work a lot. He has a fabulous book on the Bengal Renaissance. I would love to make films about their work.

Have you experienced any jealousy in Bollywood?

Look, I think jealousy is a natural human emotion. It is not a mark of a bad person or something like that. It exists everywhere. Even in a village when someone else's son gets a job, one feels why did my son not get one? It's natural to be jealous sometimes. Having said that, I came very late to Bombay. And wherever I have reached today is only because of my friends. They were the ones who supported me. Imtiaz Ali went to watch my film *Anaarkali of Aarah* and stood up and clapped for it in the theatre. Then he called me up and asked me to direct a series for him. I think Bombay is the only city where if you tell someone that you want to make a film, they won't discard you. People here believe in you. Try telling someone in Delhi or Patna about your big dreams and they will tear you apart or look down on you. Bombay accepts you. It is an amazing city in that way!

You used to run a literary blog called Mohalla Live, which was very famous back in the day. Tell me how you took to blogging.

I am an anxious, unstable person. And I always want to do things and try new things. Way back in 2005, when I was working as a journalist, blogging was very, very new. There were many English bloggers but very few Hindi ones. Even a few Hindi bloggers would write about food and travel and stuff like that. There was a person called Sunil Deepak who had published some of my poems on his Hindi website. He lived in Italy at the time. He was the one who told me how to create a blog and also gave me a tool to write in Hindi. Then I started a literary blog. It mostly focussed on Hindi literature and sometimes cinema as well – opinion, criticism, everything. I invited many writers to contribute. One day, I told Ravish (Kumar) and he started writing there every day. Anurag (Kashyap) contributed a lot too. In fact, in *Gangs of Wasseypur*, he also promoted Mohalla Live, which by then was a website.

Who are your favourite film-makers and what are your favourite films?

I think Steven Spielberg is my favourite film-maker in the world. And then Christopher Nolan too, who has his way of making films. In India, I like Shekhar Kapoor a lot – his *Bandit Queen* is fabulous. Even *Mr. India* is a film I quite like. I love Bimal Roy too. I have always loved the cinema of Ritwik Ghatak. Also I always liked Rituparno Ghosh's work. In modern times, I love Nagraj Manjule a lot. I think he is an amazing film-maker. I like Anurag Kashyap's work a lot – especially his work till *Gangs of Wasseypur*. In those days, I used to think of him as a marvellous film-maker. Then I have always admired Vittorio De Sica who made *Bicycle Thieves*. Then, of course, who doesn't like Satyajit Ray? These days, even a lot of new Malayalam cinema is fabulous.

Who are your favourite poets?

There are too many. Nagarjun, Nirala, the greats. Then also a Hindi poet that nobody knows of in the so-called mainstream of Hindi literature – Kailash Gautam. He wrote outstanding poems even about a subject like the court and law and order. I like Arun Kamal, Alok Dhanwa, Rajesh Joshi, and Vinod Kumar Shukla. Among the new poets, I like R. Chetan Kranti and Firoz Khan. These are people who are writing different kinds of poetry.

Could you name one film that you wish you had made?

Schindler's List. I think if that was made by me, I would die in peace. It's not a film. It's an epic. Probably my favourite film of all time.

Do you think art can really change the world?

The world can only be changed by people. And art can change people. Art cannot directly change the world. Time is like a lake. And art is like a stone that you fling into it. That's why art can create ripples in the world. Yes, art is a tool, sometimes even a weapon. But only people can change the world, art can't.

FIVE

Biswapati Sarkar

Biswapati Sarkar is the writer of shows such as *TVF Pitchers, Jadugar, Barely Speaking with Arnub, Permanent Roommates,* and many others. He is also the man who wrote what is probably India's first scripted viral video on YouTube – *Rowdies* – which is an iconic spoof of the TV show *Roadies.*

I met Biswapati Sarkar at his office at Mount Mary in Bandra. He was extremely kind and humble in his demeanour and what stood out to me was the amazing discipline with which he goes about his work. He knew every word of what he was saying, and he came across as a person who thinks through everything.

When and how did you first think of becoming a writer?

I would say the fantasy was always there. When you grow up in a small town, you don't know what exactly it is to be a professional writer. But I used to read a lot. There was this government library where I used to spend a lot of my time reading books like *Alice in Wonderland, Famous Five,* books by Tom Hardy, also a few literary books. But only when I went to IIT did I come to know about writing professionally and some of the opportunities it offered. That's where I started writing plays. At that time, most of the plays that would happen in college were not contemporary. So, when I wrote a play, a lot of people attended it. It was a 1000-seater auditorium and people were sitting on the stairs as well. They were responding to the jokes and I think about 70 per cent of the jokes did land. So as a first-time writer, it was a big deal for me.

Eventually, some of my seniors were talking about starting a YouTube channel. YouTube had just started becoming a part of popular culture in 2010-11 and at that time, it was a very different world. In 2011, I came down to Bombay to explore if I could make a career as a writer.

It was an interesting time because there were very few or no references for sketch comedy back then. There was the *Saturday Night Live* show or *SNL*, or there were some news articles by Onion, and then a vague reference was *The Great Indian Comedy Show*. So, there was this thought, why don't we do sketches? So, one of those nights, I wrote a sketch called *Rowdies*. That video went insanely viral at that time. It was probably one of the first scripted viral videos in India. At that time, there was no paid promotion. When we put it up, our ambition was to get 50,000 views, and guess what, it got one million views. At that time, one million views were unthinkable. Imagine … this was a time when there was no 'share' button on YouTube – people used to share the links on email!

That was probably the first time even my parents thought that something could be made of what I had chosen to do. Nowadays, of course, YouTube is a legit career option but this was a very different world. So, I think that was the time when writing graduated for me from a mere fantasy to a genuine career option I could be serious about.

You have been one of the core members of The Viral Fever or TVF team and TVF has been one of the foremost channels for original YouTube content in India. Was the journey of the company, in terms of the direction it took with content, well-planned from the beginning?

Well, I'd say, there was a vision from the beginning that we wanted to make something for the youth of India. Because the youth of India was not represented in any mainstream content at the time. For instance, when *Rowdies* came out and became a rage, there was also this kind of fear because we were making fun of something so mainstream and popular. But you know, I always found what they were saying stupid … and not just me but my friends used to laugh at them as well. So, I was sure that there were people in other colleges who also found it stupid but nobody was talking about it.

Many people talk about making content for the 'Indian youth'. What really is the sensibility of the Indian youth that you guys at TVF got so right?

It's very difficult to answer that question because 60 per cent of India is youth and we're talking about around eighty crore people. So, it's impossible that anyone can cater to all of them because it's just a diverse audience. I think that most of the Indian youth need representation of some kind and by that, I mean the experiences and the problems that they must deal with. Some regional films in India have done that well but Hindi cinema or Bollywood is so far behind. I think regional films are successful because they understand the audience better. The way youth is portrayed in Bollywood films does not exist in reality. That's a fantasy. The reason why most young people don't connect with Bollywood films is that those films don't surprise them anymore. What they want is freshness.

When we made *Permanent Roommates*, the idea was to treat live-in relationships in a casual everyday way – the way they unfold in this country. When we did *Pitchers*, it was because startups are a subject that a large section of Indian youth is interested in. Similarly, we did many such shows based on the several worlds that the youth inhabits and are all around us but were never really shown on the mainstream. I think that was our idea and we stuck to it and that's how we tried to see and then portray Indian youth.

You know, in earlier days, the majority of the people I used to meet, the people who wrote and made Hindi shows, did not watch

Hindi shows. I think everyone was doing it for the money. The kind of things that used to be discussed in meetings were like this: '*Baroda mein athaarah saal ki Pinky hai.* (Eighteen-year-old Pinky lives in Baroda.) Will she relate to this story?' I used to be like, 'Man, I don't know how this Pinky from Baroda thinks. But Biswapati from Rourkela can relate to this story and that's why I think some others will as well.' After a point, you can't take the opinions of 100 crore people, you have to do what you think is right.

How much of a role has IIT (Indian Institutes of Technology) played a role in your journey?

I think a huge one. I studied engineering because at that time for someone like me engineering and medicine were the only viable careers that we knew of. So, tenth-twelfth standards and engineering were like the basic things to do. But in college, I met so many smart people and suddenly got exposed to so many ideas and content. I must have seen around 3000 movies in those five years at IIT. That's where I got acquainted with world cinema.

TVF *Pitchers* is the first piece of long-form branded content in India. Could you walk me through its journey?

There was this idea that Arunabh (Kumar) had discussed with Amit (Golani) sometime. They had gone to Bangalore and they saw these guys discussing startups over a beer and they were talking about pitching some ideas. So that's where the name *Pitchers* came from. It was always a story of four people. I remember the first briefing for *Pitchers* where we cracked how to integrate Kingfisher as a brand. I said what if the character is drunk and he says, '*Tu beer hai … tu beer hai, bhen*****' (You are a beer … you're a beer, ****).' Eventually, the scene was cracked and it became very popular. The way we went about *Pitchers* is that we wrote two episodes and we shot them. Then we wrote two more and shot them. And then the finale was written and shot. At that time, production was not quite our strength and we figured a way, thankfully, to work with the budgets we had.

Over the last seven years, do you think the quality of branded content in India has reached where it could have been after a great start with *Pitchers*?

No, I don't think it is where it could have been. And I think it's largely because brand managers are usually scared. They want to save their jobs, and rather than thinking of doing something crazy, their first priority is damage control. This is the budget; this is the logo that needs to increase in size – that's all they want. At the end of the day, for them, it is a screenshot on their PowerPoint. Neither are they interested beyond that nor do I think they really understand the potential of branded content. Also, I think most of them see it differently. They want the brand name to be said thrice, for instance, without understanding that it would put off the audience and maybe it's better to say it once and say it well. Even from a creator's point of view, I'd say if brands are going to dictate the writing so much, you'd rather get dictated by Netflix or some other OTT, who at least understands the business of content.

One of my favourite series of digital stories in India is *Barely Speaking with Arnub*. Could you tell me what made you write that and then act on it?

So, we did this video called *Bollywood Aam Aadmi Party*, which became a rage at that time. I had written it and the actor who was supposed to play Arnub in it got a paid shoot on the same day. So, Amit (Golani), who was directing it told me that I should play Arnub. I was quite apprehensive but eventually did it and that video became very popular. Then I think *Happy New Year* was coming out and Red Chillies had contacted us saying that we could get a one-hour with Shah Rukh Khan if we wanted to do something. The idea was that I'd write something and then we would improvise on that set. Shah Rukh was late to the shoot – eight hours late – and I was a little pissed about it. But then when he walked in, everything changed. I was in awe of him and still absorbing the fact that I was sitting across from Shah Rukh Khan – the Shah Rukh Khan! And let me tell you, he is such a nice guy! I have not met one person in my life who has met Shah Rukh and has had bad things to say about him.

Within five minutes, he was a co-actor and very, very cooperative. I remember, when we started shooting, I fumbled the first line because I was shooting with Shah Rukh Khan. So, someone behind the camera shouted, 'It's okay, Bisso. *He is* just human.' So, Shah Rukh turns around and says, 'Now you're pushing it.' That's it. The ice was broken and I remember at one point, he delivered a better punchline than the one I had written. So, that's when I stopped looking at the script and then we just improvised. After that video, it kind of became an idea that we should do it with more celebrities and I was increasingly reluctant because it's very mean, it's rude and I hate insulting people like that. But then as you know, it happened!

What's your process of writing?

You know, even when I meet younger writers, the only thing I tell them is to stop thinking of this as art and think of this as work. When it comes to writing shows, I think it makes sense to develop a season arc. However, I am not a big fan of character sketches. In fact, I actively tell people not to do character sketches. I recently had a fight with someone who studied in film school who was making a sketch where he was writing everything about the character's past, his father – but then I thought how is that relevant? A character exists within the pages of the story. I don't need to know his childhood trauma in advance for instance. If while writing the story, at some point, I feel that giving this character a particular childhood trauma will serve a purpose in the story, I would do it.

How did you handle your failures?

I think one particular thing that comes to mind is *Bisht Please*. This was in 2017. Nidhi (Bisht) was doing this show and I was really excited about the idea but unfortunately, the show didn't do well. That kind of broke me for two or three weeks because this event was after a string of successes. But then you sit and analyse what went wrong and you realize a few things. I think sometimes writers tend to have knee-jerk reactions like the audience didn't get it and stuff like that. But I think that's not the best way to process it. As they say in Hindi, this is a kind of 'Sadhana' and beyond a point, the results don't say much at all. As a writer, your only goal should be to tell the story honestly. We are part of a generation that is trying to do global stuff, we don't have any mentors, and we don't have anything to learn from at least in our proximity so we are bound to make mistakes.

What is your greatest strength as a writer?

I would say probably sincerity. That's the only thing.

What's your biggest limitation as a writer?

I am wondering which one to start with. I would say I am slightly better now but I need to be more disciplined, giving work definite hours every day. Then I would say procrastination. I used to be very jealous when I was starting out but now, I am jealous in a very good way, I think. I genuinely call up writers of the films and shows I like and I buy them lunch just to understand their process – I have made some very good friends in this process. Then I would say I want to read more than I do right now. A thing I want to do is to travel within India and pick up dialects that are spoken in different parts of the country. Some writers are very good at writing how they speak Hindi in Goa for instance or how they speak in a particular district in UP (Uttar Pradesh). I am not very good at that.

What's your favourite work?

I would say it would be between *Pitchers* and *Jadugar*. I think *Jadugar* because it was such a mammoth story that we could pull out and that too during the lockdown, and *Pitchers* because I think at that point, I was not sure how to handle a show and I thought we ended up doing a good job. Had I not acted in *Barely Speaking with Arnub*, I would have enjoyed it a lot more but that one remains a crowd-favourite.

Which films, shows, and books have influenced you as a writer?

There is this writer called William Goldman who has written films like *Misery*. I think when I read his books on cinema, I can relate to his world a lot. Then (Akira) Kurosawa's work, I think I can watch any day. I love *The Wire*, the show. Then in comedy, I love *Seinfeld*. Then I love books by Stephen King. That way there is so much good work happening. Of course, the bad stuff outnumbers the good stuff. But because of the internet, you get access to the good stuff as well.

If you had to describe in a few words your journey so far, what would you say?

I think I have tremendous gratitude. That's what I'd say. Writing was my fantasy. To be a writer in this country and to be able to make money from it is a privilege for sure. Today, I am in a position where I could just take two months off and explore a subject if I wanted to. I have a loving family, I am married to a great woman, and I work with excellent people – I think I have a lot of gratitude.

SIX

Chaitanya Tamhane

I consider myself extremely fortunate to have met many, many people across different fields and walks of life due to my work in advertising and poetry, and due to my travel and my general curiosity about worlds different from my own. Out of all those fascinating people, there are very, very few who, I thought, were touched by genius. Chaitanya Tamhane is one of them.

He is the writer-director of the internationally acclaimed Marathi films *Court* and *The Disciple*. He won a seat at one of the toughest programmes in the world of cinema to crack, the Rolex Mentor and Protégé Arts Initiative, and got mentored by none other than Alfonso Cuaron.

Chaitanya is an auteur, a thinker of enormous ability, a person with a phenomenally nuanced eye for looking at the world, and a man who has mastered the craft of film-making while finding his language of cinema.

I met Chaitanya at Independence Brewery in Versova one evening, on a day, when he had, 'Exactly one hour.' Not only is he a film-maker of very, very high standards, but he is also a supremely skilled mentalist.

I think that if Chaitanya continues to work with the same uncorrupt approach that he has managed so far, a few years from now, he may go on to achieve the prowess and the stature in world cinema that no Indian except for Satyajit Ray has ever achieved, and a spot in cinema history that is reserved for the best of the best.

You've quoted somewhere that you are on an artistic journey of your own. Can you tell me what that journey is?

The artistic journey is: one, finding my truth as to how authentic I can be in my expression, and two, it is about being pleasant because a human being is not static. We all change with our age and experiences. With every project, I try to capture my concerns, worldview, and feelings at that particular time of my life. It is also about how I make my work more me. Now, I have been working for two years on a new script. I have been at it for two years and I fail every day. I haven't written a single word yet but I am convinced that this will be more me than my last two films. On one hand, I would like to push my imagination and explore directions that I have never explored before and on the other, I want to express my personality, my experiences, my inner worldview, my fears, my vulnerabilities, and my nightmares with more and more honesty. In a way, these two things may not seem to go together but that's the idea and that's my attempt.

Do you think cinema, for you, has to be personal?

I would never say that cinema has to be anything. I can only talk about my particular artistic goals and my pursuits. Also, it is tricky to say what is personal because the person keeps changing. I went through really dark times but what's come out of it is much lighter, way more buoyant. Now, the personal expression has to be of the person I am now and not of who I was or of some narrative I had made up in my head to tell myself. And also, it's always a marriage with imagination, right?

Personal storytelling does not mean that I have to only tell the story of what I have seen or lived. In a way, all fiction is autobiographical. You could be projecting that in a fantasy land or in a superhero film for all you know but it is always coming from a certain lens. So, for me, the general anchor has always been the truth. Not any objective truth but my truth. What I create should have some thematic resonance for me. Instead of just trying to impress an audience or just working with a circumstance or a situation. I mean, even though I sometimes feel immersed in situations and plots I generally tend to work at it the other way around.

On your unusual journey in cinema, what's the purchase that you are looking at?

The journey is the purchase. I mentioned that one changes as a person. In a way, the people who made my first two films or even my short film were different people from who I am today. Also, somewhere, when you are younger you are trying to prove a point and trying to declare that hey, I exist! In that sense, the success and the failure of your projects and the way they are received might end up influencing you and what you end up chasing. But right now, the world has changed since I started working when I was seventeen. There are many different mediums now and sometimes the most profound of ideas can be condensed in a meme and you don't have to read a thousand-page novel to understand everything.

So, right now one of my goals is also communication. I am trying to explore how not to be stuck in a twentieth-century idea of expression and how to be present in what is happening around me. It's also about finding how to use contemporary tools and find newer expressions rather than being insular and being in a bubble considering what has worked in the past for me. Also, for a fact, it is trying not to be in the arthouse bubble. I am a little bit done with that and want to explore new directions.

Can you tell me what attracted you to cinema and when?

I think ever since the time I remember, I wanted to be an actor. My exposure was TV, Bollywood films, and Marathi theatre. I used to watch a lot of the mainstream Bollywood films as a child but I don't remember watching any film whole. I used to only watch the comedy parts. I only wanted to laugh and experience the happy parts. So, I wanted to be an actor and one day, I don't know why, I wrote this piece called *The Autobiography of a Commode*. I must have been nine or ten years old then. So, writing in that sense came to me naturally.

Now, I think, on the other hand, I try to overcome the fear of failure and it is difficult for me to write but back then, it was very different. I have been writing since I was a child. I have written a one-act play, I have written a full-length play, and so on. The film thing, however, happened differently. Honestly, I identified myself only as a writer. The reason why I directed those projects is because I didn't see anybody else fit enough to do so.

The one-act play for instance that I wrote … at that time I was working at Balaji Productions and I gave it to somebody else to direct. When I saw the play, I was devastated. We had submitted it to a competition and we also won an award for it but I thought what I had written and what the guy made out of it were two entirely different things. Even now, although writing is something I really hate – it's the most dreadful, scary, time-consuming process – if you ask me if I could live without directing, I think I very well can. But can I live without writing? I don't think so. It is one of those major forms of expression that I understand.

Being a Bombay boy and having worked with the likes of Balaji at an early age, how did you manage not to get lured by the fame and fortune of Bollywood?

I think it's a matter of circumstances and luck. So, for example, in my late teens, when I was at Balaji, it was a game for me. I was getting paid for what I like doing and I was like wow, this is great. So, I did skirt around Bollywood in those days. In fact, I actually did work as an assistant for a few days on a project that was supposed to be a sequel to the film *No Entry* and I gave them some ideas about the wives of all the protagonists being pregnant at the same time and they liked that idea and all of that happened.

But then of course there came a point when I discovered world cinema and I developed my taste. Nobody was making me any offers to work with them anyway so I thought I'd be on my journey. In those days, I had sent out applications to some fifty advertising agencies because there was pressure to earn money but nobody really hired me. Nobody even called me for an interview. And it was a very difficult time mentally for me. So, then I made my short film which nobody paid attention to in India but was received well internationally – a pattern that I see with my work to this day.

One day, Vivek (Gomber) just told me to write my script and offered me a monthly salary of fifteen thousand rupees to do that and that was the turning point in my life. I think Vivek should get a lot of credit for all my work. So, yes, but having said that, even back then I never really had an ambition to make it big in Bollywood or something like that. I just wanted to do good work and I wanted to do my work.

Could you please take me through the journey of writing your breakthrough film *Court*?

For me, the theme is more important than the plot. The plot kind of happens on its own. So, in the case of *Court*, the main idea was observing the courtroom players outside of the court and then going into their personal lives. The idea was to set up a court case and then subvert expectations by going in a totally different direction. But I didn't have the case for the longest time. That was the last thing that fell in place.

I had a lot of stuff ready about the public prosecutor, the lawyers, the judge, and his personal life – things that came to me by purely observing various court cases that I would attend during the period of my research. I was also very inspired by Bong Joon Ho, especially

Memories of Murder. So, I was like what if he made a courtroom drama? What would it be like?

That was also the time when I was trying to find my politics. Ramu Ramanathan was a huge influence on me and has been a great mentor to me. He would take me to watch *Gadar*, he would mention Sambhaji Bhagat to me, and so on. Then I read an article by S. Anand on sanitation workers. So, things kept brewing and it took me a long while to find the right kind of case but fortunately, I did find it. In its making, in its treatment, *Court* is also a manifestation of everything I was not happy with in Indian cinema. They would make a so-called subtle film and then the messaging would just be vomited in the end and everything would be spelt out. There would be some nagging exposition in the film and I said I don't want to do that. Then there were other things about Indian cinema such as all the films I was watching were tonally inconsistent or the characters never rang true or it wasn't the Bombay that I had seen. So I tried not to do everything that I wasn't happy with.

So, some of it also came from that place of disagreement because I was young and cocky and wanted to rebel. I know a lot of writers who would outline everything that's going to happen in the film but I can't really work that way. I have my scene ideas and my characters ready but a lot of times I let the film come together by itself. I observe a lot and I observe non-judgmentally. By this, I let a subconscious form around the subject, and the imagination automatically seeps in. That is the process I have tried to follow.

Also, at the time I was writing *Court*, I was getting a salary from Vivek to write the script and I lived with my folks in one BHK (Bedroom-Hall-Kitchen) in Andheri. There were four of us in that small little space and for some reason, I wanted to write at 7 in the evening when they wanted to watch TV. The computer was in the hall and I get distracted very easily so all of them had to be quiet while I was writing. I was that spoilt brat in the family and they would be thinking, what the hell is he writing? I came from an insular family; my school was next door and we were typical middle-class.

Was your next film, *The Disciple*, in some way, an allegory to your own artistic journey and struggles?

Quite directly it is, yes. *The Disciple* is a spiritual adaptation of a play I had written called *Grey Elephants* in Denmark, which Vivek Gomber had acted in. That was the story of a magician who wanted to break away from his father's cheesy, outdated magic and wanted to do some contemporary, crazy magic, and wanted to pursue magic as an art form but art does not love him back. I had written this when I was twenty-one. So that concept stayed with me and it was a personal fear for me that what if I turned out to be an artist who just didn't have it in him?

The Disciple is, of course, a more grown-up, more mature version of that concept. And the film is also a counter to this fake, fairytale narrative where always only one person is celebrated and we are all made to feel bombarded and anxious and everybody is only looking at those 1 per cent of successful people but nobody is looking at the 99 per cent in any field who don't really make it that big or aren't that gifted. A part of the story came from this guy who used to be my granny's neighbour where I used to spend summer vacations. He lived in a one-room chawl in Mahim – Guruji's house in *The Disciple* is an exact replica of that house. This guy was so serious about cricket and he had this ball hung in a sock and he would keep playing at it with his bat. He would go for the Ranji Trophy and so many tournaments. There was no other way for him, he just wanted to be a cricketer. The next thing I knew, seven years later, he was working in a bank. That journey fascinated me.

Also, while making *The Disciple*, it was a deep philosophical exploration for me as to what is success, how we define excellence, what values are important in life, and how big a victim I am of this capitalist framework that we live in.

Now tell me how did you end up working with the great Alfonso Cuaron and what was the experience like?

I have never really had a proper mentor in film-making. There was a program that I knew existed for a long time. It is probably the world's most difficult arts program to get into. One, because you can't apply for it; you need to get invited for it. I always wanted to get into it and one year they invited me to apply. I learnt that Cuaron was going to be the mentor so without thinking for a second, I applied. This was the time when *Court* was getting international reception but I thought I wanted to learn more. So, I was lucky enough to be in the top five and then Cuaron interviewed me and I got selected. Yes, it was a crazy experience. A whole different level that those guys operate on. It was brilliant to see Cuaron work on *Roma* because I was there for the shoot, the grade, the sound, and sometimes for the edit. He and his entire team were such a wonderful bunch of people to work with and learn from. The scale, and the craft that he was operating with changed me forever as a person and a film-maker. Also, Cuaron did so much for *The Disciple* – he was even kind enough to present the film.

Who are your influences as a screenwriter and a film-maker?

Right now, my influences are authentic artists. The people who weave poetry in their work like Agnes Varda for instance. She is one of my Everests. Then, Abbas Kiarostami, the way he understands human emotions and the world is mind-blowing. Then some graphic novels sometimes make me feel that that is what I want to be – not literally but artistically. I saw *I May Destroy You* by Michaela Coel and I was blown away, then I saw Bo Burnham's *Inside* and found it brilliant. I think their nuanced expression and the way some people interpret the world fascinate me. Then there are films that I think are Everests like Fellini's *8 and a Half*, *Underground* by Emir Kusturica. There are films that have blown me over like a lot of Chaplin's work and many others.

But if you ask me about the kind of work I would like to do, it is more in the zone of *Taste of Cherry* by Kiarostami or *The Gleaners and I* by Agnes Varda. It's creating poetry out of the very ordinary, out of something very simple that attracts me.

Do you look at screenwriting and film-making as a profession?

No, I look at it as a hobby. In fact, I am in search of a profession. I have very seriously learnt and performed magic. And I am seriously considering becoming a travelling magician for a living.

SEVEN

Chandan Kumar

Chandan has worked on several YouTube sketches in his life but, as I write this, he is singularly known as the writer-creator of the show *Panchayat*. *Panchayat* has attracted rave reviews from critics as well as audiences.

I met Chandan for the interview on a Zoom call. Chandan is an easy-going man who is easy to like and befriend, and that's exactly what happened during our conversation. I particularly admire the pragmatism in his approach to writing.

How did the idea of *Panchayat* come up?

The idea came to me in 2017. I started writing it in 2018. What happened is that I had a job at TVF where I worked on many sketches. Then came a point when I thought it was time to graduate to a longer format. So, when they needed a second writer on *Humorously Yours*, I contributed to that as well. Then I had this feeling of developing a show of my own. At the time, I was exploring the idea that an educated guy from a city goes to a village for some kind of job. So initially, I had thought of the protagonist as some kind of an officer working for the government. At around that time, while I was researching this idea, I happened to come across a YouTube video where a panchayat was happening and someone was scolding the Panchayat Sachiv. I found it very funny and I also thought that this was so real. Some things are naturally funny. This was one of them.

My character was an officer. I bounced this Panchayat setup idea with some people in the office. They found it interesting too. So, I started researching about the Panchayat setup. There were some things that I knew already. I was acquainted with the Sarpanchpati Culture and stuff like that, but before this, I had never seen the Panchayat setup as a setup or a world for a show.

A good thing that happened to me at the same time when I was exploring this idea was that at TVF, Arunabh (Kumar) was thinking of making a show set in rural India. So, when I shared the idea, people in the office started liking it and then they asked me to develop it. So, I got a go-ahead in a way. That's how it started. So initially, the character of Abhishek, played by Jeetu (Jeetendra Kumar) was not a Panchayat Sachiv but the overall graph and the spirit of the story always remained the same.

Does any of *Panchayat* come from your life experiences?

See, it doesn't come from a direct life experience. Not that any of my parents was in the Panchayat or anything like that. But yes, some of the members in the family did hold positions in our village ward. Since I grew up in the Patna district, I had an idea of these things. I went to school and college in Patna city, but, where I grew up and my family lived was in a village close to the city. With an upbringing like that, you do have an idea of these things. You know, when you write a scene, you think of your own village … that you're walking down a street and what you see around you. So, you write like that. And this is such a common setup thankfully that when we went for the recce, we found it easily. And then, of course, at the end of the day, this is fiction so we created it.

What do you think makes *Panchayat* stand out so much among Indian OTT shows?

I think when you start writing any show, the first thing you do is to construct the world. And the world gets made after a point. The trickier part is to decide the conflicts in that world. I was aware that there have been a *Swades* and many other films and some international shows that are in a similar space or let's say in a similar world. Stories that have explored going to the countryside. I was very keen on keeping the episodic conflicts fresh. I didn't want anyone thinking '*Arey yaar* (oh man), this is like a copy of *Swades*', or something like that. So, I was very clear that first and foremost, my show should be fun. It should be entertaining. And all the social commentary has to be in the subtext. If you look at it, there is a lot of social commentary in the show but I have consciously tried to conceal it behind the foreground of humour and entertainment.

I believe in doing that. For instance, if I were writing a story about deaddiction, I wouldn't necessarily have to show a deprived kid who is being beaten up by his alcoholic father. There is a section in *Panchayat* where a character running a deaddiction programme is himself drunk. You know, so at the frontal layer of the story, there is no social commentary in this. It is in the subtext.

What's your process of writing?

You know, I take my time to build the world and write my characters. I don't like to rush things. If you're writing eight to ten episodes, you need to take your time to think through stuff. I am a very firm believer in the fact that if something goes wrong on paper, it is very difficult, almost impossible, to fix it on shoot or in any other stage of film-making. The medium is very unpredictable anyway. I believe getting something right on paper is getting 50 per cent of the show right. So, I took my time on *Panchayat* to design the episodic conflicts as well, in deciding how the story plays out over so many episodes and which threads connect where. I think it took around two to three months in 2017 when I had the show idea. Then when I started writing the show in 2018, I think I took around eight to nine months to have the first draft of each episode ready. After that, fine-tuning the draft is a process that is ongoing till the shoot is done.

You are the only writer on *Panchayat* although many people prefer having multiple writers on a show. Where do you stand on writing in collaboration?

I think collaborative writing is great. You know, in the case of *Panchayat*, it just so happened that I managed the whole writing for the show by myself. If you look at it, it's not that I had to write 600 pages! Thankfully, the episodes were short. But if one is to write ten episodes of, say, fifty minutes each, like it happens on some other shows, it might just be very difficult to do that alone. Another thing that collaborative writing helps in is scaling up the project. So overall, I think, collaborative writing is great and I am up for it.

How did the second season of *Panchayat* happen?

When I wrote the first season, obviously, the focus was on the first season. But honestly, since the time I had this idea, I had a feeling that this wouldn't be a one-time thing and could last long. If you noticed, there already are a few threads that were left hanging in the first season. Rinki going to the tank or Manu Devi symbolically carrying the flag suggests that even she might start having a say and not just Pradhan-ji and some others. Of course, the second season was not fully thought out in advance. But after the first season, when I started working on the second one, I picked up from the hanging threads and developed the story from there. Some ideas like the character of Bhushan were thought of after writing season one.

What was your childhood like and how did writing begin for you?

You know, honestly, I was never keen on writing when I was younger. I lived a normal student life in school. I played a lot, hung out with friends, studied when the exams neared, and fared well at my studies.

In the tenth standard, I concentrated more and got good marks. Then I thought I'd study engineering. In the twelfth standard, I did not do too well so my IIT dream never materialized. But then I left Patna to study at an engineering college in Dehradun called ICFAI (Institute of Chartered Financial Analysts of India) University. It was a private university and the fees were on the higher side so all through engineering I had one major objective that I should get out of this college with a job in hand. Luckily, in my fourth year, some good companies came over to the college for placements and I got a job with an IT company, which was in Bhubaneswar.

After starting to work that job, for some time, I started thinking seriously about what exactly I wanted to do in life. Not that I had an answer. But in those days, and I am talking about 2011-12, there was a website called Faking News. So just for fun, as a pastime, I started writing and sending some articles to them and they started publishing me. I used to only do this on weekends for fun and did not get paid for writing at all but it was great to see myself published on a website like Faking News. So, I got more regular. And when your friends see you published, you also get some validation that you seek. At that time, all my friends were thinking of an MBA or a master's in technology and all that. So, I thought that was the time for me to decide if I wanted to stay in tech or move into something else.

Since this Faking News writing was happening and I had started finding it interesting, I was keen on writing. So, at that time, I thought I'd get into advertising and try my hand at copywriting. But then I realized that there is no money in copywriting. So, it was a turn-off for me. Because for me it was very important that I earned some money regularly and I didn't want to break the flow of money I was getting from my engineering job. Luckily what happened around the time is that Faking News was acquired by Network 18 and then they had a couple of job vacancies. And since I was a contributor, they offered me a full-time job. For me, all I needed was for them to match my salary, which they happily did.

So that's why I moved to Mumbai in 2013. I had told myself that I would give writing a try for about a year or two and if I don't find it interesting enough, I will go back to my tech job. The first six months in Mumbai were really difficult, to be a professional writer in a new city, and the process of settling in. But then I started liking it and in 2015, I decided that I would make a career out of writing and now I should also get into screenwriting. By that time, I was already following TVF as an organization and its shows. One day, I came across a vacancy there. I applied and got through.

One more thing about growing up is that obviously, Bihar is not as prosperous a part of the country as many others or the metro cities. I come from a middle-class family in Bihar but maybe a middle-class family in Bihar would be called a lower-middle-class family in Delhi so there are many differences like that. When you grow up in Bihar, you also get to experience and hear a lot of negative things around you, which affects you. At the same time, I am not saying that everyone there is living a terrible life. There is a pace and momentum of their own for people there. But yes, I came from a background like that. All through this, I think my family somewhere had this faith in me that I would do something worthwhile in life. They knew that I was a person who would not turn out to be completely useless even if I took some risks or failed a couple of times.

I think one thing worth mentioning here is that somewhere the protagonist of *Panchayat*, who is a dissatisfied guy and is always thinking that he is going to get out of where he is, has a lot to do with where I was in life after engineering. So, in a way, to add to one of my previous answers about some parts of *Panchayat* coming from life experience, this is certainly one aspect that did.

What's your take on other Indian OTT shows?

I think the best thing that is coming out of the OTT scene is that everyone is getting to express themselves. There may be seventy-five mistakes and not everything will be great but that is precisely the point. Whatever you understand and you think is right can be done now, which I think is a phenomenal space to be in. The nature of this work is experimental and OTT is providing people with a platform to experiment. For example, I wrote *Panchayat* but before that, I was writing whatever I could understand on the TVF YouTube channel. You may hit it big or may learn from your mistakes but it gives you a chance to assess yourself and your ability. You get a sense of your metre and of what you can do and cannot. The audience may praise you or thrash you but you get to try, you get to experiment. And you get a report card from the audience, which without OTT, you would never get. If you don't have a budget, you make it on YouTube; if you get a bigger budget, you may make it on bigger platforms. So, I think overall, it's a fascinating time. I also believe very strongly that as more and more talent comes in, things will filter out and the overall quality of Indian shows will get better.

Now, the second part. Currently, if you ask me personally, most Indian shows don't really cater to my sensibility. It's rather simple to evaluate this. How many Indian shows from the last few years do you remember? There aren't many shows that I have liked a lot. I liked *Family Man*, I also liked *Paatal Lok*. And there may be a few others too. *Scam 92*, for instance, is good. But overall the number of good shows is small.

Some creators blame the Indian audience for the general lack of quality. Where do you stand on this?

I think the audience owes you nothing. They have neither an affinity for you nor a rivalry with you. The audience doesn't even know you. Especially if you are behind the camera. Who knows us? Why would they hold a grudge against you? If they had to have a grudge against someone, they would have it against Salman Khan or Shah Rukh Khan. You, as a writer, are a nobody. I think what we should do as creators is try and make a palatable story and stop blaming the audience. And you know, okay, we don't have a European sensibility in this country, we don't. So what now? What's the point of cribbing about it? At the end of the day, you make a story for the audience. So, it's your job to understand the Indian sensibility and make a story accordingly.

Now, I wrote *Panchayat* and thankfully the audience liked it. Maybe tomorrow I will write something that they don't understand and they might thrash me. It's all part of the trade. That doesn't mean I will start blaming the audience. I will tell myself that maybe the audience didn't feel anything, they didn't have fun. It would be my failure, not theirs. Imagine making a comedy and nobody finding it funny or making a horror film and nobody getting scared. I think it's the creator's failure. Also, I think, if you can understand these things and write something rooted and real, the audience will like it. It's not as complicated as people make it out to be.

You mentioned 'The Indian sensibility'. What is the Indian sensibility according to you?

Well, let me give you an example of two shows – *Friends* and *Seinfeld*. *Seinfeld* is more highly rated but *Friends* is more popular in India. I think it's because *Friends* has a little bit of family, romance, and those aspects, whereas, *Seinfeld* is more in the space of dry humour. I think emotions appeal more to the Indian audience. Also, I think in India, people like things a little bit more direct. If you get too subtle or too obtuse, it might be an issue. I would say just a little bit of spoon-feeding, too, is required sometimes. In India, you are addressing big numbers, really big numbers.

And you must keep in mind that everybody is not as much into content or films or shows as you are. It's not that everybody in your audience is watching two shows a week. Many people watch something because they heard about a show from someone and they sample an episode or two. If they think the show is too high-concept or something that they have to struggle to understand they're surely going to move on to another one. I think that's what I understand about the Indian audience and the Indian sensibility so to speak.

On the age-old conflict between making something for the masses and making something for yourself, where do you stand as a writer?

I think my attempt is to lie somewhere between mass appreciation and critical acclaim. I want to be somewhere on the border of the two. I would obviously like to retain some sophistication but only enough that it doesn't go beyond the reach of the masses. Consider some successful projects. *Dangal*, for instance, is a huge hit among the masses and it is critically acclaimed as well. I think not just me but everyone would have the same goal. However, people might say that they are only making something for the audience, everybody likes a little bit of critical acclaim and the reverse is true. After all, who doesn't like praise?

This industry is synonymous with struggle for outsiders. Tell me a little bit about your struggle as a writer.

I think struggle is different for everyone as everyone's journeys are different and unique in their own right. You can't fit everyone in one blanket. As far as I am concerned, thankfully, I didn't have to see days when I had no money and I had to sleep on the streets and stuff like that. Because in my case, I was switching from one job to another. From my tech job, I switched to Faking News and from Faking News, I switched to TVF for a full-time job. So, I was always getting a salary and I could afford to live a basic life in Mumbai.

Now that is about the monetary aspect. The other aspect is to gain confidence and fit into a new system. I think a lot of people have to struggle hard to earn other people's trust. In the beginning, you have no work released so people don't trust you easily. Once you have a release and in case it flops, people won't trust you with the next one. In case it succeeds, people will give you more work. Most people get stuck in this trap and don't get a chance to produce their pages. People don't understand where to start from, or whom to pitch an idea to.

Most studios have their inboxes filled with scripts and concept ideas and some new writers just don't get a chance to start working. I was lucky as I was already a part of a set system which was TVF. When I joined in 2015, there already was a team of good, hard-working people established at the company. Their first sketch came out in 2012. Biswa (Biswapati Sarkar), Golu (Amit Golani), Arunabh (Kumar), Mishra (Deepak Kumar Mishra) and many others together made an excellent and clear-headed team. One of their shows, *Permanent Roommates*, had already come out. And since I thankfully got to be part of a running system like that, I came in and I got a chance to do my experiments. I started small, of course, and wrote five- to seven-minute sketches initially but my work started coming out immediately. So, I was really lucky that I did not have to go through a phase where I was writing page after page and nobody was reading them.

Do you think films can change the world?

I think films definitely influence people. When you are travelling on a bus and you listen to your favourite film song, it does affect your mood. Films can and do make people good, bad, sad, angry. They do affect people's emotions. So, I think films definitely have a lot of consideration in people's lives and in turn the world. However, how much of actual change they bring about is something I am not sure of. For instance, *Rang De Basanti* was a huge success. But did people start revolting against the government or corruption after watching it? So, I doubt if films can actually bring about an on-ground change. And honestly, I am fine with that. A person cannot change his life after watching a film.

Do you think that every screenwriter has to take a political stance through his work?

Well, I am afraid, I don't think so. I mean, every writer has a political point of view whether he expresses it or not. But there cannot be a rule like that for sure. It's not physics where someone can say force is equal to mass multiplied by acceleration. If you think that in a particular show, you just need to do nonsense, you should be allowed to. And I think that is the most fun part of this medium. Anyone can do whatever they want to. If we started having rules like this, everything would start looking the same and that's not fun. You won't have every flavour. You want a *DDLJ* (*Dilwale Dulahnia Le Jayenge*) to be there and a *Lagaan* to be there as well.

What are your favourite films, shows, writers, and film-makers?

If we speak about the Hindi film industry, I like films that are called massy and good. I would say films like *Lagaan, Rang De Basanti*. Even *Gadar* and *Mohabbatein*. I like *Veer Zara* as well. You know, my palette is such that I like all these films and this is what I had seen earlier. But you know eventually, when I started watching films by people like (Anurag) Kashyap, I started liking those as well. When I watched *Gangs of Wasseypur*, I was floored. I was already excited because it was set in Dhanbad which is in Bihar. That's when I realized that if you have some fun with your work, you can make some good stuff. I started watching Hollywood and American shows as well. I liked *Breaking Bad, Friends*, and *Seinfeld* a lot. I think *Breaking Bad* is one of my favourite shows. I also like *Game of Thrones* a lot except for the last couple of seasons. Another show I love is *The Wire*. It's a show that I did not like initially because I was not a very mature watcher but then I started loving that show. Then I watched and loved many Tarantino films, Scorsese films, and Spielberg films.

Is there a show that makes you jealous?

Breaking Bad for sure. And also *The Sopranos*. In India, I think when I watched *The Family Man*, I thought it was such a nice setup … how could we miss it? On one hand, in his life, there is a family story happening, and on the other a thread of crime. I think the setup is so ripe that on one hand, you can do comedy or deadpan stuff and on the other, you can do high-drama stuff and in both cases, the audience sticks with you. That's why I like *Family Man* so much.

If you got 100 crore rupees in your account tomorrow, what would you make?

I think an epic or a period drama. Something like *The Gladiator* perhaps. I am interested in exploring how the world was around a thousand or a thousand and five hundred years ago. Today, we have a society and some order to things but in those days a tribe would just attack another for food and basic needs – it was very normal then. I think that animal instinct and the quest for survival is something I would love to explore. The very primal nature of human beings.

EIGHT

Charudutt Acharya

One of the most easygoing, genuinely charming, and naturally funny people I have met is Charudutt Acharya. His eye for the everyday and an eternal optimism for life comes across in his work and this conversation. Charudutt Acharya is the writer-creator of *Aranyak* and a long-time writer of *Crime Patrol*.

I met him at a coffee shop inside Inorbit Mall in Malad where the fragrance of perfumes from the Shopper's Stop nearby mingled with the aroma of freshly baked cookies to enhance the experience of our conversation.

How did writing begin for you?

I never thought I was a 'writer' writer. I was more interested in directing. But even that started later. As a child, I was not at all a reader. I had hardly read any books. Some James Hadley Chase and stuff like that are all about it. I grew up in Juhu Gaothan, which was two minutes away from the beach. I remember, one day, my schoolteacher had given me a book by Tagore and told me I should be a writer.

I took a fancy to the idea and I would carry a bag with a notebook to the beach and started scribbling something. Instead of playing football on the beach, I spent a few evenings writing. I only remember the title of the first poem I wrote, 'I love it when it rains'. Then, I remember writing an article for the school magazine which got rejected because I wrote something about three or four school kids bunking and going to the bakery, or something like that. After that, for a long, long while I never wrote anything.

I was an avid movie-watcher. I watched whatever films I could right since childhood. Then I joined FTII (Film and Television Institute of India) – for the direction course – and there were a lot of people who used to be working on films all the time, so I used to help them with writing.

I think I had a knack for dialogue writing. I could write in Hindi and did the dialogues for some student films at FTII and worked on some story ideas as well. I think I always had this ability to narrate stories. Even in my school, I was known as a storyteller. But I never wrote them down. At FTII, so many people would wonder how I always had so many stories to tell. I think, although I was never an avid reader, I had a lot of life experiences from a very early age. Many people and many experiences.

My dad was a very interesting person. He once told me in school that I should go and see all the railway stations in Bombay! He used to give me some money and I used to go to a railway station alone, eat at a restaurant nearby, and sometimes watch a film. One day, I'd go to Navy Nagar, another day to Bhaucha Dhakka, another day I'd watch flamingos. He wanted me to find out what different areas in the city are like. I think that contributed a lot to my liking for people and places. I was deeply interested in finding out how real people speak and the many different dialects that exist in this city. I found the 'Apun-tupun' speech which most of the films used as a Bombay dialect quite stupid. I used to think they could do better because real speech is nothing like that.

What was it like to enter the film industry after FTII?

That's quite a story. In 1995, I graduated from FTII. In 1996, I got married. And in 1997, I met with an accident. By that time, I had finished assisting in two films – *Albela* and *Jab Pyaar Kisi Se Hota Hai*. I had landed these two projects immediately after FTII. Their schedules were in Europe so it was a lot of fun. I used to also do a lot of work for Plus Channel, which was quite a big production house back in the mid-1990s. After that, my friend, Onir, asked me if I could write something for Kalpana Lajmi. The project did not go on the floor but I got paid for it. And I realized that for writing one episode, I got paid as much as my whole month's salary at Plus Channel.

I also did some work on commercials. There was something called Asian Sky Shop that used to be aired on cable TV in the 1990s. I did some work on that as well. But then while I was doing that, in 1997, an accident squashed one of my legs. I was going for an edit in a rickshaw and some vehicle crashed it. It was quite a dramatic time because I was newly married, my wife was pregnant and I thought now with this accident, I wouldn't be able to work. I had no money and no insurance. It was a messy situation. I had huge medical bills. And directing and being on set was not going to be possible any longer. So, the only thing I could do sitting at home was write. And I turned that into my full-time profession.

Quite literally, I became a writer by accident! I used to write, save money, get operated, and spend money on raising my children. I spent a lot of my time writing for television. *D Line* was one of the first shows I wrote regularly amongst many others. I had studied cinema in FTII and initially, it was not easy to write for television. TV writing has its own rules. I learnt on the job that you can't have, say, one scene at Starbucks and then not have three more that have Starbucks in it. Also, you can't suddenly have a scene on TV where two people are conversing and behind them, four clowns pass by. TV writing is a very specific skill and eventually I got a hang of it. Cinema is 'Show, don't tell'. In TV it is 'Tell and only when it is necessary, show'. Then, I got to write shows that became famous like *Haqeeqat* and much later, *Crime Patrol*.

Tell me about your days in England.

I had written a script. A short ninety-minute personal story that had elements from my childhood. And there was something called the Script Factory where it was selected. When I went there, those guys told me that there was something called the Charles Wallace Fellowship. They said that if I got selected I could do an MA in screenwriting from any university in England and the fellowship would pay me for going there. All I needed to do was apply, which I did. And then I got it. Their age limit was thirty-five and I was thirty-four at the time. I discussed it with my wife and family and then I went to Royal Holloway, University of London, to study. I had already written more than ten shows and a film so I was the most experienced person there. But they conducted very good workshops. Suddenly, I was away from Bombay and the TV world, which was a great break for me. I quite enjoyed my stay in England. After I came back, there were two film scripts that I was trying to pitch. But somehow, they were not happening. So, I continued writing for TV as it a source of sustained income.

What was it like writing your first film, *Vaastu Shastra*?

Saurabh Narang, who unfortunately is no more, was the director of the film. This was back in 2002. Ramu (Ram Gopal Varma) had told him that he wanted to do something along the lines of Stephen King's *Pet Sematary*. Saurabh told me a one-line idea. I was a co-writer on the film. It was not my original story. We used to jam and then we developed the story. Ramu was a very bright mind. I had great respect for him because I had seen *Satya* and other films he had made. At that point, he was a hero to me. So, I obviously wanted to work with him. There were lots of things in the film that even we weren't sure of. But we just went ahead and did it. Also, the film did not pay me much so I had to continue writing for TV.

And the film did not take me to the next level of film writing. I stuck to TV.

Can you walk me through the journey of writing *Dum Maro Dum*?

It was Shridhar (Raghavan) who had written the script. I used to sometimes go for *addabazi* at Sriram's (Raghavan) house. So, Shridhar and Sriram knew me. Also because of the FTII connection. I had worked on a TV pilot with Sriram long ago. One day, I got a call from Shridhar that he would like me to write the dialogues for the film. I was on set most of the time and it was fun. I had a great time with Rohan Sippy, who produced it. Also, the film had stars. It was almost ten years since I had worked with stars. The last time I did it was on *Vaastu Shastra* which had Sushmita Sen. So, after that I wrote a film that got selected at the Mahindra Sundance Script Lab. Rohan told me that he would produce it. It was called *Sonali Cable*. I made the film but it bombed. So, I was back to writing for TV.

How did *Crime Patrol* affect your career?

I wrote *Crime Patrol* for many years. From 2009 to 2019, I guess. The show was a huge success. It had become part of my routine. I used to write every day. I used to write the dialogue for it. Every day, I used to wake up at 4 a.m., and then by 9.30 a.m. or 10 a.m., I used to be done with one episode. Writing it became like muscle memory. It was regular and fixed income. Even if films or nothing else worked, I knew I had *Crime Patrol* to bank on. I was known as the *Crime Patrol* writer. And it helped me immensely to survive.

What do you enjoy writing the most?

I have written for several shows and TV and some films as I told you. But one of the things that I enjoy writing the most is Facebook posts. In fact, someone had offered me to publish a book of my posts. Now, I am also working on my novel. TV writers are not very valued. And films never really took off for me. I was in fact in a bit of a shock when *Sonali Cable* bombed.

Aranyak was a big hit. Did that change a lot for you? Also, walk me through the journey of creating Aranyak.

The two most defining projects in my life are *Crime Patrol* and then after OTT happened, *Aranyak*. The idea for *Aranyak* came to me in 2013, when, after *Sonali Cable*, we took a family vacation to Manali. Near Shimla, there is a pass – I forget its name. You could ride horses there. My wife's saddle was a little weak and we told the guys from whom we booked the ride that we need it replaced. They said it works like that and nothing would happen. Ten steps later, my wife fell off the horse. I was scared and I told them that we couldn't do the ride. They said we won't get the money back. At that time, it was not a small amount for me. So, we argued. They didn't budge. I decided to file a police complaint.

After a while, we found a quaint police station at a nondescript place. I went inside with my wife and kids. In the police station, there was a woman who was teaching maths to her children while cutting some vegetables. She asked us, '*Kya hua, ji? Kya hua?*' (What happened, sir? What happened?). I explained the situation to her. She seemed very kind. She took my wife inside and gave her some clothes, had someone wash her clothes. She ordered tea and pakodas for us. It was good but I said, I am here to make a complaint. She kept saying, '*Ho jayega, ho jayega.*' (It'll happen, it'll happen). Then she settled my kids down and switched on the TV for them. After a while, she got to a room and sat across the table to write the complaint down. I asked her, '*Achchha, aap SHO hain?*' (Oh, so you are the SHO?). She looked at me and said, '*Kyun? Dikkat hai koi?*' (Why? Is there any problem with that?)

Suddenly, there was a switch in her character. She started acting very professionally and then got one of her constables to get those guys. The guys were brought in and were shivering to see her and she slammed each one of them with a rod and asked them to return our money. They did. She kept their licences with her for a day. I thought now she would ask for a bribe for helping us out. But she didn't do any of that. She told me, '*Yeh hamara kartavya hai.*' (This is my duty.) She also said if you take tourism out of Himachal, only drugs will remain. And she wanted family tourists like us to keep visiting the place.

This incident stunned me. The character fascinated me. Her name was Kasturi Dogra, which I used for the protagonist of *Aranyak*, whose role was played by Raveena Tandon. That night, in the hotel room, I started writing about this character. At that time, I had no idea how I would use her. But my wife told me, you could make a film about it someday. Then, on the same trip, we went to the Hidimba temple. And the place is surrounded by charas. Everybody there was smoking up. It was an 'epiphany' moment where I had seen this world of drugs and a few days earlier, this character of Kasturi Dogra.

On the same trip, there was a guy who was telling children some stories about a character in the forest who's half-man and half-leopard. My children were freaking out but I was fascinated by this myth. One night in the hotel, I was drinking my rum and I thought what if I fuse these stories? There was another real unfortunate incident I read about which happened in Goa where a British teenage girl was raped and murdered. Her mother was being judged by everyone because she was into drugs with her boyfriend. The mother said something like just because I do drugs, it doesn't mean my daughter doesn't deserve justice. I remember feeling bad for her. And I wanted to write about this incident as well.

Many years later, all this came together as *Aranyak*. Initially, I thought of doing it as a film. Rohan Sippy was interested in producing it. Then as a mini-series. Then we started taking it around. We went to various production houses. In fact, Jio signed us on. Everything was falling into place. It had a different cast at that time. Three weeks before starting the shoot, Jio pulled the plug on all their shows. It was a huge shock for me. I didn't know what to do. In a few months, Siddharth Roy Kapoor showed interest. After that, Raveena Tandon came on board. Then, Netflix bought the rights from Jio and *Aranyak* became what it is today. *Aranyak* is my original idea and the whole show is written by me. Every episode, all screenplay, and all dialogue. Rohan was my producer all through this. So, he became the showrunner.

How do you see TV, film, and OTT writing differently from one another?

Look, on TV, there are two distinct kinds of writing. One is the soap opera, which is like the BJP of TV because it is in the majority. Say, around 80 per cent of the work that happens on TV is soap operas. The rest 20 per cent where people do crime shows and other stuff is something that I have been involved a lot with. I could never do soap operas because I don't think I know how to write them well and I wasn't very interested in them either. Even *Jassi Jaisi Koi Nahi*, on which I was one of the writers, is not really a kitchen-based soap opera. Soap opera has a different grammar. Also, you get paid more on soap operas than on the other 20 per cent of the work. But I never did a soap opera. I did more episodic TV and mini-series.

That, now in the time of OTT, works in my favour. Because many film writers find it difficult to crack OTT. But since I have written episodic TV, it is somewhere midway from a film to OTT. So, I found it relatively easier. OTT writing has its challenges. Nowadays you have Korean and British and so many other shows to watch. So as Indian OTT writers, you really have to, as Billy Wilder once said, 'Grab them by the neck and hold them tight.' I also think we are missing a trick or two in OTT writing.

In trying to shock the audience, we are losing out on the authenticity of our stories. Most of the best international shows are rooted in their country and culture. We are still trying to copy the West. We are using sex and abuse for the sake of it. I mean, of course, if the story requires it, it's fine. But sometimes, we just try to do that. For instance, the idea of a liberated woman on Indian OTT is one who goes out and has four shots of vodka or has sex in the car. These are things that have come to us from shows from the West. It is aspirational but not real. Middle-India cannot relate to this. We don't take pride in our culture or our reality. That's one of the reasons why Indian OTT shows are not watched widely in India let alone outside the country. You are living off Korean and Latin American films, you are working in advertising or something like that and living somewhere between Lokhandwala and South Bombay. How will you cater to a larger audience? I think we lack talent in writing.

I have seen a lot of half-baked stories getting into production. We usually don't think beyond templates, we think formulaic stories. I think *Panchayat* is a show that is rooted in the country. Even *Paatal Lok* to an extent, although, it is fiction. *Aranyak* is rooted in India as well. We had taken the call not to use sex and abuse at all in *Aranyak*. I guess, it worked.

How much of a role has FTII played in your journey?

See, FTII has played a role. It's a place that exposes you to a lot of cinema and also teaches you a lot about the craft of film-making. In that respect, it has been beneficial for sure. In terms of writing, however, I am not too sure. At least when I was there, back in the 1990s, it did not have a great writing department at all. I think we didn't have a course in writing. We just had a professor who had his own ideas about what a script should be and stuff like that. Also, there was a huge disconnect with the industry. FTII was very unapologetic about wanting to cater to arthouse cinema. The Mumbai industry did not need an FTII. It has always produced writers directors and cameramen who are equally competent in doing their jobs. FTII always focussed on creating independent cinema. Of course, some FTII directors have done well in the commercial space as well, like Raju Hirani and Vidhu Vinod Chopra. Personally, I think it definitely helped me. I feel privileged I was there. But I feel that I was exposed to so much there that I couldn't absorb at the time. It's like you are grappling with grammar and someone exposes you to poetry. You watch a lot, your expectations of yourself are high but your ability to reach there is not enough. So, at FTII, you struggle.

What are your favourite films, film-makers, and shows?

In Hindi cinema, which I grew up watching, my favourites are Vijay Anand – *Guide*, *Johnny Mera Naam*, *Jewel Thief*. I definitely like the work of Sai Paranjpye. I like the work of Hrishikesh Mukherjee and

Basu Chatterjee. I like some early films of Shyam Benegal. Also, some films by Govind Nihalani. As a child, I also liked films of Manmohan Desai but I can't relate to them anymore. I was in fact very influenced by the TV of the 1980s. I quite like *Malgudi Days*, I love *Tamas*.

In terms of international film-makers, I love the Japanese film-makers Yasujiro Ozu and Akira Kurosawa. I love the work of Satyajit Ray. I love the work of the Latin American film-maker Alejandro González Iñárritu. I also like the American directors like the Coen brothers a lot. And the work of Alexander Payne who made films like *Sideways*, *Election*, and *About Schmidt*. I also like the early films of Ridley Scott. I love Alan Parker and, of course, Hitchcock. I like a Chinese director called Zhang Yimou. I like the Iranian Majid Majidi a lot.

Among OTT shows, I like *Breaking Bad*, and *Better Call Saul*. The British show *Broadchurch* is a huge favourite of mine.

Name a film and a show that you would like to have written.

Amongst shows, I think that would be *Broadchurch*. Then there was one episode of *Better Call Saul*, I think the third, which I saw and thought if I could manage to write and direct one piece like that in life, I'd think I had done something worthwhile. I get this kind of feeling on some films like *As Good As It Gets* as well. And *The Shawshank Redemption*.

Given a chance, which director in the world would you like to write for?

The Coen brothers. I think they are brilliant directors. And Walter Salles, the guy who made The *Motorcycle Diaries*.

In India, if you ask me, the guy whose work I really, really like a lot is Shimit Amin. I'd love to write for him.

NINE

Durgesh Singh

Ifirst met Durgesh way back in 2015-2016 when I was invited to read my poetry at a private gathering. Durgesh read his poetry as well and I remember enjoying it. At the time, both of us worked at different advertising agencies, and that too was some common ground for us. Since then, he went on to write *Gullak*, which is a show rooted in an Indianness that he had experienced while growing up in UP.

However, we could not meet for the following conversation in person as he was travelling around the time and we decided to do it by email, which is to say that I emailed him the questions and he responded with his answers.

One of the biggest successes of *Gullak* is its unusually usual characters. Which part of your mind and life do they come from?

For half my life, I have been around unusual characters. For example, there was one Pappu bhaiya who remained unemployed his whole life. I always wondered how someone could afford to be unemployed his whole life but there he was. I always liked him. He had a Yamaha

RX100 bike and he always parked it near the khatiya where he slept. He used to tell us stories, stories wilder than imagination. Like, once upon a time, an eagle grabbed him by his hair and flew. The eagle took him to Iran via Afghanistan and finally stopped at the top of the Eiffel Tower where they both shared a cotton candy or *budhiya ke baal*. Another time, he went to Ashok Talkies (a local theatre near my village) to watch *Sholay*. After the film ended, he found Gabbar Singh outside the theatre, and Gabbar shared a beedi with Pappu bhaiya. Then Gabbar Singh gave his tamancha to Pappu bhaiya, with which he killed Kaalia. We believed this story for a long time. Pappu bhaiya is the biggest storyteller in the world for me. The phrase from *Gullak*, '*Aapko nahi pata*' (You don't know), came from Pappu bhaiya's world.

How did the journey of screenwriting begin for you?

Thanks to advertising. A writer doesn't get any room to write much in 30 seconds. And a story is a story, long stories, good stories, the stories from big writers that make you feel. I had written short stories for a long time, first for magazines and then for radio but then I got bored. Boredom always pushes you to do something new. When I got bored with advertising, I started writing *Gullak*. My screenwriting journey started from there.

As a screenwriter, did you have to make any compromises in terms of ideas and even money?

For me, screenwriting is a different kind of literature altogether. It is not 100 per cent pure but still close to my heart. I don't think of it as a compromise, but you are bound to write economically. Having said that, you also have to be a fighter. You have to fight for your most beautiful ideas. Of course, the person who puts his money will also give his own ideas, but you have to be smart, especially in the Hindi film industry, where finding people with a connection to Hindi is a rarity. You have to fight for this language, for these ideas, for money and this is only possible when you are very confident about your own work.

How has OTT changed life for writers, if at all it has?

OTT has given writers both respect and money. The story of the show starts from the bible (TV series pitch) itself. Thanks to the platforms that do not entertain just a one-pager anymore. However, there is still a long way to go as far as change is concerned but OTT has led to a rise in demand for writers. But there is an alternative perspective to it which is the herd mentality.

What's the kind of cinema that's influenced you and what kind of work do you intend to do in the near future?

Human stories. Stories of humans, not of machines. Bong Joon Ho, Asghar Farhadi, Fatih Akin, Abbas Kiarostami, Ursula Meier, Susanne Bier, Wong Kar-wai. The list is endless.

In the Indian film industry, I admire Malayalam cinema. I always wait for their new release, because they have lived their stories. They tell their stories, out of their lived realities. For example, a few days ago, I shot with Nimisha Sajayan (*The Great Indian Kitchen* fame). In between our conversations, I discovered that the director of *The Great Indian Kitchen*, Jeo Baby, is a house husband who takes care of complete household chores. That's why he was able to tell this kind of a story. The writer of *Nayattu* was an inspector in Kerala Police, that's the reason he was able to tell that story about policing. Stories born out of lived realities amaze me every time, which Malayalam cinema does wonderfully.

You have written and published short stories in the past. How do you see them differently from the ones you write or pitch for the screen?

My short stories are really close to my heart, the stories you are watching on screen are very close to the world. Both are different, but I am trying to blur the difference between the two. Even going forward, the stories that I write will remain close to my heart. After writing *Gullak 2*, my belief only grew stronger in the fact that if you create something that is closest to your heart, it will resonate with people the most.

Why have you never published the poetry you've written?

I was never able to find the courage, I always thought they were bad poems. What will people say? Because the poets that I read or read growing up were all mesmerizing. Their metaphors, and their thoughts were amazing. Alok Dhanwa, Kedarnath Singh, Shrikant Verma, Ashtabhuja Shukla, Vinod Kumar Shukla. I believed that one's poetry should be at par with these poets. That's why I buried all the poems, some in my heart and some in a box somewhere.

When and why did you decide to be a writer?

It all started during my days of graduation at Allahabad University. In the Ramakrishna Mission library of that campus, I came across the beautiful features written in *India Today*, *Aha Zindagi* and *Outlook* magazines. I aspired to write that. Later came books. The writers who impacted me the most were Phanishwar Nath Renu, Dr Rahi Masoom Raza, and then came Nirmal Verma. These three names changed my life completely. Nirmal Verma's writing especially left me spellbound. Even now, I can turn to any page, pick any paragraph, and start reading his work. Then I came to Bhopal. There, Bharat Bhavan played a huge role. My understanding of cinema and literature matured there. I still remember the Sunday I watched *Kanjeevaram* in Bharat Bhavan and met Prakash Raj. That day my perspective towards watching cinema changed.

According to you, for a writer, what is success?

To do the work close to his/her heart, to live in the city or village of his liking, to meet his close ones, to plant a mango tree on his land, to water the tree, to pluck that mango and just eat it, to watch a bird sitting by the glass window and that bird hitting the glass after seeing her face, to sit by the *puliya* near the canal and drink whiskey and using the canal's water after the water you have brought for your drink gets finished. A writer should never leave his roots. A writer should always come back to the world where he came from.

How political do you think your writing is or should be?

How can someone write without politics? I know my politics, but that does not mean I have to shout it out loud. You can decipher my political understanding in *Gullak 2* and *Gullak 3*. And how can someone do satire devoid of any political understanding? And if the writer does not talk about politics, who will – politics of relationships, politics of emotions, politics of childhood, politics of adulthood, politics of break-ups and affairs, politics of running a house, politics of building a house. Politics of living in this world, politics of exiting this world. You have to write everything after understanding all this.

You grew up in Allahabad which is now Prayagraj. Apart from the name, what else has changed from then to now?

The *amroods* (guava) are not the same as we used to get before. The quality of bun maska and chai has degraded a bit but nevertheless, I like the city. In our hostel, one dadi used to serve dahi-jalebi. She is not there anymore, that's the reason I might like it less, but I still like the city. Civil Lines Bus Stand is a bit organized now. The lying Hanuman-ji at Sangam is still lying, however, the water at Sangam does not stop now but I still like the city. Even after the construction of the bridge from Chungi to Medical Chauraha, the traffic is still moving slowly. Thank God some things have not changed.

Screenwriting, short stories, advertising, and poetry. How do you see the forms you have handled differently from each other?

Screenwriting is something I am still learning. I was never able to learn poetry. Understood it a bit, but still trying to grasp it. I have learnt insights into the world through advertising. How do people think, when do they laugh or cry, how do they speak, how do they eat, how do they dress? Advertising taught me that. But I never wanted to get lost in that world, that's why I left it. Another difference among these forms while you handle them is that screenwriting is a slightly more restricted territory and also, it's collaborative. It is amazing to see your writing converted into the screen in somebody else's vision. It's a unique experience. Short stories on the other hand are a much wider area. You can tread through it as you please, with fewer rules and regulations. In advertising, there are different kinds of restrictions and rules at play when you write for a brand. Poetry, as I said, is a mystery to me.

Tell me a little bit about your writerly utopia if you've ever imagined it?

The writer within me wants to go to the Czech Republic to meet Nirmal Verma and borrow his overcoat. To take one puff of Mohan Rakesh's cigar, to bump into Swadesh Deepak at some street corner, and to ask him to come to this world, where his anger is needed the most because writers are becoming spineless. I also want to make a film on Swadesh Deepak's life in my utopia. I don't want to meet Dharamvir Bharati at all but I want to meet Pummy from *Gunaaho ka Devta*. I want to ride around Allahabad with Pummy on a bike. My utopia is to stay in that bungalow where Renu and Raj Kapoor lived while writing *Teesri Kasam*. Why did he deny staying in that sea-facing bungalow? I want to ask him that. I want to go to Sankar's Shahjahan Hotel with Rajkamal Chaudhary on which *Chowringhee* was written. My utopia is to make Vinod-ji (Vinod Kumar Shukla) younger, I want to make him an eighteen-year-old so that he can roam around and see whether people can understand *Deewaar Mein Ek Khidki Rehti Thi* or just roam around with it.

If we were to speak again after five years, what would you like to have written by then?

Maybe you would find me teaching somewhere. In some school, college, or university. I want to write a big fat novel someday. Maybe in the next five years, I'll be able to do that.

TEN

Imtiaz Ali

The body of work of writer-director Imtiaz Ali of *Jab We Met*, *Highway*, *Rockstar* fame explores love and relationships with an undercurrent of Sufi romanticism. I met Imtiaz at his office in Versova on a weekday afternoon, on a day when his schedule ran haywire, and our interview started over two hours after the scheduled time. But when he finally came out to meet me, he came across as one of the humblest and the most gentlemanly people, apologizing for the delay and making sure that I was well-fed in his office with delicious mutton cutlets. As our conversation carried on, he forgot about his next meeting and offered his mind to me uninterruptedly for over an hour.

The Jamshedpur of the 1970s would have been an interesting setting to grow up in. What was your childhood like and how did writing begin for you?

I think the first kind of writing I ever did was poetry in English. It was back in my school in Jamshedpur. I think when I was in the 9th standard. It was a sort of anti-establishment poetry. There was also a relationship-sweetness type of thing in it. I used to show it to my English teacher, Deepa Sengupta, who was kind enough to go through it and sometimes give me a review of it. I still remember some of her comments on my work. That's how my journey as a writer started. When I was writing, I felt happy. I also enjoyed the attention that I sometimes got.

With writing, I started knowing myself more. I became aware of somebody else who was also me. After these small poems, I started writing small skits, which I think have a role to play in bringing me here today. These were skits for school, for Teacher's Day, for somebody's welcome. I remember the Rotaract Club asking me to write some plays whenever they had some delegates over for a meeting. I used to write them and then make them with my friends. Those tended to be musicals and involved a lot of poetry as I was coming from that space. I also remember this one time when the principal of our school walked into our rehearsals and after watching what was happening, asked, 'Whose play is it? Who has written it?' And I said, 'I have written it.' She looked at me for a bit and said, 'Maybe you should write more then.' So that encouraged me. This was my life in Jamshedpur and in my school as a writer.

The place poetry holds in my mind is something I can describe with that sher by Momin: *Tum mere paas hote ho goya, jab koi doosra nahin hota.* (You remain with me when no one else does.)

How did your idea of art change from Jamshedpur to Delhi and then from Delhi to Bombay?

I think it changed a lot. And that has to do with the kind of theatre I was involved in – not just as a writer but as an actor or a director as well. When I was in Jamshedpur, we were doing archaic English theatre. We were trying to enunciate old English and get that dialect in. That's the kind of theatre that has a lot of rules like an actor's shoulder blade shouldn't cut the line of the audience or an actor should never show his or her back to the audience. Till the time I was in Jamshedpur, even my writing was like that because I was writing for, let's say, that mentality. Flowery, maybe a bit high-brow, and only in English.

One of the biggest things Delhi did for me was introduce me to experimental theatre. This is also when I started writing in Hindi. Although Hindi is what we always spoke at home, till the time I went to Delhi, I always wrote in English. I still think in English.

At Mandi House, I started doing experimental Hindi plays. Now the shoulder blade could cut the line of the audience, I could have an actor showing their back to the audience. Experimental theatre is more liberal and open. It also has rules of its own but it allowed me more freedom. I also started writing and directing nukkad natak (street plays).

Delhi became an important city for me also because Delhi is a rough city. It attacks you. And you tend to hit back. And the age I was – early college days – there was a roughness. So, I found an expression in the city. In fact, when I came to Mumbai, almost all my stories were from my time in Delhi. For example, *Highway* is one of my early stories. Originally, the script was much harsher than the way I made it. I had that story since the 1990s. Maybe since 1996-1997. Then in Bombay, I wrote a play when I was at Xavier's Institute of Communication which at that point, as a theatre person, I was very proud of.

How important is a lived experience for the writer in you?

I think my take-off point is lived experience. But nothing is autobiographical either. You can say, for me, it starts with lived experience and then takes a flight of imagination. For example, *Jab We Met*. Now, a girl on a train. This is a fantasy for any guy who travels by train from Jamshedpur or any small town. Mix this imagination: What if she and I were to miss a train together? Then we might be walking down the lanes of Ratlam. This is how the story started unfolding. That never happened in reality. Unfortunately, I never missed a train with a girl. But it started because I must have seen a girl on a train in my early days. The reality is the trigger; the rest is imagination.

Many people talk about the struggle that the Hindi film industry can be for an outsider. Especially one who wants to tell original stories. What was it like for you?

Well, I feel that anybody who came to Bombay around my time to become a director was, at first, a writer. Anurag (Kashyap), Sriram Raghavan, Tishu (Tigmanshu Dhulia), (Anurag) Basu, (Rajkumar) Hirani – we would all write. I think writing created a chance for most of us to become directors. I think we were a desperate lot. Not that we wanted to tell our own, or original stories. We had no fanciful notions. We wanted work and money to survive. I wanted money to pay the rent and get married and start a household and stuff like that. We were all middle-class small-town boys. We had our own experiences and gradually, we found a way in.

Tell me about your television days in the 1990s. Especially *Star Bestsellers*. I don't think shows like that are made any longer.

I agree. Unfortunately, shows like *Star Bestsellers* aren't made any longer. All of us wanted to make films. At that time, the difference between a TV story and a film story wasn't as clear as it is today. I made one film for *Star Bestsellers* called *Witness*. It was a great opportunity for someone like me to tell a finite story, with a definite beginning, middle, and end. Otherwise, the other TV shows that I was working on, like *Imtihaan*, were endless sagas. For instance, in *Witness*, I went crazy recording sounds from the atmosphere. That's when I realized the importance of ambient sounds. Television was very important to my journey because it taught me to write quickly and shoot quickly. I think TV is the only film school I ever went to.

How easy or difficult was it to pitch your first film *Socha Na Tha*? Could you talk about that journey?

I had been writing and directing television for years. When I was working on *Bestsellers*, that was for Star. So, the team there approached me one time and said that they were working on a new segment which would have a feature film but in three parts and this was to be aired on TV. And they were looking for a story. So, I told them a story. They said they liked it and they would want to commission this to be the first one. They wanted it done quickly. So, I went underground and wrote it in three nights. The only time I went out of my house in those days was to go to the bank because I had no money to buy food either. When I finished it, the team said, for some reason, they were not going ahead with their plans, and the show was cancelled.

I had just written a full script for a film! So, I approached a friend of mine called Sanjay Routray, who now heads Matchbox Films. Then we tried to pitch it and ultimately, we landed a meeting with Sunny Deol. I went to Shimla to meet him. Imagine, I was telling an action hero a romantic film where the hero himself gets slapped. I was wondering if he would find this as a sissy plot for his action-hero self. But he listened with rapt attention and then two hours later he said, '*Khana kha lein? Bhookh lagi hai.*' (Shall we eat? I'm famished!) So, I said, '*Sir, thoda sa bacha hai.*' (Sir, only a little bit is left). He said, '*Picture main kar lunga, bhai. Khana toh kha lein!*' (I'll make the picture, brother. But first, we must eat!). That's how it happened. He just heard the story, loved it intuitively, and asked me to direct the film.

In 2008 came *Jab We Met*, which found its way into the hearts of many people, especially young lovers like I was then. How long did you take to write it and then make it?

Well, writing was very, very quick. I write to get rid of the job. You might be surprised but I don't really enjoy the process of writing, especially film writing. So, I want to get done with it quickly. And I think I enjoy direction more than writing. Writing allows me to have more fun as a director. I wrote *Jab We Met* in two nights. That was the first draft. And then only one major change happened in the screenplay before the film was made.

There's another interesting thing about *Jab We Met*. I had a friend, Joy Banerjee, who was rather depressed at the time and said he needed work. So, I told him to write something. I told him that I would come up with one idea, he could come up with another one and then, we could put the two together and write the story. He came up with the idea of 'A man who wants to kill himself'. What I came up with is 'A girl on the train'. But then my friend wasn't really interested in taking it further. So, I combined the two ideas and wrote the film in two nights when the time came.

One of the things I love about writing *Jab We Met* is that the idea of Krishna becoming Radha and Radha becoming Krishna comes through in the script. If you notice, throughout the film, Shahid's character slowly becomes Kareena's, and Kareena's character becomes Shahid's.

Is it true that the bigger the budget of a film, the lesser the creative freedom for the writer?

Ha ha! I won't say that it's entirely true. In the film industry, only when the script is complete do you get into budgeting. Till the time the script is being written, there is usually no money involved. And that is unfortunate because it puts the writer in a place where he is not guaranteed to get paid for his work. Only when the project is greenlit, does he get paid. We're trying to change that. I think what this industry lacks the most is good writers. We don't need more actors or more directors or more musicians in the industry, we need more writers. People will have to realize that everything that has ever worked in the history of cinema has been well-written!

A recurrent theme in your films is finding oneself while finding love. Does that come from an early personal experience or a deep subconscious emotion?

Nothing conscious about my writing, ever! Everything comes from my subconscious or unconscious mind. Nothing follows a set design either. If I realize that there's a design, I try to change it. I don't try to belong to it. But yes, I see that the theme you talk about exists. Shahid in *Jab We Met*, Alia in *Highway*, Ranbir in *Rockstar*, yes, I notice the theme. But, it's not a conscious play. It must be coming from a deep corner of my mind.

In almost all your films, the music has been brilliant. Do you look at film music as an integral part of the script itself?

Yes. I totally do. In fact, I write the songs in my screenplay. I mean, I don't write the lyrics. But I describe the song in the scene where I see it playing out. I also believe that songs give you the liberty to express things that cannot be written in dialogue. Sometimes, the articulation of an emotion is not all that you want. Cinema allows you the liberty to have music that articulates the mood or the emotion in a unique way. Music can also allow poetry to come in. So, the songs in my films always have a purpose.

I find a hint of a kind of Sufi romanticism in your work. Do you think that's correct?

I am not a practising spiritualist. But incidentally, the first book of philosophy that I ever read in my life was the Bhagavad Gita. It was a book that was available at book stalls in Jamshedpur at a discounted rate which I could afford and access easily. I would read it on my train journeys to Patna or Bhubaneswar that I used to frequently make alone when I was in the 6th or the 7th standard. Some things in the book started making so much sense to me! It is very straightforward, and I still think some of it is a great philosophy. I didn't know Sufi spiritualism at the time, but I did know the Bhagavad Gita. Then, when I got acquainted with Western philosophy and Sufism, I found many similarities with the Bhagavad Gita. In some cases, even the words are the same. The 'spirit' in spiritualism is the same.

Much later in life, I found Rumi being present at many junctures of my life. Like, for instance, in *Rockstar*, I was doing a scene and somebody sent me a message which was a Rumi quote that I found so relevant to the film and my mind then that I eventually used it in the film. It was like whatever mental zone I was in, this guy, Rumi, had already been there or thought about it. Even '*Nadan Parinde Ghar Aa Ja*' somewhere, coincidentally, is a reflection of Rumi's writing. It was this strange connection I made with the man.

Why did you choose to be a film-maker and a film writer and not, say, a novelist or a poet or a playwright considering you are interested in all those forms as well?

Because most of these instincts and desires are satisfied in film. I think cinema allows me to do all kinds of writing that I ever want to do. Having said that, I often think about a novel. Early in college, I thought I'd be a novelist. But now I don't know whether I'll ever be able to write something without being conscious of the visual of it. I still have the fancy of writing a novel. But I'll only write a novel that I think cannot be made into a film. And my novel, if ever there is one, will definitely not be anything like the films I make.

Everybody's talking about OTTs changing the game, especially for writers. What do you think about that?

I'd say OTT is not changing the game but upgrading it. Just like television did when it first came in. Back then, we did not fully understand the difference between writing for television and writing for film. Now we do. Television was supposed to kill cinema. But did it?

OTTs are certainly a great new avenue but they will have to coexist with cinema. OTT requires a different type of writing. Because of the length of a show, it allows for more details than a film. We are still discovering the potential of OTT and we will soon learn more, and along the way, it will also further define the way films will be written.

Who are your favourite poets?

Shakespeare, Ghalib, Faiz, Neruda. Five or seven years back, discovering Fernando Pessoa was a revelation. I think Pessoa speaks more directly to me than anyone else.

Who are your favourite film-makers and writers across the world?

Emir Kusturica in the Bosnian language; Wonk Kar-wai in Cantonese; Sergei Bodrov, a Russian film-maker who has made a film called *Prisoner of the Mountains* and another one called *The Rise of the Mongol*; the great Spanish film-maker Pedro Almodovar; and almost everyone from Iran including Asghar Farhadi, Majid Majidi, Abbas Kiarostami. In the commercial old space, I like David Lean a lot. In India, I like Bimal Roy a lot. I also like Vijay Anand a lot. Then Raj Kapoor and more recently, I like Mani Ratnam. And of course, Satyajit Ray. Shyam Benegal is a huge influence in my life. His cinema is intellectual but it is still cinema. It's not ever boring. Even Satyajit Ray was never boring. I like cinema being cinema.

Is there ever creative jealousy among big film-makers in the Hindi film industry?

Fortunately, for my generation, most of us are friends. We talk for long hours, call each other, and many times, not for work. Thankfully, it's not a finite piece of the pie. If my film does well, so can yours. We don't have to compete with each other that way. Among us, there is no creative jealousy. We are on great terms and also help each other in many ways. Like, for instance, (Anurag) Basu can pick up the phone and say to me, 'You've done such a wonderful scene. I hate you for that!'

Which of your films is your best work according to you and why?

I can't say. I feel there are things that I like about some of my films. For instance, I feel that *Jab We Met* is my most consistent film. It has a beginning, middle, and an end. It is smooth. It has a very good shape. But the depth at which *Rockstar* hits you, in its purity, is something I like a lot as well. There are portions of *Rockstar* that I feel are more precious to me. One can argue that *Jab We Met* does not have that level of depth. The *Jab We Met* fans are very different from the *Rockstar* fans. I also think that certain parts of *Highway* are utterly fulfilling. Like, I can give my life for some of those scenes and moments in *Highway*.

Define success for the writer in you.

Well, I think there are certain things that Shakespeare writes or Ghalib writes and you feel you should have written something like that. That level of relatability is aspirational for me. I'd also say that to be truthful as a writer is a success for me. It's not easy to be truthful.

I wanted to say this last thing … while I said I sometimes write to get rid of the work, I'd also say that writing is my doorway or my comforter. Writing is something I can hide behind. I think writing takes care of me. It keeps me sane, keeps me alive, and takes care of all my problems. I can't survive without writing.

ELEVEN

Ishita Moitra

I met Ishita Moitra on a Zoom call. She was candid and funny and came across as someone who embraces her journey in Bollywood in every way possible. She loves the mainstream and unabashedly so. It seems like she knows exactly what her audience wants and has the talent to give them that.

Her work includes films such as *Rocky Aur Rani Kii Prem Kahaani, Mere Dad Ki Maruti, Half Girlfriend, Shakuntala Devi,* and the Amazon Prime show *Four More Shots Please,* among others.

How and when did you start writing?

My dad was in the army and every two years, I went to a different school, in a different city. I have lived across the length and breadth of this country. Somehow, I think it was when I was in the 3rd standard or something, I started writing. I remember winning an essay-writing competition in school and other writing-related competitions, and then when I won it in another school and then in another school, I realized that I might be good at it. Another thing that happened is that since we were moving around, I picked up many languages at a young age. Since we are Bengali, we speak Bengali at home. My father was in the Jat regiment so I understand Haryanvi very well. He was posted in Punjab at a time so I can not only understand and speak but also read and write Punjabi as well. In fact, I can read and write the Gurmukhi script too. I was very passionate about Hindi poetry as a student, so I know Hindi very well. As a student, I used to fare equally well in English and Hindi. Essentially, I always loved languages and I always hated mathematics – though eventually, I went on to work on a film called *Shakuntala Devi*, which has a protagonist who is a math wizard. So, I just knew that this was something I was interested in.

I was good at studies and all the people who were good at studies used to take science. My parents, in fact, told me that I should take humanities – it was the opposite of what usually happens to people – but like a fool, I took science because all my friends were taking science. So, in 11th and 12th, I took PCBC (physics, chemistry, biology, computers), which sounds more like a swear word than a vocation. But eventually, I realized what I had to do and did my journalism honours from Delhi University and then mass communications from Jamia MCRC.

So, yes, I knew that I wanted to write but wasn't sure what kind of writing I wanted to do then. I interned at the *Asian Age* and at the India Today group. All this while I was studying journalism. Then, I interned at *Outlook* magazine, which back in the day, I loved a lot. So, when I reached there, I realized that I wanted to write newspaper features. That's where I met Namrata Joshi, who was the editor then and she urged me to consider films as a profession and join Jamia Millia to study films. Namrata used to take me to film festivals and introduced me to world cinema including the work of Godard. Then I took the Jamia MCRC exam, which was very tough to crack, and happened to get admission there. So, between the ages of eighteen to twenty-one, things got crystallized. One thing led to another and at twenty-two, I moved to Bombay. In Bombay, I knew that I was either going to write films or write about films – one of the two. I had decided that much by then.

Did you have to struggle a lot as an outsider coming to Bombay and trying to find work?

There was a film festival called CineFan that used to be held in Delhi back in the day and they used to have a talent campus where they would invite students to send in their short films and they would choose some people from there. I won the talent campus and I got an opportunity to attend the festival. There, I met people from the Bombay film industry. I met Rajat Kapoor and Abbas Tyrewala there. In fact, even Christopher Nolan had conducted a session there. It was a very good experience for the students at a young age. So, when I came to Bombay, I had some confidence. In fifteen days, I ended up getting a job at Nadiadwala Grandson. This wasn't a plan, it just happened. And then on the same day, I met a girl, whom I knew from Delhi, who was looking for a flatmate. So, in one day, I got a job as well as a house to stay in Bombay. I took it as a sign from the universe. I decided not to go back and I never took my MA final exam – a decision I still regret. But at that time, I thought if all this was happening to me, why should I go back to Delhi, take an exam, and then come back to do the same? I just wanted my life in Bombay to begin and I thought it had begun by then.

I started working. I didn't know too many people in Bombay. And I was still learning the ropes of the industry. My first film was called *Kambakkht Ishq*. I was the junior-most writer on it – there were many writers on the film – and I had no idea what I was doing. But it was a great learning experience for me as it was a big-budget film and I realized how a big production works. Although I had very little contribution to the film, the production house was amazing in the sense that they took everyone on the team to Los Angeles for months. Everybody stayed at the same hotel. So, Nadiadwala is amazing in that way.

After that, I started finding my path. I went to Yash Raj Television, where I wrote the TV show *Khote Sikkay*. From there, I got to Y-Films and worked on the film *Mere Dad Ki Maruti*. I think that was the time I found my voice. For the first time, I got to write something that I enjoyed writing and something that was totally up my alley. I did dialogues for *Mere Dad Ki Maruti*. The film changed my life in more ways than one. One was obviously the creative satisfaction I got while working on the project. I started getting many calls after that film, so professionally it was a huge milestone in my life. And number two, I met my husband, Neeraj Udhwani, in that film. I was the dialogue writer and he was the one who did the story and the screenplay for that film. Both of us had a red Maruti car while we were working on that film, and we were working on a film called *Mere Dad Ki Maruti*. So, during that time, I made a stupid joke with him, I said, 'We had car-ma.' And guess what, it came true! Things got better and bigger, and it was a much smoother decade post the release of that film.

You have done both screenplay and dialogue on some projects and then there are some on which you did just the dialogue. Do you think it requires a special kind of skill to write dialogue in Hindi cinema considering that there is no such thing as an exclusive dialogue writer in the West or anywhere else in the world?

We've had specific dialogue writers in India for a long time now. And I think it's somewhere got to do with the oral traditions that we have had. Our epics, for instance, had been passed on orally. All our jatras and folk theatre have a strong element of oral tradition. Even in our daily lives, I think, there is a lot of *dialoguebaazi*. Even in our political speeches, there are punches that are very particular to India. I think as a country, we enjoy the spoken word a lot. Our theatre has a lot more dialogue, with many long monologues, than the theatre of other countries. I think all that has permeated into our cinema. While screenplay writing requires a very rational and analytical mind, dialogue writing requires spontaneity. The best dialogues that I have written, in my opinion, are the ones that I wrote within no time, one after the other. If you think too much before writing dialogue, it will sound constructed. And people don't think about what they have to say next for thirty minutes and then they say it. People speak spontaneously, and I think, good dialogue on the screen has to be spontaneous as well. Dialogue has to be as spoken and as real as possible.

So, yes, there are writers who specialize in dialogues but at the same time, there are people who do all three – story, screenplay, and dialogue. Even Salim-Javed used to do all three and their screenplays used to have great scenes and amazing dialogue. I think, if you are writing dialogues for your own screenplay, it could be slightly easier because you know the characters very well as you have written and created them yourself. I think most dialogue writers would prefer that though it is not a necessity.

How is the screenwriter placed in the film industry today in terms of money, respect, and creative power?

I think it depends on the production house that the writer is working with. The situation is not uniform across the industry. A-list production houses pay writers well. I think OTT has changed the scenario for the better. TV pays writers well. TV has always paid writers very well as you get paid per episode, every day. So, you'd find TV writers to be way richer than film writers. In OTT, writers get paid pretty well. But having said that, there are so many smaller producers who will ask you to write an entire screenplay for just 5 lakh rupees or something like that. And there are so many people in India who are just looking for an opportunity so some of them end up taking up such projects.

We don't have a basic minimum contract system in India, which says that a writer cannot be employed below a certain minimum wage. And since we don't have that in India, there are people who are ready to work for as little as they get because, for a new writer in the city, the opportunity counts more than money. So, there are market forces that will exploit writers, particularly new writers. Once you get established as a writer, these things don't happen. But new writers do get exploited. The Writers' Association is full of complaints with the settlement committee.

What could established writers do to make this a fairer playing field for all writers?

I think the Writers' Association is working very hard to make things fairer. They are pushing for the basic minimum contract. They have been negotiating hard with all the Producers' Guilds to put that in place. They are trying to do this in a Trade Union to Trade Union way. But the challenge is that everybody has to get on board for it to happen.

The thing is that I can't really put the blame on a new writer who is roaming around Bombay and looking for an opportunity. I can't tell them that they should not work below a certain amount. They are the ones who are powerless so it's not about the writers, it's about the market. The market has to change, not the writer.

How does the gender of a writer affect their work in the film industry?

When I first came in, gender used to matter a lot more because, at that point, there weren't too many women screenwriters. Back then, I didn't see too many top films written by women except for Shibani Bathija, who wrote *Fanaa* and *My Name is Khan*. All the big films used to be written by male writers. But that is not the case any longer. I have literally seen the transition. Now, most Writers' Rooms have a gender ratio of 50-50. Now a woman is not a woman writer. She is just a writer. And women are now writing every genre and every kind of film and show. It's pretty positive. That's one thing I have seen change and I am very happy about it. Not just writers, but even in the crew, even in the people on the sets, there are several women now in every department of film-making.

Can you walk me through the journey of writing the dialogue and co-writing the screenplay for *Rocky Aur Rani Kii Prem Kahaani*?

The film was Karan's (Johar) idea. I happened to be working on another project for Dharma and I was a Delhi-Bong who happened to speak both Punjabi and Bengali. The film was set in Delhi and it had the Chatterjees and the Randhawas. Somen Mishra, who is the head of development at Dharma and also a co-producer on this film, introduced me to Karan. It was again a case of the universe putting me in the right place, at the right time. This is the most important project I have ever worked on. It was like a dream, you know. I was growing up in all these small towns, in army cantonments, and I was in school when I watched the likes of *Kuch Kuch Hota Hai* and *Kabhi Khushi Kabhie Gham*. I always enjoyed watching mainstream Hindi cinema. It is my first love. I remember coming back from school and watching mainstream Hindi films on Set Max. You know, when people used to ask me in Delhi, 'Where do you see yourself in ten years?', I used to laugh and say, 'Oh, I'll be writing for Karan.' And when it really happened, it was really like living a dream.

The project started in late 2020, during the pandemic, so the world outside was challenging and this was the positivity that I needed at that time. We did not even know if people would ever go back to the theatres or if they would get used to watching everything on OTT. Things were changing. But it was eventually just about doing what we loved doing and we did it. I genuinely love the Karan Johar brand of cinema which makes me feel good every time I watch it. I mean, I can literally watch *K3G* (*Kabhi Khushi Kabhie Gham*) from anywhere to anywhere and enjoy it.

So, the idea was that if what we were doing was bringing us happiness, it would bring happiness to those who watch the film as well. That was the faith we wrote the film with. I think Karan had mentioned in many interviews that he was anxious before the release of the film. Thankfully, we got a lot of love. That was really the best part – the kind of reactions the film opened to was just mesmerizing. I have seen it in the theatres a few times and after the first couple of times, I was not just watching the film but also watching people to see when they were smiling and crying. And you know, the experience of a wholesome Hindi film used to be exactly this back in the day.

You have written *Four More Shots Please* – a show that has been fairly popular among a certain kind of audience. What was it like working on it across three seasons?

Devika (Bhagat) and I have written all three seasons. She has written the screenplay and I have written the dialogues. *Four More Shots Please* is a project where everything just aligns, and you find the perfect fit in terms of everything for yourself. There were women who were producers, each season was directed by a female director and there were many women behind the camera along with the ones in the star cast which was led by four women. So, that brings a certain gaze into the story, and we could talk about topics that a group of girls would chat about on a given day. A lot of it is about how girls feel. It is a very real emotion – not just superficial. And we wanted to capture that in this show. Many woman-woman conversations exist in the show.

Also, it wasn't something that had been done in India. It was one of the first shows that Amazon Prime India had greenlit, and it has done pretty well for them. It's one of those shows that whenever a new season drops, there is like a tsunami of messages in our DMs about how people love it. And you know what, it's not just watched by women, but it's watched by many men as well. It all started in 2016, the early days of OTT, so we didn't know back then what to expect but the idea was to push the envelope and explore what we could do with a subject like this. If you look at it, the tone of the show is not very serious although what the characters are going through are challenges of life. We have tried to keep it humorous and entertaining.

When you look back at your career, is there a film you shouldn't have written or should have written differently?

Yes, there are some. But, you know, I feel that had I not written those projects, I may not have met some of the people I met on those projects who led me to much better things. So, I don't know how it would be if I were to remove that from my life. I think every experience teaches you something and there are always good things in everything. The Buddhists say, 'There is good in bad and there is bad in good.' Eventually, you find out the good in everything. So, I think I am very happy with where I am today. I just know that whatever I have done, I have given it my everything. And I think I did what I did on some such projects because those were the choices that were available to me at that time.

What's your best work of all that you have written?

I feel it's definitely *Rocky Aur Rani Kii Prem Kahaani*.

What are the films and shows, and who are the film-makers that have influenced you?

I have many. This is going to be long. I think I am a very influenced person.

In India, I'd say the film *Mughal-e-Azam*. I have seen it many times for its dialogue. I think every line coming from every character is so well-written that it sounds like music. Then, of course, I love Salim-Javed who have influenced every single screenwriter in India. I am a very mainstream person that way. I love Gulzar – I just love the way he has written dialogue. There is something so conversational about his dialogue that I love that quality about his work. I think I generally sway towards saying things in a comedy, slice-of-life way. So, I like films that tend to do that. And for that, I genuinely enjoyed films such as *Mili* and *Anand*. These are super-hit films and the issues they deal with are very serious but the way they have written those is something I really appreciate. So, when to punch up the drama and when to keep it real are things that really interest me. When I was growing up, of course, film such as *Kuch Kuch Hota Hai* and *Dilwale Dulhania Le Jayenge* were favourites. And even *Dil Chahta Hai* is very special to me because I had never heard characters speak like that before. I also really loved *Vicky Donor*. I love Juhi Chaturvedi's work in *Vicky Donor*.

Then outside of India, I like *Fleabag* a lot. I love Phoebe Waller-Bridge and whatever she does. Even what she did with *Killing Eve* is amazing. Then, I really like Aaron Sorkin, of course. I like Tina Fey. I also love Shonda Rhimes. She is a very, very big writer. She has written *Grey's Anatomy*, *Scandal*, *Bridgerton*, and several other shows. When I see something written by Shonda, you don't have to tell me that it's written by her. I can tell that she has written it. Then, there is Richard Curtis whose work I like. Honestly, the list would just go on.

Now, after having established yourself as a writer in the industry, what would be success to you in the next ten to fifteen years?

So, now I am a mother. I have a daughter who is a year and a half old. And I think the way I look at the world has changed. I was making her listen to the song '*What Jhumka*' and I was telling her, 'When you grow up, we will watch this film together that mumma has written.' Now I want to do stuff that my daughter will be proud of or at least would like to watch. I want to keep getting opportunities to do good work and want to continue to be in a position to choose what I want to work on. I want to enjoy the process and hopefully leave some legacy behind. I hope to be able to find an identity as a writer, my own signature style that hopefully people will like and remember.

TWELVE

Jasmeet K. Reen

I met Jasmeet at a beautiful café called Joshi House at Pali Naka not long after *Darlings* was released. She came across as a smart, sophisticated, and well-read woman who knew the importance of hard work and perseverance in the film industry.

I can only wish that a writer-director like her – not only because she is a strong and much-needed woman voice but also purely for her sensitivity and awareness – gets to work with growing budgets and on all kinds of films she wants to.

Tell me about your childhood.

Childhood was figuring out what I wanted to do in life. I am a Bombay girl. I have a lot of family in Delhi and Chandigarh since I am a Sardar but I was born and grew up in Bombay. As a child, I used to read a lot of books and watched a lot of films – both Bollywood and Hollywood. My dad used to watch a lot of classics so I grew up watching films by Hrishikesh Mukherjee and Guru Dutt and people like those. Good cinema. Also, some commercial films like *Sholay*. My dad was also a huge Sahir fan. He used to listen to the radio and read books. He was a rooted man. I enjoyed watching films with him a lot but I never really wrote anything in my childhood though I was aware that there was a creative side to me.

I used to fare fairly well in my studies. So, I started studying commerce. And then I began to study to be a CA. Then when I was working at Ernst & Young as an intern, I remember speaking to my boss, who's still a dear friend. I told him I couldn't see myself doing this for the rest of my life. I thought, what else? And I tried my hand at advertising. I worked with McCann as well as with Ogilvy. But because I went with a CA background, I worked in client servicing and not in the creative department. I had joined as an intern but then they hired me.

This was when I could witness ad film production. At Ogilvy, I used to sometimes write ad films as well although I was not working there as a copywriter. I got a freehand at that time. I remember writing dialogues for a Kodak. This was when Mahesh was still alive. Mahesh V. and Rajiv (Rao) were the creative directors on it. They wrote the ad but I was tweaking dialogues here and there. That must be the first thing I ever wrote – not counting the several love letters when I was growing up. Then I quit Ogilvy and started assisting on ad films, which my mother was rather upset about because one couldn't see a career as an AD (assistant director). Then I realized that advertising AD is great but to make a career, I need to start working in Hindi films.

Now, Hindi films, for outsiders, could be an alien territory. So, you won't believe this, I had a random gym friend, who gave me some contact. Through him, I met someone over a cup of coffee and got the job. It was that random. I started assisting on feature films for a while. Then again, I thought, wait, enough is enough, I want to make my film. So, I stopped working as an AD. To make my feature film, I knew I had to be able to write. Advertising was great and I learnt a lot from assisting on ad films. But I knew I wanted to direct and I also knew that I didn't want to direct anything that comes my way. I did a couple of short films and some music videos and I guess I screwed up. The ideas were not mine; I was only directing. That's when I realized that the voice has to be mine. And to work on my voice, I had to write. So that's when I stopped everything else, took a break, and started writing.

This was also around the time I got married. So, I took a two-year break just to write. The first script I wrote was about Sahir Ludhianvi and Amrita Pritam's story and I really, really wanted to make that film. It was a Sahir Ludhianvi biopic. I put my heart and soul into the project. I took Urdu classes, I met a lot of people, one of whom was Khayyam Sahab when he was alive – he was fabulous. I spent evenings with him and many other people. I read a lot of Sahir's work and basically spent a lot of time in research. I finished that script and wanted to direct it. Initially, Sanjay Leela Bhansali was one of the people supposed to produce it. But then it didn't work out and the film was never made. But people really liked my script, it was an ambitious project. Although the film wasn't made, I started getting a lot of writing work. And I enjoyed it a lot. So, that's it. After that, I started writing full-time.

What kind of books do you like to read?

I read fiction mostly. Milan Kundera. Knut Hamsun – I am very old school that way. Manto, for sure. Sahir, for sure. Murakami, I like a lot. I also read poetry. I like Bukowski, I like Neruda. Lots of Hindi poetry as well. Growing up, it was more Hindi books than English because more of them were at home. So luckily, I started reading in Devanagari. Then of course, in college, I was hungry to explore other writers. A lot of Henry Miller, and Fyodor Dostoevsky followed later.

Was it a struggle to first get in and then fit into Bollywood?

Yes, it was. You know, when I joined advertising, I wanted to be a copywriter but I worked in client servicing. Because I did not even tell myself that I was a writer. I was not sure. When I worked as an AD, the only way to get work was to prove yourself. As a writer, especially a film writer, you need to get people to read your work. You know, even if the script you're approaching people with doesn't work out, some other conversation will. And of course, things take time. That is the struggle. But I think almost everyone has to do it. I assisted in five-six films. *Zinda* was one of them. Also a film made by Hansal Mehta. And with my first film script, the one about Sahir, I went door to door. Things here don't happen immediately. You have to be patient. Something that this industry has taught me is to be patient. And I have learnt it the hard way. My film on Sahir never got made but here I am today. And I believe, in a way, I am just starting out now. When you're waiting for that first thing to happen, you can either wait or you can just keep writing. I chose the latter. One thing is for sure that if you can wake up and write every day and if you're getting paid for it, there is no bigger joy than that. I feel I am lucky that way.

Do you think the industry is still partial against female film-makers and writers?

No, I don't think so. I am sure there are challenges. At least in my experience, and I can't speak for others, I don't think I have ever faced something gender-related. Just because I am a woman, I won't get work or would be judged a certain way – it has never been that way. You know, a lot of it is about how you see yourself. There is a problem if you get into a room, for instance, and think, 'Hey, I am a woman. How can I narrate an action film?' But I never thought that. I have written action films too. My first film that ever got released was *Force 2*! So, you have to first accept that there is no problem and go about your job. And even if there occurs a problem, you deal with it. In my experience, this industry's beauty as well as its problems are more or less the same for both male and female writers and film-makers. It's quite democratic that way.

With *Darlings*, you have arrived. Run me through the journey of the film.

You know, *Darlings* is fully fiction. In the sense that it definitely doesn't come from my life, nor is it based on anyone I know personally. But growing up, you have seen violence here and there and the shocking part is that everyone is okay with it. And this happens across social strata. I would never say that this happens only in a chawl in Byculla. So, I had this idea back in the day. I started speaking to different women about it. I would bring it up in conversations and understand people's experiences and stories. That's when I realized this problem is so common. Almost everyone knows a neighbour or someone who has suffered something like this.

Another interesting thing happened a long time ago. If you meet my husband, he is a very sophisticated, polite, well-behaved man from an army background. When I got married, there was a distant aunt of mine, who just walked up to me one day and out of the blue, asked me, 'Does your husband hit you?' I was shocked. I was like, 'What did I or my husband do to make you believe that?' For her to ask me this question was bizarre. Then I thought about it and realized that the problem was not me or my husband but her. This is certainly coming from one of her life experiences or from someone she knows. People's inability to leave a bad relationship is certainly a thing.

So, in *Darlings*, I knew that the daughter had to decide to either stay or let go. It can't be anyone else deciding this for her. Also, a lot of dark humour naturally found its way into the script. I didn't want to preach anything – I knew that for sure. I just wanted to start the conversation about this subject and yet I wanted to make an interesting film. I don't think my film is going to change the world. I don't think any film can change the world. It's too much pressure on a film, honestly. So, I just wrote the story. I spent a lot of time working on each and every character. Even the parlour lady's character which is small but very important to me was there from the beginning.

After I wrote the story, I approached Parveez (Shaikh), who I have written with before. I asked him if we could write the script together because comedy is a nice genre to collaborate with other writers on. He loved the idea and we wrote it together. Once the script was ready, I took it to Red Chillies and then we met Alia (Bhatt). We narrated the script to her. This was just pre-pandemic. Must be December 2019. Alia liked it immediately and she wanted to produce it too. I was super happy. For Alia's husband, I always had Vijay Verma in mind because there were so many layers to that character. And then once Alia was on board, she once asked me on a Zoom call, 'What do you think of Vijay?' I said, 'Fab!'

Initially he was a bit scared but when he heard from me how I was seeing it, he liked it and agreed to do it. Even Shefali. The moment she heard it, she liked it. And we have seen her in so many roles with depth. She is a serious actor. But when I met her, I realized, she had so much spunk and she was perfect for the character of Shamshu. And then, one by one, things came together and you have the film to see.

You mentioned films can't change the world. Do you really believe that?

Well, what I am trying to say is that you don't make a film to change the world. But of course, you hope that a film you have made is something that people relate to and absorb. Films can and should stimulate people. I have been stimulated by the books I have read and the films I have watched. For instance, *Guide* and *Abhimaan* are films that have stimulated me but they were not made with the expectation of changing the world. It was a reflection of society at that time. Well, in a way, you look at it, yes, films can change the world. I am only saying that can't be the objective that you make them with. After *Darlings*, which is fiction, so many people have written to me saying something like this has happened to them. So, people are talking about it. And that itself is change enough for me. When you reflect on society in the most correct, rooted manner and when you show people the mirror, they can see it. And that, in my view, is the job of a film, at least the job of films that I make.

Do you have a favourite genre or are you okay writing pretty much everything?

I don't think genre specific. I think it is the story that should determine the genre. I love everything, even a period drama, for example. Having said that, I love dark comedy, which is one of the reasons why *Darlings* became what it did. But the story should have a voice. Even if it's a hard-core entertainer, it still has to say something.

Let's talk about things that did not do too well. What made you write something like *Force 2*?

See, when you write for people, a part of the vision is theirs. And *Force 2* is what Abhinay (Deo) and Vipul (Amrutlal Shah) wanted to make. Parvez and I had an idea and they liked it. And the film was made. I respect Abhinay's vision. He wanted to make that film that way and he did. Also, I think as a writer, I take full responsibility for everything I have written. And as I said, you are collaborating with people on a film, especially when you are only writing and not directing it. *Darlings*, for instance, is my voice because I have also directed the film. Of course, Parveez wrote it with me, and then Vijay (Maurya) came in with dialogues but it's my voice and I take 100 per cent responsibility for it.

What drives you to write films and not, say, poetry or fiction?

I love poetry. I wish I could write it. But I don't know if I can. I read a lot of poetry. Maybe someday, I will write a novel too, who knows? The thing with cinema is that I just lose myself in it. I thrive on it. One of the main reasons why writing films appeals to me is also because I want to direct them. I love watching films and that's why I want to make them. It's simple that way.

Where do you stand on the OTT evolution?

I think it's a great time for so many voices to come in. Because of OTT, so many writers and directors have found so much opportunity. You can see so many different kinds of stories because of this. New talent gets introduced, new writers get a chance and because of it all, it gets highly competitive. So you're inspired to work harder. I think it's great.

Say, ten years ago, we were still making a lot of films but there were only a few production houses. Right now, there are many production houses to pitch to. There are more players. And it's advantageous for writers, especially new writers, to have them. Talking about the struggle, that still exists. I mean it's not easy now just because OTT is here. But I think people should struggle a little bit, right? It only adds up eventually and makes them stronger. One should just focus on work and build, build, build, build, build. It will surprise you in ways you can't imagine.

Do you think Bollywood lacks creative ambition as an industry?

I think one should make the film they want to make. You might get less money for something or more money for something else. But who's stopping you? Of course, there will be some struggle involved but I am sure one can eventually make what they want to. And I think we have so many different film-makers who do make what they want to. Look at Anurag's (Kashyap) films. He makes what he wants to and how he wants to. Same with Zoya (Akhtar). Even Imtiaz Ali, Raju Hirani. These guys have a voice of their own. So, if anyone believes that they would like to see something else, they can attempt to change that by making it. If you want to make a *hatke* (different) film, write it. I am sure, not everyone would buy it or maybe then you would want to make it in a certain way. But *Dev D* was made, right? That, too, with Abhay Deol.

With *Darlings*, I was lucky that someone like Alia saw merit in the script. And she is also a good actor. *Darlings* is not a conventional film. For her to back it was great because once you have someone like Alia on board, the producers feel more secure to put their money in.

Some advice you'd like to offer to young writers.

Write, work hard, take risks. It's simple. Respect your voice, and trust yourself. Sometimes, you write a script that you feel is coming from within but then you tweak it considering what is working at the moment. Don't do that. Because nobody knows what the audience will like or won't like. So, stick to what you've got. Also, always remember that nothing is easy.

Do you think screenwriting is better self-taught or studied formally?

Well, I think both ways work. I, for one, never went to a film school. And learnt mainly from watching films. But you know, there is a lot of material. Syd Field and so many others. And I would say one must read as much of it as possible. You can't reject something you haven't read. So get exposed to everything and then figure out what's working for you. I mean, you can learn so much by reading screenplays or even interviews with writers like Aaron Sorkin for example. I also did a short summer course at FTII, which I learnt a lot from. Education is great. Just remember that you have to learn so much on the job as well. In the art world, there is a lot to learn on the job. So, if you assist writers, and work with people, you get to learn a lot about not just writing scripts but also pitching them. You gain confidence and lose your fears.

Do you think the gender of a writer influences their work?

See, I feel representing women in a certain way, for sure, has nothing to do with gender. Through the years, we have seen many male film-makers beautifully representing women. However, maybe the gaze of looking at any character would be different for a woman. When I met women, for *Darlings*, I felt maybe they would be more open to talk to me. Maybe as a woman, I would understand and empathize with some of the things in a different way. It's a patriarchal society and maybe women can sometimes see things that men don't. I mean, why Alia would hold on to Vijay Verma despite the violence? She has grown up without a father or strong male presence so she holds onto the first man she is with. These are things that I am not saying a man cannot see but maybe because I am a woman, I can see sooner. If a man makes *Darlings*, he would make it differently but that's true for any film. In essence,

I don't think artists have genders. Men have a feminine side to them and women have a masculine side as well. I mean look at Guru Dutt, for example, for the way he handles women characters or the character of Charulata that Satyajit Ray has developed – how utterly beautiful is that!

What are your favourite films and shows and who are your favourite film-makers?

Earlier, in college, it was more of world cinema for me. Federico Fellini, Krzysztof Kieslowski, Stanley Kubrick, Jean-Luc Godard, and these guys. Kubrick is all wow for me. *A Clockwork Orange*, *Dr Strangelove*, *Eyes Wide Shut*, everything. But at the same time, I used to also watch Hrishikesh Mukherjee, Guru Dutt, and Satyajit Ray. Then I started watching a lot of Hollywood films. I love the Coen brothers. I love Tarantino. *Pulp Fiction* is a film I have watched many times over and admire it. I also love *American Beauty*. I like Sam Mendes's work. I love *Revolutionary Road*. *Who's Afraid of Virginia Woolf* blew my mind. It is as dark a comedy as it gets. Then recently, I loved Asghar Farhadi's work. *Hero*, his latest film, is what I watched last and it was out of this world. I like *A Separation* and *About Elly* and his other films as well. Then of course there are gurus like Spielberg and Scorsese that you learn from. Elia Kazan's classic *A Streetcar Named Desire* is what I love a lot. I liked *Parasite* a lot. A lot of Paul Thomas Anderson's work. Noah Baumbach's *A Marriage Story*. And who did I miss? I could go on.

Among shows, *The West Wing* is the best thing I have ever seen in the world. I like *True Detective*. I love *Better Call Saul*. I think it's a very good show. I love *Black Mirror* and *Fargo* as well. Then *Mad Men*, *House of Cards*. I like a lot of HBO shows. I like *Squid Games* as well. It was fun to watch. *Succession* – that's a show everybody likes. It's like the film *Eternal Sunshine of the Spotless Mind* – I don't know anyone who doesn't like it. What a film!

Is there a film you wish you had written or made?

Well, you know, there are films I love as I told you. But no, I don't wish I had made any other films because if I did, I would make them differently.

If you had 100 crore rupees, what would you make?

I'll make the film I am working on. I would not make a film just because I have 100 crores. I would make what I want to and if I don't end up using all the money, I'd give it back.

THIRTEEN

Kamal Swaroop

One of the most fascinating conversations I have had about cinema – not just for this book, but in my entire life – was with Kamal Swaroop. He is an original thinker and quite unlike anyone else. His path-breaking film *Om-Dar-B-Dar* remains a cult classic of Indian arthouse cinema and there is nary a serious film-maker in Bombay who doesn't rate it phenomenally highly.

I met Kamal Swaroop at his apartment, which is just a few buildings away from where I spent some of the most thrilling years of my life. Kamal Swaroop is unpredictable, unabashed, terribly complex, and amazingly honest about his ideas of film, his life, and the world in general.

What was your childhood like and how did films happen?

It's been too long since my childhood. I am not sure if I can remember it all. I was born in Kashmir, and spent a few years there. Then, I moved to Rajasthan with my family. We lived in many small villages there, tribal villages as well. I completed my graduation from Ajmer. We have been a big, happy family for as long as I remember. My childhood was a happy place.

When did writing and your love for films begin?

In my childhood, I had nothing to do with writing or films. Yes, I used to read a lot. A lot of Hindi literature and some Western books. I vaguely remember reading every day, in fact. But as a skill, I had nothing. I used to copy some stories from some magazines and tell people that I had written them. That was the only skill I had. The worth of a cut-paste artist.

I started writing when I came to Pune to join FTII. At that time, there was no such thing as a professional writer in films. Nobody knew what film writing was about. People used to rely only on books and literature. From there, they used to make some kind of a production script and would use it for films. In commercial cinema, people wrote dialogue but nobody had an idea of screenplay writing. Art cinema, at the time, was controlled by English-speaking people. They didn't know how to make a film in Hindi. So, if anybody was from the north, he or she could find work as a dialogue writer. And those art cinema guys would pick up anybody who knew Hindi. People used to work for free for them as well. The idea of payment didn't exist.

So, some of us were cast as writers. I could be useful to them. After I graduated from FTII, I did some writing for Mani Kaul and Kumar Shahani. I wrote the dialogue for Kumar's film *Tarang*. I started my career with the Indian Space Research Organization (ISRO). There I did writing, direction, and production for two years. We used to make science programmes for children and made some documentaries.

Why did you join FTII if you had no interest in film as a child?

Purely because I wanted to get out of the house. And FTII was cheap. That's the only reason. I knew about FTII as it would get mentioned in newspapers. And in those days, people like Mani Kaul and Kumar Shahani were becoming famous. Their films were getting talked about. The first avant-garde film was Satyadev Dubey's *Shantata! Court Chalu Aahe*. Then films like *Uski Roti* and *Sara Akash* got noticed. In *Dharmyug* and *Madhuri* and magazines like those, there were a lot of write-ups about *Uski Roti* and these small films. Those guys were from small towns like me. I thought even I might get lucky with films and I applied to FTII and got through. Who doesn't want to be famous? Today, I know the cost of fame. But back then, in your early twenties, you think it's going to be easy.

How important has FTII been in your journey? Did it make you fall in love with cinema?

I won't say love for films and all. I am not sure if I can call it love anymore. But it is the only profession I know or perhaps don't know. But it was a matter of luck and chance that I landed in FTII. It was a gamble. And I don't know if it paid off. I haven't made a great career or money, you know. I am not saying it was the right decision to join FTII but that's what I did and here I am. I won't romanticize being in FTII. Also, I was very young, just nineteen years old, when I went there and graduated when I was twenty-two. I don't think that's an age when you understand what you're seeing.

The problem with FTII is that it makes you believe that you could be one of the greats and that greatness is very much possible. You read great literature and philosophy and aesthetics at that age. You get affected by FTII's grandeur. And that creates complications in life because most of us don't understand what we are encountering but are smitten by its aura. You tend to roleplay greatness. And then get cut off from your family and friends because you start thinking you are special and living with the greats. You develop a certain contempt for your people and your ordinary friends. Like everyone, I experienced all of that as well.

What was it like after working for ISRO?

I wanted to make films. So, we opened this cooperative called Yukt where we made films like *Ghashiram Kotwal* and Saeed Akhtar Mirza's *Arvind Desai Ki Ajeeb Dastaan*. I wrote dialogues for *Arvind Desai Ki Ajeeb Dastaan*. The four of us, Saeed Akhtar Mirza, Mani

Kaul, K. Hariharan and I, directed *Ghashiram* which was based on Vijay Tendulkar's Marathi play.

You are still associated with FTII as a teacher. How has the institute changed over the decades?

Well, today people have access to world cinema and so much material even before they join FTII. Kids now are intelligent. Also, today, there is a lot of promise. You could get a lucrative job and there's a lot of value to the FTII degree on paper. At our time, we had no clue and there was a sense of depression, you know. People used to stay alone, locked up in their rooms, studying, and reading. Cinema wasn't a business then. We lived there as if there was no future. Also, at our time, a lot of older people used to come there. People at the age of thirty or thirty-five even. I was an aberration at nineteen. People used to come there and meditate. It was an opportunity to be away from the world. And there was no politics. No sense of crowd and groupism. People were more individualistic back then. No party politics, no group identity. A certain kind of depression and being resigned to life is how people were. Having said that, people were sensitive. They may not be as smart as today's generation but they were sensitive.

Did you, at any point in life, have the will to make a hit Bollywood film? How did you survive with arthouse cinema?

No, no, I never had the courage. There was a certain flamboyance and robustness to that business which always scared me. I was very thin and shy, and I was afraid of approaching those guys. Of course, there was a sense of romance back then. I had read novels about the industry and there was an attraction I did have but never really had the guts to be on that side of things. I somehow saw a possibility in art cinema. So, I got into that circle. This art cinema kind of guys used to come to FTII. They were the middle-class intelligentsia. Somehow, either by policy or by natural process, the commercial guys were looked down upon by the art circle. A differentiation was created between the masses and the classes. This differentiation started not only in FTII but in the magazines like *Filmfare* as well. We happened to slot ourselves into the classes. And then we began operating in that world.

Arthouse cinema was a very small world. Although, in reality, a lot of the FTII people also worked in advertising and in commercial cinema because it was lucrative to do so. They used to mint money during the day with some heavy-duty commercial stuff and at night, after getting drunk, they used to talk about Tarkovsky and philosophy and whatnot. Some people also tried to break that barrier between these two schools. But there was no use in breaking that image. Because the projection of purity, romance, and art benefitted them.

I, for one, had no desire to get into commercial cinema. I was okay not making money. It's still a mystery to me how I have survived so long without working in any of that. I would do the odd writing job for someone but I have no memory of working regularly. I have worked in foreign productions as well. I assisted Richard Attenborough with *Gandhi*. I was the person who was in charge of handling the crowd. I think I had the skill of handling a crowd. This affected my film-making as well because on a very low budget, I managed to create a spectacle by playing with crowds. *Gandhi* was a six-month-long project. Then I also worked on *A Passage to India* and some other films. I didn't have too many monetary needs so even if I worked on one such project it would facilitate my survival for a whole year. I lived like this till I made *Om-Dar-B-Dar*.

Please tell me about the journey of writing and then making your cult masterpiece – *Om-Dar-B-Dar*. How did you reach the idea to begin with?

The idea occurred to me when I was working on *Gandhi* and when I told stories to keep the crowd busy. Also, I was always interested in folk tales and mythological stories. *Gandhi* paid me well as it was a foreign production. So, after I got my cheque, I took a house on rent for a year and started working on *Om-Dar-B-Dar*. It was not written as a single idea. I used to have a register back then and I would scribble stuff in it. One idea from here, another from there. I didn't know what the whole story was. You can imagine the process to be like how David Lynch operates. You get ideas from different places fuse them in a pot and let them all cook together. It is a surrealist work.

Sometimes what I wrote made sense. Sometimes, I told myself what I have written is bullshit and would discard it. So sometimes I felt happy, some depressed. The process itself was terrific. I was alone with the subject. Small bits of information would sneak into the draft. The idea was to load the script with information. The information then crystallizes into small ideas. Sometimes, I would write about what is past. Sometimes about what is class. Then I'd crack them into seeds, different abstracts, and then gather them.

I had a friend called Suresh Jindal, who was also the producer of Satyajit Ray's *Shatranj Ke Khiladi*. He told me it had been too long since I was living with the subject and I should now start to make it. His nephew had a typewriter and we started putting all the story ideas I had written in one document. For three nights, I narrated the story and he typed it out. In three days, we had the script. I submitted it to NFDC (National Film Development Corporation). And eventually, it got approved. But the script was written in English. So, after it got approved, I had to spend another year and a half on dialogue. Because you can write anything in English at a script level. When you go ahead and make it in Hindi, the dialogue work starts.

It got into a more surreal zone. I, in fact, always work like this. I cannot follow a plotline or the 'hero journey' structure. I always have multiple ideas, sometimes five to seven of them and I fuse them together. I always think why waste the whole film on one single idea?

I find all these middle-class films terrible. Husband-wife and plotline and stuff like that. I can't stand them. I try to make things more and more complex for me and more and more difficult. I tend to create greater hurdles for myself to the point that it's almost impossible to make the film. And then try to overcome them. It's a form of self-torture. I don't know what enmity I have with myself!

Do you think this unique process is one of the reasons why *Om-Dar-B-Dar* is such a special film which is like no other? How did your life change after *Om-Dar-B-Dar*?

Yes, maybe. Because it is dense. It is not a fixed pattern or an idea. It is generative. At no point can you say that you have understood the film. It does not have a definite meaning. It generates multiple ideas. The film is a living object. And just like living objects, you cannot and need not fully understand the piece. My process is more of an anarchic activity. I destroy the film. That's why I faced a lot of mental violence. At that time, some people said *Om-Dar-B-Dar* was not a film at all. It didn't get into Panorama and didn't get any awards. It got rejected by everyone when it came out. NFDC almost banned it too, you know, because they thought the film was very different from the script I presented to them. They felt cheated. They also felt there must be some hidden messages in it, so even the censor board gave it an 'A' certificate. The film was doomed.

What happened is that one of the copies I had made got leaked and eventually it started getting distributed underground. Then in 2012, twenty-four years after I made it, it got revived because Neena Gupta noticed it and drew attention to it. That was the time it was restored and finally got accepted. But for twenty-four years, I lived as a loan defaulter. I had compound interest accumulating on me and NFDC banned me from working with them. I couldn't find any work. Now, they have taken over the film and they are minting money from it.

What you call my special film or masterpiece ruined my life. People used to laugh at me. They'd tease me saying '*Darbadar ghum raha hai, dekho!*' (He's going door to door, look!) As an artist, you need to be cast. You need some protective system. I didn't have any of it. People won't miss a chance to make fun of you. Especially if you're a film-maker or a celebrity. If you show the slightest vulnerability, you are doomed. And I was vulnerable all through my life. In some ways, I am still paying for *Om-Dar-B-Dar*. Yes, I got accepted after 2012 but honestly, it was quite late. I was already sixty by then. I had started to lose faith. I had almost given it up. I was manically depressed for many years after that. Yes, I made a couple of documentaries during this time but I was never accepted. My situation after *Om-Dar-B-Dar* was I was neither the masses nor the classes. I was simply rejected.

I now think some of it was also self-created, you know. I could have shifted in another direction and redeemed myself. But I didn't. You cannot be a cult figure for cheap. It comes with a heavy cost. I now know a lot of people who would die to have made a cult film like that. But what you need to bear with that is something nobody wants or even understands.

There's a new thing in society and cinema. Too much emphasis on correctness. Where do you stand on that?

In the clutches of correctness, there is no expression anymore. Everyone will soon come to a sterile consent where there is no individuality left. Or they will create a common invisible hate object on whom they can take off their anger and rejoice in it. But that hate object is abstract, very abstract. Everybody is looking for a hate object where they can come together. Hate is the only place where they will arrive at consent. You can't openly speak anymore. I think it's really stupid. A person's life is dynamic, you know. It's paradoxical and ironical and sick and so many other things. But you can't open up about those things anymore.

Some people want this to be overcome but they don't want to do anything about it themselves. They want another person to take that fight and get beaten up but don't want themselves to be that guy. Nobody wants to volunteer. Who wants to bear with so much, right? This is taking society and cinema down together.

Any film-maker that you were influenced by or admired the work of?

See, when I was growing up, in the FTII days, we were trained to dislike Satyajit Ray and Ritwik Ghatak. We were foot soldiers trained to dislike everything except the old masters. I don't think any film influenced me. For me, it was the kind of life I was living that inspired my films. My life in Ajmer and Kashmir and everywhere else. I wanted that to come out. I didn't want my film to look like another film. Having said that, sure, you do get attracted to some films. I was very fond of (Luis) Bunuel and his surrealist cinema. Now they call it experimental cinema. I was more into that zone. The conventional dramatic narrative never attracted me. In fact, now that I teach, and after all these years, when I know film-making, I have begun to appreciate the difficult process of film-making.

When I made *Om-Dar-B-Dar*, I did not know film-making. Today, when I look at Ray, some of the scenes he's created are stunning. But I would personally still be more attracted to the David Lynch kind of cinema. Also, I don't get anything classical. Before this, I did have a sense of cinematic rhythm but I don't think I knew the craft.

How political should cinema be?

Our very existence is political. *Om-Dar-B-Dar* is a political film. But it's not about party politics. These days, when people say they have a political stance, they actually have propaganda. Be it the right or the left. Most of it is propaganda. Nothing comes from individuality. The people who call themselves political film-makers run around in groups and have no political stance of their own. Their personal politics is zero.

You have had an extremely eventful life. Anything that you'd do differently in life if you got another chance?

Of course. First and foremost, don't get into this business. Given a chance, I would go back to the time when I joined FTII and tell myself not to go anywhere near films. I'd pick up a government job, do it well, and then live off the pension post-retirement. That would be a good life.

I don't know if my journey was worth it. You know, for the last thirty to thirty-five years, after *Om-Dar-B-Dar*, whenever someone asked me what I was up to, I told them that I was working on a film on Dadasaheb Phalke. I have done lots of research. Also wrote a book on Phalke. But I haven't yet made the film. Now, I don't know how much is left in me. But you know, if I am able to crack Phalke before I go, I'd say this was all worth it.

FOURTEEN

Mohinder Pratap Singh

Understated, often underplayed, and in many ways, underrated, Mohinder Pratap Singh is the writer of the shows *Undekhi* and *Apharan* among others, and the writer-director of the short films *Jutti* and *Salt 'N' Pepper*. He has also written the feature film *Happi* and has been a co-writer on *M.S. Dhoni: The Untold Story*.

Mohinder Pratap Singh is a quiet man who reads and writes for leisure and does both with great dedication and acumen. The perseverance with which he has made the journey of writing is commendable.

I met him at Alfredo's in Malad, where we met many times before and after this conversation. It was an evening that matured into a night quite beautifully as his journey of about twenty years in the film industry flowed like a river.

How did you develop an interest in literature?

If not the sole reason, a rather prominent reason why I became a writer is that I was born to my father, who is a professor of Hindi literature. So, a lot of literature was available to me when I was growing up. You know, there were times, when you were not allowed to go out and play as a young boy. At those times, the books came in handy. I took a liking to a lot of poetry and fiction. I was more or less an introvert as a kid and I didn't share my thoughts with too many kids around me. I was also perfectly average in school. Far from the lot of the toppers but also, fortunately, far from the bottom lot in my class. I was a sixty-seventy per cent kind of a student and that made me a little under-confident and reluctant to interact with too many people outside. I found my peace and self in literature. So, when I read Sarveshwar Dayal Saxena, Shrikant Verma, Kedarnath Singh, and Premchand, they all spoke to me and became my childhood friends.

What was college like and how did words find a way into it?

As I said, as a child I was surrounded by books and wasn't particularly sharing a lot of my thoughts with people around me. But as a child, you have a lot to say. And when you don't want to speak to people, you start speaking to the page. That's what got me writing. Soon, I wrote a poem that got published in a local newspaper called *Darpan* which used to be published in Karnal. I went to their office one day with my written pages and saw a man smoking a beedi who read it and said, '*Theek hai, rakhke jao. Chhaap denge.*' (Very well, just leave it here. We'll publish it.) And in the next few days, it was published!

Let's talk about your move from Haryana to Mumbai and how geography played a role in the development of the writer in you.

I was born in Ambala and went to school there. Then my family moved to Karnal where I went to college. It was here that I started to write to change the world. My father was a professor in the same college, which as you might guess, takes away a lot of joy from college life. Especially, for a person like me who wanted to go out and explore. Whenever I bunked a lecture, my father used to come to know of it by evening.

How geography affected my writing is that Karnal was part of the Mahabharata. The city is named after Karna. Kurukshetra is just forty kilometres away where Krishna gave Gita Gyan to Arjun right in the middle of the battlefield. So, growing up here made me fall in love with the Mahabharata and its characters. To me, the Mahabharata is the greatest tale ever told. It left a lasting impression on me and shaped the storyteller that I would eventually become.

Tell me about your advertising days in the 1990s and what they taught you.

I think advertising is a very different form. I started working in advertising when I came to Mumbai. This was back in 1994. I joined Leo Burnett, which was at the time called Chaitra Leo Burnett. At the time, I lived in Mira Road and the office was at Kemp's Corner. Advertising found some value in me because I could write in Hindi and at that time, there weren't too many good Hindi copywriters in Mumbai. Advertising is a much shorter format and you have to write for brands. It doesn't always allow you to tell the stories you want to.

I worked very closely with Aggy (Agnello Dias) and Chaks (K.S. Chakravarthy), who are both stalwarts now. Aggy was my immediate boss and I loved working with him. I spent four years in advertising. One of the great things advertising taught me was how to think of great ideas. Advertising is an idea-led industry, or at least was back then. To filter out bad ideas and arrive at good ones is what I learnt from those years. I'd say, somewhere that learning is still useful to me while I write films and shows and the longer format in general.

What was the experience of writing for TV like?

Though I have written about 400 episodes of television, I don't think I have much experience in that world. I recently wrote 176 episodes of a show called *Kaatelal and Sons*. Honestly, before I started writing it, all my life I had looked down upon television. However, an important thing that I learnt once I quit advertising and started writing for TV is that advertising does not teach you a sense of drama; television does. In visual storytelling, in this medium, you need drama. Without drama, you can't even mount a single scene. And television taught me this. Another thing I learnt about TV is that if I don't enjoy watching TV, I probably am not the audience for it. So, I should not say that television is bad. And as a writer, you don't necessarily have to write what you'd like to consume. Just like TV, I wasn't the audience for Ghadi detergent powder either but I still wrote for it.

Tell me about your days of struggle.

Struggle for me is with an objective. I wrote ads, wrote TV, then got to write cinema and now shows. But all this while, what are you trying to do? You are trying to tell the story you want to! And the process of getting to that is what some of us call a struggle. Some people take too long to get there, some people take a shorter while. It's not just about talent but also how you handle yourself as a person.

Another thing is how you know if and when you are ready. All these years are not wasted because you have always learnt something from the experience. I have learnt the craft that I know over the years. I may have thought I was ready twenty years ago, but probably I wasn't. I truly believe that writing is a journey. You know, in my younger days, I wanted to change the world with my writing. I had a lot of passion but not much craft. Today, if you ask me, I know a thing or two about craft but I don't have that passion, that aggression I had when I was younger.

Both your short films *Salt 'N' Pepper* and *Jutti* were critically acclaimed and were ten years apart. Why and how did you decide to write and direct them, especially considering the lack of commerce for short films in India?

I made *Salt 'N' Pepper* with Nawazuddin Siddiqui and Tejaswini Kolhapure. It was a story I wanted to tell. Now, I couldn't produce my feature film, didn't have the money to. Hence a short film seemed like the best way out. I invested my own money in the film. But it was an idea that I wanted to work on because it combined two ideas: young people committing suicide over heartbreak and the state of the farmers in the country. Nawaz was not as big a star back then as he is today. But he has always been a fabulous actor. I am very glad that the film was received well.

Ten years later, there was another story I wanted to tell. Once, I was travelling on a train from Mumbai to Haryana. And next to me was a young couple. We talked about the long journey. And they told me that the guy owned a shoe shop that the girl would visit often and then the two of them fell in love. Their story fascinated me. The germ of the idea of *Jutti* came from there – a part of my lived experience. Yes, I made both films with my money and yes, I haven't even recovered the amount I invested but guess what, I have recovered half the amount! Also, I don't think the return from a short film can only be measured in terms of money. That work is there to stay and the satisfaction I gained from it is priceless.

When and how did you get your first break in films?

While I was working in advertising at Leo Burnett, everybody knew that I wanted to write and make a film. Because that's what I talked about over drinks. One day, a colleague of mine called Manohar, who was then the 'Language Head' at Leo Burnett and who now owns the famous recording studio Shankh, introduced me to a friend of his who was looking for a Hindi writer to work on a feature. This man was Gaurav Pandey. Gaurav had written a film called *Aastha* for Basu Bhattacharya and he was planning his feature. We started writing the film. At the time, I stayed in Mira Road. I used to leave my house at 6 in the morning, take a train to Kandivali station, and then a bus from there to reach Thakur Complex at 7. From 7 to 10, I used to work with him on the film. Then from there, I used to go to Kemp's Corner for my job.

The reporting time in office was 9.15. But there was no way, in this setup, that I could reach before 11. So, I requested my boss to give me such permission for a few months till I was writing this film. The permission was granted. When you entered after 9.15, it was considered a half-day. And for every four-and-a-half days, a day of your monthly salary would get cut. So, I was pretty okay with losing around four to five days of salary. I think it was a minimal cost I had to pay to learn scriptwriting.

Gaurav changed my life. He changed so many things for the writer in me. One, he introduced me to international cinema. He had studied cinema in France. It was at his house that I got to see Kieslowski's *Three Colours* trilogy and many other films. In those days, international films were not as freely available. Gaurav had those DVDs he had bought from France. Gaurav shaped my thinking and taught me the nuances of writing. The film I wrote with him called *Ek Boond Aasman* eventually got made as a one-hour-long episode on Zee TV's *Rishtey*. The process of it taught me a hell of a lot. Then I wrote another episode of *Rishtey* called *Sahil*. After that, the first feature film I got to write was *Mr Lonely Miss Lovely*. It was a silent film directed by a Telugu star called Aditya Om. It starred Nandana Sen (daughter of Amartya Sen).

Although I think the first good film I wrote was *Happi* directed by Bhavna Talwar and starring the great Pankaj Kapoor in the lead. It was his story. And I used to go to his house every day in that phase to work on the script, which was a great experience for me. How I got to work on that film is an interesting story itself. One day, Bhavna's husband, who was in advertising as well, asked Aggy if he knew a Hindi writer for a film his wife was directing. Aggy suggested my name. I met Bhavna and started writing a film with her. After writing the whole script, Bhavna and I approached Pankaj-ji (Kapoor). When we met him, he asked me, '*Chai piyoge?*' (Do you want tea?) I was rather confident about the script and said, 'Sir, script *suna dete hain. Agar aapko pasand aayi toh chai pi lenge.*' (Sir, let me tell you the script first. If you think it's good, we'll have tea.) He thought for a moment and said, 'Risk *kyun lete ho yaar? Chai toh pi lo!*' (Why do you take risks, dude? First, let's drink some tea!) It all seems quite funny now.

I read the script out to him. And he rejected the film! He liked the script but thought that there was not much for him to do in the film. Then we went back home. But as fate would have it, Pankaj-ji called Bhavna and asked her if I would like to develop a story he has with him. I said yes and then *Happi* happened. I even attended most of the shoot. All this happened in 2008 but then the film got released in 2019! The wait was long. All this while, I wrote a TV show and did some more script and dialogue work. Then there was another film which I got to write dialogues for. It was Sada-ji's (Sadashiv Amrapurkar) story that he was going to make for Rajshri Productions. My friend Raju (Parulekar) had written the screenplay. And I got a chance to work on it. I was quite excited. I remember it was an honour for me to narrate a script to Raj Barjatya. He was one of the best listeners of scripts. He listened to me for sixteen hours at a stretch without taking a single phone call or attending to anything else. He told me, 'You have a bright future.' I was ecstatic. Ranbir Kapoor was supposed to get launched with that film. But as fate would have it, that film never got made and my struggle continued.

Did things change for you dramatically after writing *M.S. Dhoni*, which was a commercial success?

Writing *M.S. Dhoni: The Untold Story* was a great experience. And I wrote it with a lot of heart. But on it, I was the primary writer. That film could not be written by one person because there was a lot of research involved. We met not just Dhoni but also his family and friends. We spent a lot of time in Ranchi, then Kharagpur and Calcutta as well. Then we gave Neeraj (Pandey) a four-hour-long draft. Neeraj, who also directed the film, compiled the final draft. My credit on the film is that of a writing associate. So, the film wasn't as transformational for me career-wise as you'd think.

I'd say my real success happened in 2018 when both my short film *Jutti* and the show *Apharan* came out. *Apharan*, as you know, became very popular and I started getting calls from the who's who of the industry.

***Undekhi* was received very well. How did you get to pitch that project and where did the idea come from?**

Undekhi is the third piece of my work that changed my life. It came out during the lockdown in 2020. *Undekhi* is a story I wrote and an idea I came up with. The thing is I read a lot of newspapers and fairly regularly. One day, I read a piece of news that somewhere up north, a dancer got shot at a wedding. The idea started there. I pitched it to Siddharth sir (Siddharth Sengupta) who made it and directed it. It is one of his special directorial talents that he can make you binge-watch something. It's very important for a writer to find the right person to collaborate with on a project.

Which of the films from the world over would you have liked to have written or made?

I think *A Few Good Men* is certainly one of them. Then I'd say, *The Newsroom*, a show helmed by Aaron Sorkin. I love Aaron Sorkin. I think that's the kind of work where words have a lot of importance. I also like theatre and some of my favourite cinema is a little on the theatrical side. For instance, *Twelve Angry Men* is another film I eternally love.

What is your imagined writerly utopia?

When I was younger, I wanted to change a lot of things in the world. At the age of fifty-four, however, I honestly don't have too many complaints about the world. I think conflict is an essential part of the world. Without conflict, there is no world. Having said that, if you asked me, what is the one quality or attribute that I would like to see more of in the world, it is justice. I'd like to see more justice in the world.

FIFTEEN

Nitesh Tiwari

Nitesh Tiwari is the writer-director of *Dangal*, one of the highest-grossing films ever in the history of Hindi cinema, and of *Chhichhore*, *Bhootnath Returns*, and *Chillar Party* among other films. He is also the writer-ideator-creative director of some famous advertising campaigns such as for *Kaun Banega Crorepati*.

I met Nitesh at his office in Santacruz at noon.

What was your time at IIT Bombay like?

I never thought, when I went to IIT Bombay, that cultural activities like dramatics would be given so much importance. And I never knew I had it in me. So, things just happened, you know. There were hostels that used to take great pride in Sports GC (General Championship), a glimpse of which you may have seen in *Chhichhore*. But, at the same time, equal importance was given to winning the Cultural GC as well. There used to be one-act plays in English, Hindi, and Marathi; there used to be miming, there used to be group miming, there used to be mono acting, and there used to be music – seniors took great interest in all these things. What used to happen is that as soon as a fresher batch came in, the first job that the seniors would do was start scouting for talent that could represent their hostel in one or many of these things.

So when it came to the sports selections, I used to be good at cricket, so I got in. But dramatics is something that not many people are exposed to at such a young age. Many freshers themselves don't know if they have any such talent. The seniors would call us and see if any of us fit the bill. I remember my senior Dhiraj Kakkad was figuring out who could enter the Freshy Miming Competition. Miming is not easy. He wasn't sure if we had anyone who could do the job well. I had not even raised my hand initially. But I had seen the miming competition at HBTU Kanpur (Harcourt Butler Technical University) earlier. So, I thought I could try something and I went ahead and did that. And he came and he hugged me and said, 'Where were you hiding?'

That year, I won miming in the Freshy Competition and after that, I won miming four years in a row in the senior competition at IIT Bombay. So that is where my interests grew in dramatics and writing.

Although you didn't work in the field, do you think the experience of studying engineering has shaped your personality and expression?

I feel engineering shapes you. When you study engineering, it helps you become more analytical by nature. Because those problems require an analytical approach to thinking. Now, I believe, or the writers I work with and I believe as a team, that there has to be a lot of analytical thinking that should go into the writing of a screenplay and a story as well. There has to be a logical reason for everything to exist. There has to be a proper flow of things. And all of this is very, very analytical. Along with creativity, writing a screenplay also involves a lot of logic and analytical thinking, especially in terms of how to structure a screenplay, how to move from one scene to another, what is your logical flow, how the graph of the characters is developed, and many other things. So, I think somewhere that engineering study comes into play. I am not saying that's the only way to do it. I am sure some writers have not studied engineering and also employ their analytical brains in writing. But for me, I think that is of great help.

That's one aspect of studying engineering. The other one is that in your impressionable years, it matters a lot who you are surrounded by. And fortunately, in my college, I was surrounded by some very, very fertile brains. Not only were they very good at academics but also creative. So, I learnt so much from them, just by being amongst them and observing them. There was nothing conventional about the way they used to think. It was out-of-the-box thinking even in the simplest of things – even in the pranks, even in the *keedas* they used to do, even in the very basic way things were thought.

I'll give you an example of a prank. Once, some guys had removed the hinges from the side of someone's door using some tools from the mechanical engineering department and put them on the top. So normally, the door opens sideways. But after doing this, when the guy walked in, the door opened straight, up-down. It came back straight on his face. And the guy, on whose door this prank was played, loved it so much that he refused to remove the hinges and put them back in their usual place – he used to always walk into his room by bending down! It was all crazy. Another time bulls were lured by chapatis and grass and taken to the first floor of the hostel. When the guy occupying that room came in, he saw two bulls sitting inside. There were many such crazy ideas that we would witness or be part of regularly. In my third and fourth years, I was directing plays for my hostel, and the kind of response I got was marvellous.

I think it's the fabulous response I got in college that drew me towards this field. However, at the time, I never thought I would make a career in this. I did an internship at RK Swamy BBDO, which is an advertising agency, while I was in my third year of engineering. I had decided by then that I wanted to give writing a shot. Most engineers do internships in tech firms or in the industry but I chose to do it in an advertising agency. Those two months in RK Swamy were something I just loved. People were coming to the office with dogs, everybody was casual, it was a great environment, nothing formal about it. I thought someday I would like to work in an environment like that.

Then in my fourth year, I got placed in a software firm. I didn't like it as much as I thought I would. Every morning, when I went to work, I used to question myself if this is what I wanted to do for the rest of my life. The answer was always a no. After some time, I thought, this is the time for me to take risks. Because otherwise, very soon, I would settle into the job, and get comfortable with the money coming my way. And I thought I didn't want to be old and regretful that I didn't give writing a proper shot. I was not sure at all if I had it in me but I still wanted to give it a shot.

There was a *Brand Equity* article that featured the top five agencies for young writers. I applied to all five. Three rejected me straight away. Only two agencies gave me a copy test. One of which was Ulka. At that time, both Ambi and Shashi, who were the top management of Ulka, were IITians. So, they called me, spoke to me, and discouraged me! They genuinely meant well and were wondering why I wanted to be a writer after studying at IIT. They thought I was coming from a misconception that advertising is all about glamour, cool people and partying. But in reality, it is a business where you have to live with rejection every day. It's a meticulously thought job. But I was genuinely interested so I told them I still wanted to do it. After that, they gave me a copy test and soon, I joined Ulka as my first advertising job at one-fourth of my salary at the software firm. Also, I remember they didn't hire me based on a copy test. They hired me based on a poem that I had once written.

You grew up in a very small town in Madhya Pradesh. Does that affect the way you write and look at the world?

I have lived in many small towns in MP (Madhya Pradesh). Ganj Basoda, Itarsi, and many others. I draw a lot from my real-life experiences. And what seemed like a burden in childhood eventually worked in my favour. My only weakness was that I was not very good at English when I came to Bombay but it turned out to be my strength because I was very good at Hindi. That gave me an edge in advertising. At the time, I was the only Hindi writer in Ulka. So, I got to work on a lot more projects than any trainee writer ever would. I was allotted to one group but I got to work on projects from all groups. So, with four groups in play, I got four times the opportunities. And very soon, people realized that I could write good scripts. I used to be briefed by everyone. I think it was quite generous of them. I got a lot of ad films out around that time.

For a junior to have so many ad films is not common, as you may know. And some of those things also became very popular. I was making very little money. But seeing my work on TV kind of compensated for travelling from Kandivali to Nariman Point in a second-class compartment and for reading the menu card like you read Urdu – looking at the price first and then deciding on the dish. Work made up for all the struggle. And once you start doing well, you get compensated. So very soon, money started coming my way too.

Also, in my childhood, I used to be troubled because my dad worked in the education department, which was a transferable job. So, every three years, I had to make new friends. But now, I think of it as a blessing because I got to experience so much life. I got to meet such fascinating people and experience such remarkable stories that wouldn't have been possible if I lived only in one town. Every town has its own culture and I got to experience it. Let me tell you, in my ninth standard, there was no English-medium school in Ganj Basoda. The closest English-medium school was forty-two kilometres away in Vidisha. Now, today, when I look at my kids, they live in Bombay and I won't even let them go alone to the shop. But in the ninth standard, eleven of us kids, would cycle for half an hour to the Ganj Basoda station, then catch an intercity train – Pathankot Express or Southern Express. Then after a forty-five-minute journey on the train, we used to get down at Vidisha station and walk for twenty minutes to reach our school.

We used to always carry a bat and a ball with us because, in those days, trains would run late regularly. So, when the train was late, we would play cricket at the station. So, these are the experiences I have grown up with. You know, only when I went to Gwalior in my tenth standard did I come to know that there was something called IIT. Till then I aimed to get into the best institute in MP. Gwalior was also the first place I saw a semi-metro. I was good at academics – I stood fourth in MP in tenth standard. And then I aimed for IIT and got in.

You have a set team of three-four writers with whom you always write. What's that experience like?

Yes, I like to write with someone and not alone. I think sometimes when you're writing alone, you may have tunnel vision. Even in advertising, I believed a lot in writing with my team. In fact, the people I write films with were all my *bachchas* (kids) in advertising – Sherry, Piyush and Nikhil. As I said, they all come from small towns as well. So together, we have a varied set of experiences. Also, their life experiences are ten years younger than mine, which gives our writing a very balanced perspective.

If you look at the characters we have in our films, most of them are borrowed from real-life characters. Even in *Bhootnath*, Sanjay Mishra's character is called Gabdi. It was the name of my father's friend back in Itarsi, at whose shop we used to drink tea. How else do you come up with a name called Gabdi? In *Bareilly Ki Barfi*, Kriti's (Sanon) character is called Bitti Mishra. That was my nani's name. They used to call her Bitti in the house. Even the life I have spent in Mumbai comes in handy while writing my characters.

One of my favourite advertising campaigns from India is the series you did for *Kaun Banega Crorepati* – 'Koi Bhi Sawal Chhota Nahi Hota' – and then the follow-up campaign, 'Koi Bhi Insaan Chhota Nahi Hota.' Could you walk me through its journey?

It's an interesting story. *KBC* was already launched and two or three campaigns had already been released, which were not done by us, but by some other agency. After a few seasons, Shah Rukh

Khan came in in place of Amitabh Bachchan and then *KBC* took a long break only to come back in 2010. I remember the year clearly because that's when my kids were born. The relaunch was when my team and I came in and worked on the brand. I must tell you that I had an excellent team of creative people working on that project and we had a lot of fun together. Ashwini's (Iyer Tiwari) team was handling it. She used to be an ED at the time working under me and I was an ECD (executive creative director). My thing was that whenever I sensed a big opportunity, I used to open it up to a lot of people on the team. I believe that rarely do you get an opportunity to do work like this which gets noticed and talked about to this extent. I believe in doing great brand work. So the idea came from me but everyone sat and wrote the scripts. One situation came from someone, another came from someone else and I just compiled everything together.

I believe that you may have a great insight but if that great insight doesn't lead to a fabulous execution, the insight is useless. You need to have a combination of both. When we opened the brief to everyone, everyone came up with ideas and of course, I was working on it myself as well. My thinking was that at that point, you didn't need to explain to people what *KBC* was – it was already very famous. What the campaign should do is romanticize *KBC*. Now, *KBC* as a platform is something that celebrates knowledge. So I thought it would be great to focus on knowledge when it came to the campaign thought. While thinking, I kept going back to my life and my associations with knowledge.

My dad did a double MA, an LLB, and a PhD. He studied so much because he loved to study. He believed that education should never stop. Then, for a very long time, he always wondered why he did an LLB. But when he became an additional director in the education department, he had to start attending many court cases between some individuals vs the Government of MP. Now, nobody expected him to know the law. But seeing his knowledge of the subject, even some lawyers were astonished. He told me, 'It is true as they say, knowledge never goes to waste.'

I thought, for *KBC*, this is the insight I should go with – 'Knowledge never goes to waste'. It was a great insight but the execution was not happening. So, the next day, I thought what if I turned the insight on its head? You are saying that knowledge never goes to waste so you can also look at it as if you disrespect knowledge, it's going to haunt you at the worst possible time. And what's the worst possible time in this context? A *KBC* hot seat. There I had it! I went and shared it with my team and I said, '*Koi Bhi Sawal Chhota Nahi Hota.*' (There is no such thing as a small question.) Then I asked the team to write about different situations. I gave them an example: '*Akbar ka baap kaun tha?*' A man whose son asks him, 'Who was Akbar's father?' The man doesn't know, doesn't care at that moment. Then he is on the *KBC* hot seat and he is asked the same question. This was my first example.

The team went to town with it and wrote many, many scripts. We chose the best ones and you have the films you said you liked. After that year, I felt the natural extension to '*Koi Bhi Sawal Chhota Nahi Hota*' was '*Koi Bhi Insaan Chhota Nahi Hota.*' (No human should ever be considered less.) So, that's how that one happened.

We spoke about my favourite campaign of yours. What are your favourite campaigns of the ones you have written and thought of?

I have many favourites. Some of the work I did on Tide is something I am proud of because I think I contributed to building that brand and did some insightful work on Tide. I always take a lot of pride in the work that helps build brands. So, the stuff that I did on McDonald's – one of which was a follow-up of a campaign done by another team called '*Purane Zamane Ke Daam*'. (The price of the olden days.) My follow-up campaign was '*Aapke zamane mein baap ke zamane ke daam.*' (Enjoy the price of your father's time, in your time.) Then there was a commercial for Happy Price Menu where a young boy and a young girl were sitting outside McDonald's. That was also the first commercial I ever directed.

Then some of the stuff that I did on Reliance Mobile – one was the T20 partnership which was '*Apun Ka Sapna*'. (My dream.) This was for the first T20 World Cup in 2007. My insight there was that although the format is now smaller, the expectation of the nation is still as big – they want the team to win the World Cup for India. So, we came up with this thought: '*Baat bhale hi chhoti ho lekin sapne chhote nahin hote.*' (Conversations can be short, but never dreams.) And it was done with small kids and there was a jingle in the execution. Then another campaign we did for Reliance Mobile around Free Talktime. The insight for that was that in India, everybody, all the time, gives free advice. But when it comes to advising on the phone, you would cut it short because your talk time was getting over – until Reliance introduced Free Talktime. That was the thought process behind it.

There are also some campaigns we did on HDFC Life that I like a lot. There is an interesting personal story behind one of the ads we did for HDFC Life. My dad was rather unhappy that after IIT, I became a writer. He and I never spoke about my work. There was a little discomfort from his end – he never wanted to know what I was doing at work. Then one day, he was talking to my brother on the phone and told him, '*Advertising mein kaam achchha ho raha hai.*' (It's going great at the advertisement job.) And then he told my brother that he saw an ad that touched him. And my brother said, 'Do you even know who's written that ad?' My father called me and told me what I had done was very good. The line '*Car badi ho gayi aur beti bhi*' (The car has grown bigger, so has our daughter) was one that my dad connected a lot with. So, that will always remain special for me. Then of course there is other work that I cherish on brands like Sony, Perfetti, and some others as well.

Did you always want to make cinema?

Never. I never thought I would leave advertising. I was doing very well and was really happy. Yes, I became NCD – national creative director – of Leo Burnett at around the age of thirty-eight. But I never really worked for designations. If I had my way, I would always go back to being a trainee copywriter because that's where I had the most fun. But films happened to me by chance. Honestly, I am a reluctant director and a reluctant screenplay writer.

Vikas (Bahl) was my client on Sab TV. We got along very well. After some time, he joined UTV Spotboy. One day, he called me and said that he had a one-line idea for a film and if I would be interested in writing a screenplay along with him. At the time, I was still working in advertising so together we would work on the screenplay on weekends, and in one year, we wrote *Chillar Party*. Then we went to five-six directors to see if they wanted to direct the film. Nobody agreed and we were heartbroken. Vikas asked me, 'Why don't you direct it?' My first response was, 'I am doing fine in advertising. I don't want to be slammed by people for making a bad film or whatever.' I had never directed anything before. Then Vikas said, 'Let's direct the film together.'

I thought to myself, 'Why am I getting so scared?' The fear was of failure. Even if it didn't work out, I always had advertising to fall back on. I took the leap of faith. I went to my boss, Pops (K.V. Sridhar), and told him about what I was thinking. Surprisingly, he seemed very happy that I was trying something new and granted me a leave of five months. He was very kind and supportive. Eventually, we made *Chillar Party*. We won three national awards as well. After that, I was not actively looking to make the next film. But things happened and I made *Bhootnath Returns*. By that time, I had to take the tough call of leaving advertising. I knew films would be full of uncertainty and quitting the job was a big decision especially since I was a national creative director and you also get used to a certain amount that you get every month. Burnett wanted me to stay back ... they would let me do films, but at that point, my kids were young and growing up, and taking up so much work would have meant that I wouldn't spend any time with them. So, I chose time with my kids and quit my advertising job.

Dangal became the highest-grossing original Hindi film of all time, which is as big as it gets. Could you walk me through the journey of writing and making it?

Dangal changed my life. It all started with Manish and Divya who worked in the content development department. They came to me with a paragraph that they had read somewhere about how Mahavir Singh Phogat fought all odds and made his daughters world-class wrestlers. At that time, there was not much written about Geeta and Babita online. But I thought the premise was very strong. So, I told Manish and Divya, let's dig deeper, find out more, and see if there's something interesting in there. Piyush, one of my co-writers, and I went to Haryana and met Geeta and Babita and Mahavir Singh-ji and we came back stunned knowing their story. It was such a potent story that I involved Nikhil and Sherry as well and all four of us wrote the film.

Then Ronnie (Screwvala) and Sid (Siddharth Roy Kapur) asked me who would I ideally like to cast in this film as Mahavir Singh? My instant answer was Aamir Khan. They said okay and we had a meeting with Aamir sir. After our narration he said that he wanted to do this film. But did not know when he would be ready to do it. He told us to wait if we were willing to do so. We thought if Aamir Khan was interested, it was worth waiting for. Exactly one year later, he called us to Delhi and told us that he wanted to hear the script again. I went to his hotel room in Delhi to narrate it. He was exhausted and sleepy. I told him he should sleep for about a couple of hours and I could come back and narrate the script to him. He said, 'No, if I like the script in this condition, only then it's a really good one.'

That was my most nervous narration ever. He heard the whole film again and said, 'Let's do it.' So, when we were flying back to Mumbai, we were metaphorically flying as well because we were on cloud nine! We started the prep and the rest, as they say, is history.

What role, do you think, does cinema play in society?

I think the primary function of cinema, especially in our society, is that it's a stress-buster. People want to enjoy themselves; they want to be moved. I put myself as a consumer, not as a creator. Why do I go and watch movies? I watch movies to get entertained. So I would always want to make sure that my films entertain people. The secondary function of cinema is that people can take something back from the film. A film that serves both the primary and the secondary functions is a great film for me. And that's why, if you see, *Dangal* may have a very serious undertone to it; *Chhichhore* may have a very serious undertone to it but the way we have written those films is that they are all entertaining; they don't sound preachy.

Where do you stand on the mainstream versus arthouse debate?

I can't separate the two. For me, either you like a film or you don't. I think there are two kinds of films. One is the director's vision; the director's story and they would make whatever they want to. The other, the one I create, thinks of the audience first. I always make films for the audience and not for myself – I am very clear about that. I want to cater to the masses and the audiences. I am not trying to prove a point by doing something else. I care about how my audience is looking at my film and consuming it.

What is success to you?

If I were to give you a philosophical answer, success is something that gives you the power to say no. That's how I would define it. Today, I have the power to say no to many projects that I don't want to be part of. Otherwise, sometimes, you work on something because you need money, and then you have to compromise and all that.

What is failure to you?

Failure is a great learning. Failure keeps you grounded and teaches you a lot of humility. Failure is something that also reminds you that maybe you should have tried harder. I don't run away from my failures. I face them. If you turn a blind eye to your failures, I think you are setting yourself up for another one. Failure is inevitable for everyone. Don't be scared of it.

Could you name some of your favourite films and film-makers for me?

Too many of them. I think the one who will always remain at the top of my list is Steven Spielberg. David Fincher is someone I really admire a lot. Christopher Nolan and Martin Scorsese. I am talking about consistency right now. All these guys have been consistent. There have been some one-hit wonders as well where someone made a great one-off film but couldn't repeat it. I give a lot of importance to consistency and the entire body of work.

In India, of course, Satyajit Ray. I mean everyone takes his name and it's almost a cliché to mention him. But his work is remarkable. I even like the kind of work that Raj Kapoor did or that which Hrishi-da (Hrishikesh Mukherjee) or Basu Chatterjee did – they knew what was required. I also love Sai Paranjpye's work – I can watch *Katha* and *Chashme Buddoor* any number of times. Also, to a certain extent, Yash Chopra's work as well – especially, *Deewaar, Kaala Patthar* and *Lamhe*.

You have achieved great success in almost everything you have done and that too pretty quickly. Is there still anything that you think you wanted to do but could not?

Honestly, no. My philosophy is that if I want to do something, I would do it. If I want to make a film, I will make that film. If you ask me, at least, as of now, I can't think of anything that I missed out on. I am very grateful to life for giving me so much. I have no ambition that's left unfulfilled.

SIXTEEN

Onir

Onir is one of the nicest, politest, and kindest people I have met. That afternoon at Leaping Windows, a gorgeous café in Versova, I remembered watching *My Brother... Nikhil* in a theatre and liked it a lot way back when I was in junior college. Onir's ideas flowed beautifully into the conversation as we spoke about his upbringing, same-sex love, the role of his sister in his life, and, of course, writing and making cinema.

When and how did you start writing and find your voice?

I started writing properly, in terms of screenplay and stuff, around the year 2000. Before that, of course, when I was in school, I remember I would note down my thoughts. Interestingly, I used to dream a lot. And I used to write down my dreams. I'd tell myself that I would use them someday. I didn't know how back then but I had this habit of writing down the descriptions of the visuals I would see in my dreams. After I worked on my first film, as an editor, in 1999, Sanjay (Suri) asked me why I don't write. And with that push, I thought my writing could be worth something. So that's when I started working on my first screenplay.

I was born in Bhutan and was brought up there. As a child, I did a lot of reading. Back then in Bhutan, we didn't have any distractions that we have today. Till I was in the tenth standard in school, I had never seen TV. There was no internet back then. So, we did a lot of outdoor sports during the day and in the evening, at home, both my sister and I would read every day. To the extent that our parents would ask us to go to sleep at a certain point in the night and we would even read books under the blanket with a tiny light on. I think we were obsessed with reading. And I feel that reading and writing are kind of connected. So, it all explains itself now.

My mother was a huge fan of cinema. So, she would make us watch movies. I remember there was a film based on Charles Dickens's novel which I watched in the sixth standard and some of the visuals stayed with me. After that, I watched a film called *Junoon* by Shyam Benegal. I didn't understand the film at all back then but it left an impression. The visuals, the colours, the faces – they all stayed with me. I somehow knew subconsciously that I wanted to be part of this whole world of film-making. In the tenth standard, I went to attend a film festival for the first time, to which my sister took me, as I had come down to Calcutta for my winter vacation. There, I saw Satyajit Ray's *Charulata* and another film called *The French Lieutenant's Woman*. That's when I was convinced that this is what I want to do in life. When my sister went to FTII, I used to spend a lot of time there. I used to tell her that I had more friends at FTII than she did.

How much of you needs to be in a story that you write?

You know, *My Brother…Nikhil*, the first film I wrote and made, is based on someone else's life. A guy called Dominic D'Souza from Goa. So, if you look at it in one way, it is his life story. But in another way, there's a lot of me in the film. I feel that world and the characters. I am not a trained writer. So, I had zero idea about all these acts and the structure of a screenplay and at what point something needs to happen and stuff like that. I just wrote and still write what I feel.

And I never write down a story before the screenplay. I directly write the screenplay with dialogue. I can't even write just a screenplay and think about dialogue later as many people do. So naturally, there is a lot of me in everything I write.

After *My Brother … Nikhil*, I co-wrote *I Am*. I wrote two of the stories in that film – *I Am Abhimanyu* and *I Am Omar*. They were based on other people but when I wrote and presented it, it was obviously with my sensibility and how I see the world. Even when I wrote *Sorry Bhai*, Shabana's character drew a lot from my mother. Or the brother's character draws some characteristics from my brother.

Tell me about the journey of making *My Brother … Nikhil*, which was a refreshing film to have come out in 2005.

My Brother… Nikhil was my fifth script. The first one I wrote had a lot of gay characters and also a bigger budget. It never got made. There were other films that I couldn't find takers for. Sanjay and I got tired of approaching people and decided that we would make a film with our own money. By then I had realized that whatever I was writing was not for the commercial space. So, we put in all we had and also borrowed from friends. I had to write something that could be made on a smaller budget. That's when I thought of Dominic and his story. I had worked on a documentary on him, so I was well-acquainted with the material. But at the same time, I didn't want to do a biopic on him for various reasons. One, with Dominic, there are different claims on his sexuality. He had already passed away and I didn't know him personally. So, I don't think I have the right to call him bisexual or anything else and define his sexuality. Even his family wasn't perfectly aware of that.

From my research, I figured that there were a lot of grey areas in Dominic's life. But I wanted to tell this story so I decided to fictionalize some parts and not make it a biopic. For instance, he didn't have a sister campaigning for him but in the film there is, which comes from my own life as my sister has been a huge support for me all through. Sanjay, Raj Kaushal, and Vicky were the principal financiers and the rest we borrowed from friends and family. The people of Goa were incredibly lovely and supportive. Also, I am thankful that because Yash Raj came in, the film got the visibility it did. And not just the film, but for me, as a gay film-maker and an independent film-maker, it was a huge thing because I got established with that film.

Every newcomer has to struggle to make his first film. But I had another kind of struggle happening simultaneously, which is to come out as gay and deal with the larger Indian society where your identity was criminalized back then.

Do you think it was more difficult for you than other outsiders to the industry?

All my friends knew about me. I have never had a tussle with my sexuality. I recognized my sexuality pretty late in the day. Initially, I was falling in love with women. But around eleventh standard, I realized, I was attracted to men. But by the time I moved to Bombay, around the age of twenty-twenty-one, I kind of knew. When I told my sister, 'I think I am gay,' she just responded saying, 'Okay.' It was that cool and that easy. Even with my parents, it was never difficult. Their only concern was if I would have someone in life as a partner. It was coming more from a place of care and companionship. So, I was never afraid about my identity. Yes, I was sometimes worried about society or the law, as it was, till recently. Now, coming back to writing and the stories I want to tell. My film *We Are* was also my way of celebrating the Supreme Court verdict, but also to say that while homosexuality is legal now, love, adoption, and marriage are rights that are still not legal.

Does a writer need to be an activist?

Today, the word activist has several different connotations. But from my point of view, I do think of cinema as a medium to empower people. And that is not limited to the genre you are working with. Be it a comedy, be it a thriller, or even a superhero film. The fact that today you have people thinking of the possibilities of Spiderman being gay or whatever is proof that people are opening up to these ideas. Today, a superhero could be a woman, gay, or trans. The awareness is more now. Having said that, I think the ability to empathize beyond your own identity is crucial for artists. I find most renditions of gay or trans cinema problematic. It always surprises me why it is so difficult – why do you have to go through so much process and workshops – to understand a simple human existence? You know recently, a woman asked me a question at a book reading: 'We are allies and what do we need to do?' I said, 'Just be a better human being.' That's it. You don't need some special human skills to understand LGBTQ. Empathy is all you need.

Some writers have told me that they are trying to imagine how gay or trans people think to write some characters. But you know, I don't have to talk to my sister or straight friends to imagine how straight people think, right? I mean writing Juhi's (Chawla) character in *My Brother … Nikhil* or so many others, I don't need to talk to people or do a study on straight people.

You are probably more familiar with thought-censorship than most people. How do you navigate it as a writer?

I got a U certificate for *My Brother … Nikhil* in 2005. All I was told is don't write 'inspired from a true story'. I said okay. I could do that much. As it is, the film is made in a docu-fiction style and anybody will figure out that it is real. In 2011, when I did *I Am*, I had to fight for it a lot. It was difficult to even get an A certificate initially. Then in 2017, when I did *Shab*, I was told by the censor board initially, about the gay characters, *'Arey inko toh aapne normal dikha diya!'* (Hey, you portrayed them so normal!) So, it was difficult. And it took me a year to get a certificate. Then in 2022, when I wrote *We Are*, it got rejected at the script level itself. The next thing I know is that my film is being discussed in the parliament. It got talked about everywhere – in TV media, even internationally. Because Varun Gandhi brought it up. The defence ministry had a problem with it because it was based on a real person – a major from the Indian army who came out publicly announcing that he is gay. Some people argue that it is dangerous for the security of the country!

I was happy to discuss with anyone if they had any problems. But they couldn't have a problem because I know I have shot it beautifully. I am not looking for controversies. I want to tell real stories. So, imagine a story that is based on a real person, who came along with me on NDTV and said that it is based on his life, and that was not being allowed.

I look at a country like Iran and the film-makers there and I think I am relatively in a better place. So, I try to navigate my way around all this. There are so many people from the army who have messaged me that they love and respect me and respect what I am trying to do and it is unfortunate what happened to the film. All I want is a conversation to start.

What is success to you?

For me, success is the fact that I am a film-maker. I had one dream in my life – that of being a film-maker, coming from a middle-class family of teachers. And I am living my dream. To me, that is a success. To be doing the kind of good, bad, ugly independent films that I want to do is success. Sometimes, I take the local train and I think of all these people, working a 9-to-5 job, travelling for hours, and I tell myself that I have no reason to complain. Even the hurdles that I face come from the choices I make. I am fortunate that I can keep making those choices. Success also is to have my own identity. I have always wanted to make a kind of cinema that I could leave behind in the world and hopefully, I am in the process of doing that. You know box office does not break me. What breaks me is that somebody watches my film and says, 'Hey, what a terrible film he has made!' That breaks me. Money is not a driving force for me. Fame for me is that when I see that my films are part of libraries and different universities around the world. What matters to me is that I can walk into a bookshop and say that I am gay and be okay with it. The identity that I have fought for being out there is fame for me. Fame is also about travelling the world with my films and discussing them with people from different cultures who connect with you. Even if they are not 100-crore-rupee films, building that connection matters to me.

What is failure to you?

Failure to me is when despite trying all my agencies I am not able to do what I really want to. I punish myself more than people and the system around me. There are times when I get frustrated.

What's the worst criticism you've ever faced?

Well, I remember, when I made *Sorry Bhai*, a trade analyst wrote something like, 'Onir is known for pushing the envelope but this is the limit. It's against the culture. How could a sister-in-law fall for her brother-in-law?' I remember, when a year later, *Mere Brother Ki Dulha*n or something like that came out, nobody seemed to have a problem. And I kept thinking that Satyajit Ray did *Charulata* in 1964! Are we really going back?

Then, of course, there are other people. I remember my sister met someone who said about me, *'Haan achchha film banata hai magar nahi chalta hai.'* (Yeah he makes good movies but they don't sell.) *'Nahi chalta hai'* is like a tag that I have.

If you could, what's the one thing you'd want to change about what they call Bollywood?

We desperately need to empower new talent. When Sushant's (Singh) incident happened there was a lot of conversation about nepotism but unfortunately, it went into a negative space so I am not for that either. But the truth is that it's the same set of people who keep making films. When OTT came out, it attracted a lot of new talent but now even those guys have become big stars and now they keep doing all the work. Of course, there are exceptions. But largely, as an industry, if you look at Hollywood, if you need a twenty-year-old actor, you'll have twenty choices; if you need a thirty-year-old actor, you'll have twenty choices. But back here in Bollywood, it's the same set of people. I was recently told by a platform: 'We don't care about the subject. You get us a star and we'll do whatever you're doing.' And that's why perhaps a lot of our work isn't smart.

Even the smallest budget independent films are denied budgets. As an industry or a system, we just don't encourage diversity, new talent, and independent voices. You know there are people in the industry who will talk about nepotism but they won't accept new talent on their projects. So how does one combat it? People have to become something to be accepted here. But becoming is a process, right? You don't become something overnight. And why is this not applicable to kids of stars or industry people? No one asks them to prove themselves, right? It's only the outsiders and new talent that have to do it the hard way.

How difficult is it to tell a story that you want to without other people changing it?

I have been fortunate to have worked with actors who have believed in what I had written or in my vision. Most of my films have been produced in-house or independently so I haven't had to deal with producers in that sense.

In this industry, most people have a template and everything you do has to fit into that template. I, on the other hand, believe very strongly that every story has its own texture and you can't go by templates. Negotiating templates is not creativity. How come a non-film-maker is telling you what to make and how to make it? That's why, if you see, after a point, a lot of web series becomes repetitive. They are all following a formula because they are made to.

Having been a voracious reader as well as a writer, what makes you choose cinema as your primary medium of expression?

Images. I think cinemas are about images. And in cinema, I can combine my love for words, music, images, colour. I could pursue each of my interests in cinema as a medium.

What are your favourite films and film-makers?

I think there are lots of films. The French New Wave Cinema is something I admire a lot. Then Tarkovsky. Also, East European cinema. Akira Kurosawa, Ritwik Ghatak, Satyajit Ray. In terms of Indian parallel cinema as they call it, Shyam Benegal's work, Ketan Mehta's work.

Also, not in college or after, but as a kid, I loved watching commercial films like *Deewaar*, *Sholay*, *Umrao Jaan*, etc. But as I grew up, I developed a different sensibility. I think, I'd say, I am more European in sensibility than Hollywood.

Of the present-day film-makers, I love Pedro Almodovar. I got to know that he was gay much later in the day. But I already loved his films. I remember watching *Pain and Glory* at the Mumbai Film Festival three years ago and I was in tears. And it's heartening to see all these big Hollywood actors open to working with Almodovar. I have been trying to do a biopic on India's first gay film-maker, Riyad Wadia, who made this film called *BOMgAY* in 1996. He eventually died of AIDS. His life has been somewhat like Freddie Mercury's – glamorous, flamboyant, and out there. But the answer that I get from the industry is that I have to wait and I can't make it now and all that. But I know that the truth is that they are uncomfortable with a story like that. There are people who'd say, 'Oh, the scenes are so intimate!' and stuff like that. They can't tolerate intimacy between two guys.

Among Hindi contemporaries, there are some films that I have enjoyed watching. I sometimes enjoy Anurag's (Kashyap) work, Dibakar's (Banerjee) or Shoojit's (Sircar) work. I quite enjoyed *Oye Lucky! Lucky Oye!* and *Khosla Ka Ghosla*. I also like Raj Kumar Gupta's film *No One Killed Jessica*. Or Neeraj Pandey's *A Wednesday*. But these films haven't influenced me because I come from a different world and identity. And the way that some European cinema or the works of Shyam Benegal have stayed with me for years, unfortunately, these contemporary Hindi films haven't. You know, *Pain and Glory* or *Call Me By Your Name* are films I watched recently, at this age, but they mesmerized me.

It's not only about films that deal with a certain kind of sexuality. For instance, *Before Sunrise* and *Before Sunset* are films that have stayed with me. You think of films like *City of God, Babel,* and so many others, the images just stay with you. Some films just have an impact, which I think contemporary films generally lack. Even films as mainstream as *Jo Jeeta Wohi Sikandar* or *Rangeela* have a massive impact. They have some unforgettable magic. I think some of these films I talked about move to a world I don't know. And cinema is also about that. The uniqueness of some of these films is what excites me. In fact, I like some films by Rima Das like *Village Rockstars* or *Bulbul Can Sing*. Even Vikramaditya Motwane's *Udaan*. These are films that last.

What are your favourite shows?

There are quite a few that I like. I like *Narcos* a lot. I love *Breaking Bad*. I also like certain elements of *Sense 8*. *How To Get Away With Murder* is so clever. In India, I loved watching the three seasons of *Gullak*. I just couldn't stop watching it. Then I quite like *Panchayat*. *Paatal Lok* is something I love. I liked the first season of *Mirzapur* but then I thought it was getting into the same trap of violence. I liked *Jamtara, Delhi Crime*: Season 1 as well.

If there's one thing you would want to change about your journey, what would it be?

Nothing. The mistakes I have made in life have taught me. No one is perfect and I accept my imperfections as a part of me.

SEVENTEEN

Puneet Sharma

I have known Puneet for about a decade. I met him through poetry and then we also worked on a project together – which did not go anywhere – in a writers' room set up by a director. Puneet's poetry has often struck me as explosive but at the same time sensitive. He is highly political in his work, especially in his poetry, and I think it's the inherent lyricism in his verse that gave way to his songwriting. Puneet is a natural lyricist and he has gone on to write some famous songs such as '*Baba Bolta Hai Ab Bas Ho Gaya*' and '*Main Badhiya Tu Bhi Badhiya*' from *Sanju* as well as the tragically underrated songs from *Revolver Rani*. He has written the film *Dhamaka* and has also co-written the show *A Great Indian Murder*.

How did a young boy who swore by the street food of Indore move to Mumbai?

I truly believed that after I went to Mumbai, two of my biggest challenges would be to get the work I desire and to get the food I desire. How the rest of my day pans out, even today, is largely dependent on the breakfast. The thing is that the food in Indore spoils you. There aren't many places to visit or things to do in Indore. So, the food stalls and the restaurants are the local tourism in Indore.

At breakfast, we think about what we would have for lunch and at lunch we think about dinner. Food is our circle of life. However, I found a way in Mumbai. I put up as a paying guest with an Indori senior from a theatre group for which I had to pay beyond my means at the time. That's when I learnt to cook so that I could keep eating what I wanted to.

Your poem '*Tum Kaun Ho Bey*' became one of the major voices of the anti-CAA (Citizenship Amendment Act) protests. Let's speak a bit about that piece and writing as a political exercise.

It was when I left college and joined theatre that I realized how writing is related to politics. That's also when I realized that politics is not just electoral politics. In fact, electoral politics is a small part of politics. Politics is present everywhere in the world. Even at the places where talking about it is the death of romanticism according to many people. So, this poem of mine was written several months before it went viral. In fact, it was even available on the internet before it went viral. But as an anxious person, I think, I can see danger from far away. Maybe that's why it takes time for society to relate to my ideas. I was bothered for a long time by the fact that some people were questioning my love for my country. I have a direct relationship with my country. That's what I have grown up with and can't understand another relationship being planted between us.

It's the same as I love my mother. Unlike other 'ideal children' I may not touch her feet every day. I don't like showing off my love. I like to hug her instead. Now my mother has never asked me to touch her feet but my relatives have taunted me about not doing it. Then I felt like they were saying to me that if I don't express it in the ways they have prescribed, my love isn't true. That's when I thought: who is anyone else to interfere between my mother and me, or my country and me? Who are they to tell me? That's when I wrote '*Tum Kaun Ho Bey?*' (Who are you, man?). I wrote '*Tum Pehle Jahil Nahin Ho Jo Kehte Ho Ke Cheekh Ke Pyaar Karo*' (You aren't the first idiot who says that love has to be screamed). Many people believe that showing it off to the world is the only way to love. Some of them are hypocrites.

But still, it's their choice. All I ask for is that they don't impose their choices and ways on me. That's how I wrote it, and said without saying it, that this is the relationship I share with my country.

There's an innate lyricism in your poetry. Did that help you to become a successful lyricist?

When I started writing, I didn't have anyone around me who would tell me about poetry. My family and friends and the colony where I grew up have nothing to do with literature. My exposure to poetry was limited to my school textbooks. The only other medium which unconsciously drew me to poetry was Hindi film music. A good thing was that my father and his elder brother were fond of old Hindi music and both had knowledge of it. They'd remember not only the singer's name but also the music director's and the lyricist's. They'd tell me stories of Shailendra and Sahir. Consciously and subconsciously, I started looking at Hindi film songs as poetry. Progressive poetry arrived in my life much later. Till then Hindi film music was my only poetry school. Maybe that's the reason for the lyricism in my poetry which you speak about.

Do you approach writing poetry and lyrics differently? If yes, how so?

Songs and poetry are not very different forms. But what separates film lyrics is that what you say in them is not entirely your poetic expression. You need to keep the story of the film in mind too which is not the poet's own story. You need to keep in mind the characters and the milieu that you've just met. You are at their service. Then you need to take inputs and feedback from the music director and the director of the film as well. You need to make the producer happy, then the actor, and then the music company. After all this what comes out might still be poetry but it's not entirely your poetry. Even if it is poetry, it is a product of this mammoth collaboration process. Just like any aspect of a film is impossible without collaboration. Amidst all this, your poetry or your own expression needs to be subtly hidden and carried onto the lyrics like a smuggler smuggles his goods. That's why I think a good lyricist needs to be a good smuggler.

Which is the best song you have written according to you?

I truly think that many of my unreleased songs are the best I have written. And I am not saying this because it is poetic to say this. I truly think so. Those songs have become more poetry than songs. And in this industry, people have a special talent to differentiate between a song and a poem and as soon as they recognize or spot a poem, they reject it. To search for one such good assignment, a lyricist has to reject many bad ones, which is a privilege in itself.

Let's move to the screenwriter in you. How did that journey begin?

I was interested in scripts for a long, long time. Especially since the time I started watching mainstream Bollywood films back in college. I found those stories interesting because I thought they were a place where imagination is respected. I remember the first film story I ever wrote was for *Spider-Man 3* after I watched the first two parts. Sci-fi was my favourite genre. And there it all began! Then I wrote plays. I started writing film concepts. I was writing everything I could. But just like I spent three years to become a professional lyric writer after I learnt to write songs, I spent three-four years honing my craft before making scriptwriting my career.

One of the biggest reasons why I wanted to move from lyric writing to scriptwriting is that I had begun to observe that lyrics are slowly moving away from the centre stage in Hindi cinema. Unless you're a top lyricist, chances are rare that you will get a variety of songs. But scriptwriting offered me the freedom to choose my subject. I came to the film industry because I wanted to have my say. That's why I chose the path of screenwriting. A good thing was that I personally believe that film screenplay and the craft of poetry are closely related. In both the crafts, there's a special rhythmic flow of images that's governed by the genre.

***A Great Indian Murder* was a success. How was the experience of co-writing it with Vijay Maurya?**

It's my privilege that I got a chance to work with Vijay (Maurya) bhai and Tishu (Tigmanshu Dhulia) bhai. Both are way more experienced writers than I am and senior to me. Both of them gave me a lot of confidence and allowed me a space where I could express myself. I could use this confidence not just in that series but also in the ones I worked on after that one.

From Vijay Maurya, I got to learn the quality of being unrestrained, unbridled in writing. Since he is an actor as well, his language of dialogue translates very naturally on paper. And when it comes to dialogue, who can forget the lines written by Tishu bhai? By now it's a well-known cliché that every small-town kid grows up watching *Haasil*. Those who love Tishu bhai's work will continue to swear by it for generations to come.

What would you have done differently about *Dhamaka* from a writing point of view?

Hazaaron khwahishen aisi ki har khwahish pe dum nikle. Bahut nikle mere armaan lekin phir bhi kam nikle. (There are thousands of desires and each takes the breath away. So many dreams fulfilled, and yet it seems too few.)

***Dhamaka* was a remake of a Korean film. Do you think remakes give you the same thrill as writing an original script?**

Earlier, I used to look at this very differently. Now my perspective about this is the same as the one I have about the adaptation of books into films. You have a particular source material using which you have to write a story, which should not look like a copy of the source material. Your story should have its own voice. If you follow this approach, every adaptation seems necessary. Yes, if one uses it just to cash on something famous, it makes no sense at all.

Who are your favourite poets, writers, and lyricists?

The first lyricist that comes to mind and the one closest to me is Shailendra. I learnt the simplicity of thought from him. I learnt how lyrics could be translated into urban folk. How ideological commitment can be so easily put up as satire. I learnt about direct conflict and learnt that whether it is the politics of love or society, your political commitment cannot change with your need. From Majrooh (Sultanpuri), I learnt how to write so well to a tune that the audience would keep guessing if the tune was composed first or the song was written before that.

Among the poets, the first name would be Gajanan Madhav Muktibodh. He broke everything inside me that needed to be broken. It took me five-six years to understand him and since then whenever I feel the need to understand myself again, his poems are what I go back to. Then come Dhumil, Pash, Kedarnath Singh, Vinod Kumar Shukla, Nagarjun, Shiv Kumar Batalvi, Faiz, Kabir, Nirala, Ghalib, Mir. The list is pretty long. Among prose writers, Harishankar Parsai was the writer who pulled me out of an abyss. He told me the most bitter truth in the most exciting manner. He was also the writer who introduced me to Muktibodh. I can add many more names to this list as well but Harishankar Parsai is like the sun for me behind whom all other names rest like stars.

Do you think that commercial writing, especially in Bollywood, is necessarily a compromise of creativity?

In all work, all work in the world that is concerned with a market, creativity walks according to the market. The market can make creativity soar to gain profit or make it sink if it thinks that is more beneficial to do. The market looks at creativity like it looks at any other product. It has turned art into 'content'. These terms may be new but the concept is not. Just like the consumption of the consumer encourages or discourages a product in the market, it does the same in the business of cinema as well. If the majority encourages cheap and easy products, who will fund deep and complex art? As Ibsen said, 'Minority is rarely right but majority is always wrong.'

How important is mass appeal and appreciation for the writer in you?

As I said, I am in the film industry to have my say and to be heard. So, I'd like it if what I want to say reaches as many people as possible. But for me to reach as many people as possible, I wouldn't start saying and writing things I don't believe in. I think till the time I can be consciously aware of the difference between these two things, my wish to reach as many people as possible is valid.

When was the last time you wrote something that did not have money involved and what was it?

I don't think I can answer this question considering my poetry because in this country, even if I want and try for it, poetry will never attract money. I wouldn't involve the songs that I have written for my theatre friends in this answer as well. Alas! There was a time when I used to do a lot of work that did not involve money. But then the needs of life took prominence and that kind of work reduced. My most recent work which I did without money was writing a song for an army battalion.

Which films and film-makers influenced you in your early days?

Satya. The film affected me a lot. That is where I started looking at films differently. Then there was a Russian war film called *Come and See*. That one touched me as deeply as no other film ever has. Then a Santosh Sivan film, a children's film, called *Halo; Singing in the Rain*. The list of directors is long. Maybe it will tell you the kind of work I enjoy. Sriram Raghavan, Ritwik Ghatak, Hrishikesh Mukherjee, Scorsese, Hitchcock, Kieslowski, Edgar Wright, Andrei Tarkovsky, Baz Luhrmann, Miyazaki, Satoshi Kon.

If you get 100 crore rupees credited to your bank account tomorrow, what would you write if you'd write at all?

Musicals. Only and only musicals.

If a hundred years later someone is getting to know about Puneet Sharma, what's the one thing you'd like them to know?

A writer who wrote what he said, what he did, and what he lived.

EIGHTEEN

R. Balki

R. Balki is an advertising legend and there is no doubt about it. As someone who has been working in advertising for close to a decade and a half, there was no way that I was going to be able to forget this while speaking with him.

I met Balki at his office in Pali Naka one morning and it was evident to me that Balki knew how to hold a brilliant conversation. We met just a week ahead of the release of his film *Chup* but we also spoke about his other films as well as some of the most iconic advertising campaigns created under his leadership in India.

Why and when did you first think of becoming a writer?

I never thought of becoming a writer, I just loved movies. So, it just went on. Normal middle-class people like me usually want to become doctors or engineers but I think those things require more intelligence. So, one day, I saw an ad from Mudra in those days – this was even before MICA (Mudra Institute of Communications) was formed. I always wanted to be in films and I knew Mudra was a Ramesh Sippy company. But then I found out it was an advertising agency. I started working there. They say strategy and all but I understood advertising from the first ad. My first ad was for a shaving cream and I had a beard even then. I thought if anything can make me shave, I am home. So, I wrote a song that plays in the ad when somebody is slowly applying the shaving cream. This was for a brand called Willman which was eventually bought over by Gillette. This was in 1991 or 1992.

For somebody who has always wanted to be a film-maker as you have always maintained, wasn't around thirty years of working in advertising and becoming one of the legends of the trade too much of a digression?

In advertising, you get to work on films almost every day. I was sometimes making three films every day. It's like when you do five thousand-odd ads, each one is a story, each one is an idea, and each one is a screenplay. So, in my head, I was always doing what I wanted. I was working with films, just that the format was different. Advertising is somebody giving you money to tell a story; in feature film-making, you tell a story and ask people for money. That's the difference.

But then you did take a hard call and stopped working in advertising to entirely focus on films, didn't you?

Yes, because I believe you should leave something when you're still interested in it. I wasn't tired of advertising; I loved it with all my heart when I left it. Besides, after a certain point, you realize that advertising is not just about my work. As you grow, there are thousands of other responsibilities that you have to manage. At some point, I thought, I just wanted to focus on my work and do exactly what I wanted. Feature films are not exactly a profession that I would advise anybody to get into. In a way, it's not a profession. If I hadn't worked in advertising for so long, it may have been difficult for me to come to terms with the unknown territory that feature films can be. It's sort of difficult for a creative person to be continuously in the realm of the unknown.

Even advertising involves some amount of the unknown but you still have protection – there are systems in place. Here, it's totally unknown. But then sometimes, you realize that you are not getting any younger so you try and do what exactly you've always wanted. Also, I wanted to test out being a film-maker. I didn't want to be distracted by a reason to tell a story – which advertising always gives you. Advertising can sometimes become like a slot machine where people are putting coins and out comes an idea. So, I didn't want anybody to put a slot coin and I just wanted an idea to come out without any coin. So yes, it was good fun.

Was there a trigger – an event where you thought enough is enough and you're going to focus only on films from there onwards?

Yes, there was one. I think it was *Shamitabh*. When *Shamitabh* didn't do well, I could have gone back to advertising. But that's when I thought, no, I want to give it all and test myself. Yes, of course, I had made *Cheeni Kum* and *Paa*, while I was still in advertising, but the failure of *Shamitabh* actually made me think and I said I want to put myself out there without any protection. That's where, in a way, I really began.

Do you see the advertisement writer in you and the film writer in you as mutually exclusive entities?

They are neither mutually inclusive nor do they interact with each other. At the end of the day, you are telling a story. There is a logical pattern that's formed by your creative thought. You are telling a story that has to be new and then you have to communicate it. If I say this, they will get this – you have to think like that. You form those algorithms right through your life. That is beautiful for a screenwriter. In my view, the best way to learn screenwriting is to go through the process of advertising because you have to get it right, you have to communicate. In screenwriting, sometimes, you might write something that people may not get at all but in advertising that's not allowed. People have to understand the ad you write, otherwise it's a failure. So that communication practice you get in advertising is invaluable and that comes into play every time I write. Can I say it with just one gesture? Can my character do this instead in this scene? I think like that and look at communication exactly like that.

Many advertisement writers have gone on to do very well in feature films. Nitesh Tiwari, for example, was very successful in advertising and then went on to write and make probably the most successful film of recent times (*Dangal*). Then there are advertisement film-makers, of course. Shoojit (Sircar), Ram (Madhvani), Amit (Sharma). Amit Sharma is a hard-core advertising director and has gone on to make beautiful films. So, there are examples aplenty and everywhere. Having said that, this industry, the film industry, is an illogical mess. Because you get rejected, you get appreciated, you get another chance – I don't know how. You know, a lot of things that people take credit for in the industry have got to do a lot with divinity. Nobody knows why something works or what will end up working.

I mean, I just made *Chup*. I think it's a nice film and maybe others will think it's a nice film but I have no idea what will happen to the film. Anything could happen. The thrill of actually living in a business when you put in two years and its fate is going to be decided in two days is a very strange thing. It can psychologically damage you. And unless you've seen enough ups and downs in life it could be difficult. Ups and downs in advertising are common too. You make an ad, sometimes it works wonders and sometimes it bombs. But you learn from that and move on to the next one. So, make sure that you don't make the same mistakes.

But in feature films, you don't learn from anything. There is nothing to learn from. Even if your last film was a smashing hit, there is no guarantee that your next one will work. Even for a star, it is true. There is uncertainty all over. It's quite a mythical industry, I must say. In this industry, skill is not enough. I think whoever succeeds is just luckier than others. The fate of your film might depend on the environment in the country, and how the mood of the masses is, if there is a cricket match on your film release day, there are one thousand things that you have no control over that affect the film. I think luck is the only thing there is. Of course, you have to work hard, write, and think out of the box, those are the basics. But the second thing is luck and that often becomes the decision-maker.

What's your writing process for both advertising and feature films?

There is a lot of laziness when I write a feature film. In advertising, there is no time for laziness. The idea for *Chup* is one that I had in 2008 after *Cheeni Kum*. I always toy around with my ideas and let them be for a while. Because I feel that you need a very good reason to spend two years of your life doing something. And the idea must be the biggest motivator. You may get lots of money, you may get big stars and whatever you have always dreamt of but it's only the idea, the core, that can keep you motivated for that long. The cruelty is the environment that I talked about. Someone is a pundit one day and a pauper the next day. Nobody knows anything here. So for one to survive this cruelty, it must be an idea that really, really motivates you.

So I take my time with the ideas I have. Once I am convinced with my idea, I open my laptop and start writing. I always write with dialogue. I like to get the grammar right and get all my thoughts right. That's how you do it in advertising. Nobody writes just a concept. You write the whole script. So, on *Chup*, I had Rishi as a co-writer, who has been writing with me for a long time now, and then Raja Sen, a critic, because I wanted a critic's perspective on this film. I can't think when somebody else is writing. I have to type myself for me to be able to think. I don't like going away to any corner or whatever. Only at the time of *Pad Man*, I went to the location where I shot but largely, I write here, where you are sitting. I write on my table.

Most of the ideas for your films are kind of wild. Could you tell me how and where you thought of them using a few examples?

I think this one again starts with luck. You don't know where an idea is going to come to you. When I was sitting and doing a Lifebuoy ad, I was struggling to crack an idea that day. So, I just went to the loo or somewhere and then I came back and went, 'I got it, I got it.' The person who was sitting with me said, 'Oh brilliant!' I said, 'No, I got a film idea. The ad, we'll crack tomorrow!' And we cracked the ad the next day. That film idea, however, was *Cheeni Kum*. In the case of *Shamitabh*, I was going to Amit-ji's (Amitabh Bachchan) house on his birthday. My driver had taken off and I was in a taxi. Massive traffic jam. I spent two hours going from my house in Breach Candy to his bungalow in Juhu. And I had not got him a gift. I was thinking about what I should buy – flowers, champagne (but I knew he is a teetotaller so that wouldn't fly). So then suddenly I thought the best thing to give him is an idea.

I started thinking. In that taxi, I thought about his voice and all that and the idea for *Shamitabh* was ready. I went to the party and whispered into his ears, 'Amit-ji, I have got a gift for you.' In a corner, I narrated the idea and he instinctively said, 'Let's do it!' That's how *Shamitabh* happened. You see, again luck! Even *Paa* happened randomly. This was during the promotion of *Cheeni Kum*. Abhishek (Bachchan) came down to meet Amit-ji. At that point, I didn't know him. But I saw Abhishek was behaving very wise that day and Amit-ji was playing the fool. It just struck me. What if there is a film where the son plays the father and the father plays the son? That's how *Paa* happened.

Do you think a sense of humour is an integral part of creativity?

Absolutely. I think a sense of humour is one thing. Another is the ability to see things differently. If you go to a funeral, for instance, you're taught to feel sad. But let me tell you, a couple of years ago, when my dad passed away, I was smiling looking at him, 'What a lucky guy! He's seen more places in the world than I have. He is peaceful. Fortunately, he suffered very little towards the end of his life. I wanna go like this guy!' I didn't have an ounce of thinking that oh my dad is not there anymore or whatever. I think he was in a good space and I felt pleasant and nice, really. Because I felt he was happy and I was happy for the life he led. So why should I be sad?

Another thing is, you know, marriage is supposed to be a happy occasion but whenever I see people getting married, I feel very sad. I look at the couple and think they're imagining a hundred thousand things at the moment but little do they know about the problems to come. I have tears in my eyes when I see people getting married. Even in my own wedding, I had tears in my eyes and I am sure Gauri (Shinde) had tears in her eyes. See, it's all fun, and it's great companionship and all that but the fact of the matter is that a marriage is not an easy ride. Gauri and I both advise a lot of people not to get married. We even offer our condolences. So yes, it's fun. I think as a person, somehow your trip has been to see things differently and to try and connect things differently. Humour always connects things differently. So yes, I do see it as a natural part of the creative process.

Do you think creativity is necessarily an act of rebellion?

I won't say rebellion. But creativity is questioning rules. There is a set of rules in society. You don't have to break them for the sake of breaking them. But if you question them, without harming anybody, it can be really funny. For instance, somebody told you that left was left. But what if there is a vocabulary in the world where the left is right? What will you do? I think that's what my trip is in life. Why? Question. Always ask why. Who said anything is sacrosanct? And remember, you're not doing it for any other reason but to have some fun. You question and break the rules because, at the end of the day, it's fun to do so.

Where do you stand on the emergence of OTT?

I think every medium is an avenue for displaying creativity or entertainment or whatever. So, I see OTT as another avenue – another screen. Somebody told me that man was a cave animal. He ventured out of the cave to hunt for his meal. Would he have ever ventured out of the cave if the food came right into his cave? Now, a lot of things are coming home. Entertainment through OTT is one of them. But the funny thing is that I think man will still venture out of the cave even if the food comes home. Why? Because sometimes, you want to see the open air. But how often is the question. Now, you can order anything from the food delivery apps but is the restaurant business dying?

I say the same thing about the theatres. Although they have to stand in the queue, buy tickets, spend money to get the popcorn, they are still going to the theatres. What's the difference? I think it's the sound. I believe people go to the theatre for the sound; they don't go to the theatre for the picture. And whichever home theatre system you may have, you can't replicate the sound in a theatre. The theatre sound is huge, much bigger. Having said that, OTT is here to stay. It may well be the way of the future but at the same time, I don't think theatres are going away in a hurry at least. Also, there is an OTT myth that it has changed storytelling and all that, but tell me something, look at *Darlings*, for example, do you think as many people would have watched it without Alia? Yes, it would have got its audience but the numbers will be vastly different. I think whether it is OTT or film, we have to evolve, as storytellers, we have to continue to evolve. OTT is changing the way of storytelling and all that are tall claims. We need to keep finding new ways to be interesting.

You've achieved so much in life. Is there anything you wanted to do but couldn't?

I don't think I have achieved anything in life. I just want to earn my right to make my next film. And yes, I would love to have been a cricket commentator, which I never did. Because I am very angry at some of the cricket commentators. I like only Harsha Bhogle. In a country so obsessed with cricket, we have somehow produced the worst commentators. There is one Harsha Bhogle and today there is one other person Dinesh Karthik, who is a beautiful commentator. But besides these two, how can you not have good commentators in a country with over a billion cricket-crazy people? I have always loved the BBC (British Broadcasting Corporation) commentators – why can't we produce that kind of people? Our commentators are embarrassing, to say the least. I don't know how they were even allowed by the BCCI (Board of Control for Cricket in India).

What are your favourite campaigns out of the ones you have written and thought of?

It's always your first campaign. I think the shaving one I told you about is very dear to me. Then I liked 'Jaago Re' (for Tata Tea) only because we started this trend of social advertising at Lowe and then many people started doing random stuff under the name of social advertising. I like some of the things we did for Bajaj. I liked Saint-Gobain when I was doing it. I liked doing ads for Havells – 'Hawa Badlegi'. I think the greatest joy of advertising is that you move on fast. You don't dwell in the past for too long. You don't have time.

Most of your advertising work is fantastic brand strategy coupled with good creativity. Though I always wanted to understand how you arrived at one of your most famous campaigns – 'Hoodibaba' for Bajaj Caliber.

It was a very simple thing. I was sitting with an account planner. And he said that the brief was 'Great Mileage. Great Power'. And he kept saying that it was what the bike offered. I asked him what's the strategy and he said it was the first bike to offer great mileage and great power. I was like: 'Why are you repeating the same thing? What do you mean by the first bike? It's not a magical thing. Who's going to believe this? You think it's like some hoodibaba or something?' The planner said, 'Balki, it's just this much.' And I said, 'Wait, hang on. What did I just say?' That's how the campaign happened. When I pitched it to Rajiv (Bajaj), he was like we have spent some two years of R and D (Research and Development) and market research and you are telling me to run a campaign called 'Hoodibaba'? But then he loved it and it became a huge success. That's it.

Tell me about the journey of *Chup*. A man killing film critics is a crazy idea.

It is about a serial killer who kills film critics. How it all happened is, long ago, back in 2008, when *Cheeni Kum* came out, on one hand, I saw people clapping for it. Then on the other, I still remember it was a Wednesday, a very popular film critic at the time had written a review of it. I read it with great curiosity and excitement only to find out that he had slammed the film. I took the review so much to heart that I went into depression. I didn't answer anyone's phone including Amit-ji's. Amit-ji was trying to reach me saying that people love the film. Then he met me and explained to me that people have various agendas, it's the public that matters. Only one person had written bad things about the film and I happened to read only that one.

Eventually, I got over it, the film made its money and I thought why should just one person's review matter? From that day till the time I wrote *Chup*, I did not read a single review. In some ways, after the *Cheeni Kum* incident, I started thinking that he was holding me accountable for my film. Who is holding him accountable for his review? I told Amit-ji around the time that I wanted to make a film about someone killing a film critic. Eventually, it became what it became.

So *Chup* is one of the most personal stories I have written. It comes from the anger and dejection I felt when someone was trashing in two hours a piece of work that I had spent two years making. In a way, *Chup* is a mockery of the whole system of film criticism. I am not saying every critic has to like my film but expressing a dislike requires sensitivity. Because it's your profession. If you're an audience, that's fine. You can say anything because you are not responsible and paying for the film. But a film critic does this for a living and he must do his job with some sensitivity and responsibility because a lot of times a review influences people. Some critics have mistaken their job as a powerful job but it's actually a job of responsibility.

I think it's a system that we have put up with for too long without correcting it. I am saying again, that I am not expecting praise. Please go ahead and critique my films but don't blast them. As a film critic, you are nobody to blast me. And as a creative person, you are taught to take everything on the chin. But I find the film critic deal quite unfair. I don't have the media. If you blast me, how do I counter it? Do I have an avenue to blast you back? Not just in films but I have faced this in advertising as well. A very famous advertising magazine used to have this thing called Best & Bekaar. All my ads used to first be categorized as Bekaar. Why? Because they had not seen anything like that. Then it turns around and becomes a thing and at the end of the year, they conduct a poll in which the same ad comes first. I was like you were the magazine that called it Bekaar and now a year later you are the one calling it number 1. Aren't you ashamed?

Sometimes I feel what authority does a magazine have to tell me how to write an ad or who is a film critic to tell me how to make a film? I don't tell them how to do journalism or how to write film reviews. I have spent the whole of my life doing what I do. I should know a little better than them, at least, right? Having said this, I maintain that criticism is very important. You cannot have a world without critics. But I always say that in a publication you must put the most intellectual, the most well-rounded people as critics because they do influence a lot of people. But most publications don't get it right.

The trailer of *Chup* made me sense some of Guru Dutt's influence on the film. Does the story of his life have a role to play?

We are talking of the most sensitive artist of our cinema, whose most beautiful film – *Kaagaz Ke Phool* – was trashed so much by film critics that he never made a film after that. Today, you call it a cult classic. I like the cheek of these people. There's not even an apology from the Critics Guild of India. Isn't that the least they could do? You have harmed an artist like Guru Dutt, for god's sake! Guru Dutt is not part of the plot of *Chup* but he is the biggest inspiration for the film.

What is your idea of success as a film-maker?

The first aspect of it is that I call my film successful if after watching it I think I couldn't have done a better job. That's one aspect of it. The second point is it should be something that people haven't seen before. The third and most important thing is that people should like it – at least to the point that nobody should say that it's a loss-making venture. Also, I can never control how many people are going to see my film but those who happen to see it, if they like it and come out of the theatres praising it, I would be very, very happy.

Could you name your favourite films and film-makers for me?

My favourite film has always been *Moondram Pirai*, which is the Tamil version of *Sadma*. It's a classic for me beyond any Ray, beyond anything by anyone. Then I caught up recently with some of Bimal Roy's films like *Do Bigha Zameen* and *Madhumati* and all of those and I really enjoyed them. All of Guru Dutt's films are my favourites. *Kaagaz Ke Phool* is one of my favourite films. I would say one of my all-time favourite international films is *Blue Valentine*. I am a huge fan of Woody Allen. I think *Zelig* is one of his best films. I think Woody Allen is the greatest thinker in our cinematic universe. I am also a huge fan of Clint Eastwood's films. Then again, at the same time, I am a huge fan of Bachchan's films – particularly those by Manmohan Desai. So, I like all kinds of cinema. I even like *Pushpa* very much. Then as soon as a Mahesh Babu film or a Rajinikanth film comes out, I watch it. Then Iranian films, of course, everyone knows of them. Who doesn't like Majid Majidi's films, for instance? I am a huge fan of Marathi cinema. I really like the film *Gabhricha Paus*, which is the most underrated, under-marketed film of our times in my opinion. I think Marathi cinema explores some layers that are just fabulous. From *Harishchandrachi Factory* to *Deool*. Then I love *Fandry* and *Sairat*. I think Nagraj Manjule is a phenomenal film-maker. I like anything he does. I also like Dhanush down south as a film-maker. Of course, I like him as an actor but I think he is very special as a film-maker as well.

If you were to meet a twenty-year-old self today, what would you differ with him on?

At twenty, I thought I was intelligent and the system was bad. Today, at fifty-eight, I think I am foolish and the system is bad.

NINETEEN

Rajat Kapoor

I met Rajat Kapoor at his office in Bandra one afternoon and as I waited for him to arrive, I felt I had entered another world through a wormhole. It was a wonderful bungalow, about a five-minute walk from Bandra station, with an old-world charm and a quietude that has gone missing from Bombay.

He was extremely articulate, sophisticated, and charming. As an actor, Rajat Kapoor is a household name but as a writer-director, he is an artist who believes in the auteur theory, a man who seeks purity from his art and would go all out to achieve his creative ambition no matter the odds. He is the writer-director of *Bheja Fry*, *Ankhon Dekhi*, and *RK/RKay*.

What did you like reading?

Fiction. But now it's becoming less and less, I must admit. These days, I am reading a lot of scripts and that takes up a lot of my reading time. But I have read a lot for about forty-forty-five years of my life. And I have read various things, everything. There are, of course, a few favourites. I started with Hindi literature when I was in Delhi in my teens. That's when I read a lot of Hindi literature. People like Rajendra Yadav and Mannu Bhandari and of course Colonel Ranjit and those pulp fiction kind of stories as well as the classics. Then of course world literature. If I were asked to pick one person from all I have read, I rate (Fyodor) Dostoevsky very highly. I have not read anybody else who writes with that kind of delirious madness. It looks like he's possessed when he's writing. Sentences go on, everything is pitched high. It's quite feverish. It's like a feverish delirium and you can't put the book down. Maybe I should make a film like that, you know, when all the characters are acting that high a pitch. That might be fun, don't you think?

Exactly how and when did you start writing?

I started writing when I went to FTII. Though, I must say, there was not much importance given to writing in FTII in those days. The direction course was good but the writing one wasn't. Even the people there didn't take writing seriously. Everyone was like 'Oh, we're film-makers!' so a script was looked down upon in a strange way. People believed that it was a medium of images and they wanted to create abstract images on film. There were two reasons for writing to be treated this way. One was the belief that we are all image-makers and the second one was that everyone wanted to run away from the hard work that is writing. It was more an escape route than anything else. Who wants to write? Let's just go and shoot something. That was the attitude.

But then you come out and realize that you have to write. Because you have to present your script to someone. That is the first step of making a film. So, I started writing. When I started assisting Kumar Shahani and Mani Kaul, I started to write by the end of my apprenticeship. I remember very well that the first script I wrote was an adaptation of a Borges story. Jorge Luis Borges, the great South American writer. My script was based on his story 'The Unlikely Impersonator'. Nothing really happened to the script, the film never got made. But I guess, years later, somewhere it came back to me as part of my film *Mithya* where somebody is impersonating someone. And then in 1993-94, I wrote *Private Detective*, which luckily got made. And I have been writing ever since.

Every year, I spend about two-three months writing. And I write and I throw the draft sometimes. Sometimes, I go back to it after two years. Sometimes, some drafts get discarded because they don't work out. But I try to give every idea a fair chance. At least two-three drafts. And if it still doesn't work out, I move on to the next one.

Do you think that enough importance is given to writing in the Hindi film industry?

We all know the general answer to this question. What has been changing is that people have started asking for bound scripts unlike before. But what is in that bound script? Good stuff? Rarely. But at least people are making an effort to write and get themselves registered with the Writers Association. But I don't think that has improved the quality of writing or scripts. You know, my teacher Mani Kaul had an interesting thing to say about it. He said that we are oral people, we are people of the ear. We like to hear things to understand them.

That's why music is such a big thing in our part of the world. Anyone can listen to a song and say that this, for instance, is Raag Todi and this is the sur (music) and this is the taal (rhythm) that go with it. That's why we have so many songs in our films. The story just meanders somewhere near all this without much attention or importance. The idea of writing a script itself was not developed. The story was just to keep the songs moving or to keep the emotions moving. It was just a ploy. Now, with the younger generation of film-makers, who are a little influenced by Western film-makers or mainly Hollywood film-makers, the story has assumed some importance. But I don't think we are pushing ourselves at all. I don't know any writers of films who are pushing themselves at all, unfortunately. I am sure poets, novelists or other writers are doing that. But film writers are not. In that, I think, nothing really has changed.

I know that it works both ways. Because if you write a good script, you never know how long it will take to get made or if it will ever get made at all. So then why bother? Might as well say, I am doing *Dabangg 8* and be happy with it. But I am not talking about newcomers here. Their struggle is valid and is another story. But what about the established people? Do you think they're pushing themselves enough? I think it's a lack of ambition to even look at ourselves as artists or to look at cinema as a medium of art. We look at cinema as a medium to make money, a trade, a business. Who made how much at the box office, who's making money, that's all we talk about. You know even if people go for a film preview, nobody talks about how they liked it. They say if it will work or not. I mean, what do you care if it will work or not? Why don't you say how you liked it? Whereas cinema as a medium is supposed to do something else. It's supposed to light up things. It's supposed to illuminate you. It's supposed to make you aware of things that you either weren't before or if you were, you weren't able to find an expression for them. That is what cinema and art are supposed to do in my view.

Did you always want to be a writer as a child? How did all this start?

I always wanted to be a film-maker. My father was a great film buff. I watched a lot of films as a child. I remember very well, in 1974, when I was thirteen years old, my father used to take us to watch all the award-winning films that were shown in Delhi at an event. I remember at thirteen, my father took me to watch Mani Kaul's *Duvidha*. Maybe something stirred within me there. Then around sixteen, I watched some films by Werner Herzog and then later Ingmar Bergman and Jean-Luc Godard. I was lucky that I got to watch this kind of cinema at these film societies in Delhi. I got to FTII when I was twenty-five, which is quite late. Because most people joined it by twenty or twenty-one. But I took some time to convince my parents. By the time I applied to FTII and got through, I was certain that I wanted to be a film-maker.

You have always written peculiar stories and screenplays, especially in the context of the Hindi film industry. Has that been a conscious choice?

I don't think it's a conscious choice. This is just who I am. I think the biggest struggle for any artist in this world is to find who they are. And to find their expression. The film I made in 1995, *Private Detective*, was so influenced by Kumar Shahani. Yes, it was a thriller that has a murder and everybody is a suspect and all of that but in the making, it was all influenced by Kumar Shahani. In the writing, it was me. It took me about ten years to become my own man. In 1996-97 I made a short film called *Hypnothesis* about clowns. I think with that I started to find my own voice.

Tell me about the journey of making *Ankhon Dekhi*.

Many scripts I have had are ideas that have evolved over time. For *Ankhon Dekhi*, I had an idea for a long time – what if a man decides that what he experiences is his only truth. This stuck with me but I didn't know what to do with it. Because an idea is not a film. An idea is not a poem. A poem is made with words. The words have to resonate, not the idea. Then, many years later, I thought of a joint family. Boom! And there I had a way ahead. The dream of Babuji flying is a dream that I have had. It was a recurring dream for me. One of my most joyous dreams. After I made the film, I never had that dream again. *Ankhon Dekhi* was comparatively easy to make because Manish Mundra, whom I met on Twitter, produced it. Albeit that was after the studios had rejected it.

All my films have had a long wait. *RK/RKay* was very difficult to make in comparison. I had to put my own money, a part of it was crowdfunded. When I was writing *Ankhon Dekhi*, I was already thinking of Sanjay Mishra. Because I had just done *Phas Gaye Re Obama* with him as an actor and I thought he fit my character very well.

And how did *Mixed Doubles* happen and how about your constant collaboration with Ranvir Shorey?

That was my first film with Ranvir. I auditioned him. He was great. In the film, I had an interesting journey. The thing is I had made *Raghu Romeo*, which made it to the Locarno Film Festival. And we were on a big high. We thought it was an international breakthrough. The film was shown in an open-air venue and trust me, nine thousand people were watching it! Nine-thousand people clapped for that film. It was unbelievable. I thought I had a hit on our hands. But then it was released here and it bombed and I went into depression. But what happened is that at the Locarno Film Festival, there was this gentleman called Sunil Doshi, whom I became friends with. He told me he had sixty lakh rupees and asked if I could make a film in that much. I said yes. He asked if I had a script. I shared two ideas with him, one of which was *Mixed Doubles*. He accepted it and we jumped into it. I didn't want to lose that opportunity. I wrote and made the film in two months.

You asked me how the idea came to me. In 2004, when I went to Locarno, I was really depressed and my ticket was bought by someone else. From Locarno, I went to Geneva and my flight back was the next morning. I didn't have the money to book a hotel so I thought I'd spend the night at the airport itself. But they said the airport was shut! I was like, how can an airport be shut at night? But then, anyway, I went back to the train station. And I ordered a coffee to stay up all night. In that café, I wrote on a tissue paper: *Mixed Doubles*. And then the story occurred to me.

How do you go about writing theatre?

Let me tell you about my process of writing theatre. It's very interesting. I call up a few friends whom I want to work with. And then we decide what we want to do. For instance, *Hamlet – The Crown Prince*. The first day we meet, we read the first scene of *Hamlet*. We destroy the scene. Finally, what we are left with has nothing to do with the original scene. But we build like that. We don't know where we are going. Yes, there is a chance of falling completely flat on your face in a process like that. But that's the risk that you run and that's where the fun is.

Then in the case of *King Lear*, we go into themes of the original play, not the text. Father and daughter and loss of youth. For days, we talk about the loss of youth. We start getting back to our own stories related to that theme and develop something. And that's why we call it *Nothing Like Lear*. Because it's nothing like the original play. Though at the same time, it's every bit the original play. The process is very exciting and very scary. There is no safety net.

By now, I have done four Shakespeare plays and in all, followed the same process. I think Shakespeare is unbeatable. It's not just his craft or his words. It's the depth. You can't go beyond *Hamlet*. And it is as modern as it was 500 years ago. Why has no one written anything better in five centuries? Shakespeare is a colossus.

Does being an actor help the writer in you?

Not really. I'd say, all it does is that it helps me empathize a little more with my actors. I understand where they are coming from.

How do you see the industry change in the last thirty-odd years?

Things haven't changed. If we look at the larger picture, nothing has changed. And nothing will change for the next thirty years either. I say that because we have been making the same mediocre stuff that we were making thirty years ago. Some changes happened in tiny spurts. For instance, when the multiplexes came in, we thought our kind of cinema would now be made. It worked for a couple of years and then the multiplexes started getting bombarded with the same old kind of stuff.

When the OTT platforms came in, we again thought, now indie cinema will get a boost. Nothing happened! They all fall into the same traps of the system. They all want to play to the system. Everyone ends up chasing superstars and stars. That's the only thing they know in this industry. And it's not just here but in Hollywood as well. It's like gambling and putting money on the horse that's likely to win the race. It's not about telling stories or making films for anyone. I would say modern Hollywood is as bad in my opinion.

One unfortunate thing that has happened is that in the 1980s, there was NFDC (National Film Development Corporation), which kind of backed out by the early 1990s. That was a terrible tragedy. Because film-makers like Saeed Mirza, Kumar Shahani, Mani Kaul, and Shyam Benegal were denied opportunities to make any more films after that. While we think that we have taken leaps ahead, actually we have regressed. Because there was state support for cinema back then, which doesn't exist anymore. The whole new wave of the 1970s and the 1980s started because of NFDC. Even in the Western world in those days, great cinema was state-funded to some extent. In France, Germany, in Austria. The great Germans like Herzog and Fassbinder were helped by the state.

Why would the so-called market be interested in a Kumar Shahani film? I think it's a matter of shame, national shame, that Kumar did not make a film in the last fifteen years of his life! What are we celebrating, man? For twenty years, I have been hearing that things have changed. We say now it has all been democratized. We keep hearing that cinema is getting better, the audience is getting better. Show me where. I can't think of one film.

Well, I remember *Court*. I'd say that was a fantastic film. *Gangs of Wasseypur* is one of my favourites. But that's it. I have to stop after that. Show me what else. Where is the progress? Some people say that it's because of the audience that we make films like what we make. But you have to make films for yourself, not for an audience. If you do the latter, you are in the business of films. Not in the art of films. But if you are interested in the medium, how can you make anything lesser than you?

However, I must accept one thing here. Any kind of art comes much later in your evolution. I mean, if 50 per cent of the population in the city lives in slums and so many in this country are below the poverty line, how can you talk art to them? We don't have basic sanitation to give them, no basic food or education. How can we expect them to come and watch what we perceive as art? They have other concerns. That's why I am saying that nothing is going to change in this country for the next thirty years. Art is a far-fetched concept for most people here where their basic needs are not met. Art is spiritual but before that, what about the corporeal?

Where do you stand on the advent of OTT?

I think I am comfortable with my ninety minutes. Just as every short-story writer needn't be a great novelist and vice versa, I think every film writer cannot be a show or a long-form writer. I think OTT shows are a different medium. At least, so far, I have never had an idea that needs more than a film. One good thing that OTT has done though is that it has made some rare films available. *Ankhon Dekhi* slipped out of theatres when it was released but it got a new life on OTT. For that, I am really thankful to the OTT platforms.

What are your cinematic influences?

The list is huge. The constant one and two have been Charlie Chaplin and Federico Fellini. I think Chaplin is the greatest ever film-maker of all time. He is incredible. And Fellini has had a lasting influence on me. Then after these two, there is a long list. Billy Wilder, Godard. There is a French film-maker called Eric Rohmer I like very much. Ritwik Ghatak, Guru Dutt. I like Guru Dutt very much. There are films I don't talk about much. Because I am very far away from mainstream cinema. But as a child, the film that impressed me a lot was *Deewaar*. I must have been thirteen or fourteen when I saw it. I think it has affected my psyche. For example, in *Ankhon Dekhi*, there might be a bit of Balraj Sahni's *Do Raaste*. These are some of the mainstream films that have impacted me earlier in my life in a deep, deep way.

I met Javed Sahib (Javed Akhtar) recently on a flight and I walked up to him and told him that *Deewaar* is one of my favourite films. I told him I still remember that scene between Bachchan and Parveen Babi, after having made love, lying on the bed, smoking cigarettes.

When was the last time you saw that on screen in a Hindi film? It's incredible. That has just stayed with me. The idea of sin is a taboo.

What's your creative purpose?

Philosophically speaking, I think celebrating life and joy. I don't relate to morbidity or self-destruction at all, which film-makers like Michael Haneke might be coming from. I am not against making people uncomfortable. That is of course a role of art. But a morbid view of the world, the gloom that a person like Kieslowski might bring in is something I don't relate to. I mean, Haneke and Kieslowski are great film-makers but I am telling you where I come from. I belong more to the Fellini world. The world of joy.

TWENTY

Reema Kagti

Reema Kagti is the co-writer and co-creator of some of India's best OTT shows such as *Made in Heaven* and *Dahaad*, and of sparkling mainstream films such as *Zindagi Na Milegi Dobara* and *Gully Boy*. Her long-term writing partnership with Zoya Akhtar makes the duo commercial Hindi cinema's most sought-after writer-creators of our day.

I am a fan of Reema and Zoya for consistently making characters that breathe and for telling sensible stories sensitively. I love the layers and the complexity they bring to their characters, which most people in commercial cinema don't manage to.

After trying to get an appointment for about a year, I finally got a chance to meet Reema at her house in Bandra, and over some strong coffee, she was kind enough to answer my questions with candidness and a sharp sense of humour, which made the evening all the more enjoyable.

What was your childhood like and at what point did you think of taking writing up as a profession?

My connection to writing developed way before my connection to direction did. I think I enjoyed reading a lot as a kid. You know, they make you do these essays in school? 'If I were a one-rupee coin' or 'If I were a plastic bag' and those things. Those were the first fiction pieces, so to say, that I ever wrote. I think that kind of set it off for me. I do remember enjoying the process of writing a lot. So, I would keep writing. I started writing a few little stories. I would write a few plays that I would enact with siblings and neighbourhood kids. Then there was a magazine called *Tinkle* when we were growing up to which you could send stories. So, I started sending some stories to them, one of which they published, and I got fifteen rupees for it. I think in that sense it validated me. Somewhere, I always grew up wanting to be a writer. The film-making part came in much later, writing for film came in later as well. All of this was happening while I was in school. Initially, I was in Carmen School in Digboi. Then I moved to Loreto Convent School in Shillong and after that, I shifted to Delhi Public School in R.K. Puram.

All through this, I kept writing. My father had a farm in Assam, and he wanted me to study business management and work with him on the farm business. I was always a film buff. I loved watching films and could have never had enough of them. I would watch a lot of Bollywood and some Hollywood as well. I am a full product of piracy. Back in Assam, in those days, there was a huge culture of VCD (Video Compact Disc). You could get a crack version of anything. So, that gave me access to Hollywood. Then, my parents were fans of Bengali cinema and that exposed me to some art films at the time. But somehow, I had never thought of making films. When I was in ninth standard, I remember, one day, I bunked school and watched Mira Nair's *Salaam Bombay*. And at the end of the credits, I thought, 'I need to be doing this. This is what I should be doing.' It was a very sudden realization. It was like a flash. I went in as a school kid to watch a movie, and I literally came out, in my head, as a director. In that sense, Mira Nair's film changed my life.

After school, I took up literature at Sophia College in Mumbai, for Junior College, which is eleventh and twelfth standards. I continued at Sophia's for graduation as well. I was always interested in literature. Because I think to be a writer, you have to be interested in reading just like to make films, you have to be interested in watching films. One feeds the other. Now, even in college, my writing continued. There were short stories. Then some novels ended up as short stories and stuff like that. In college, I joined a film club. One of my subjects was advertising. So, in college, I wrote ads, which turned out to be the first scripts I attempted. After college, I applied to FTII and was rejected three times. But by that time, after my graduation, I had started working in Bombay. My father wanted me to have some formal education in media if I wanted to pursue a career in it. So, after getting rejected at FTII, he suggested I try SCM (Supply Chain Management) at Sophia College which was a media course – they still have that course – so, I did that for a year, and then when you finish the course, you're supposed to intern for a month. So, that's how I met Rajat Kapoor who was working on a film called *Private Detective* at the time. I just started working. I did a film with Rajat Kapoor and then met a few more people along the way with whom I worked on other films.

I just started AD-ing (being an Assistant Director). I moved to First AD. In this process, I was working on Kaizad Gustad's *Bombay Boys* where I met Zoya (Akhtar). We became friends. So, on the side, Zoya and I started having conversations about making something of our own. We were both compulsive writers. We wrote stuff. We wrote a short film together. We would encourage each other to write. And from there, came up our first film together. It just happened. Though we have not officially credited each other, both of us had a role in writing *Luck by Chance*, which was her first film, and *Honeymoon Travels*, which was mine. For example, on *Honeymoon Travels*, I did the bulk of the writing, but there are scenes that Zoya wrote, and vice-versa on *Luck by Chance*. But since those were our first films, we just decided not to credit each other. But then, since we had begun writing together, we just kept doing it. We didn't have a plan. We were just sort of two compulsive writers who had started compulsively writing together. We did it once, we did it another time, and then we just kept doing it.

How did being an AD help you in your journey as a screenwriter and a film-maker?

I think being an AD was a very conscious move and a stepping stone. I did not have any formal training in film, and I didn't have the luxury of going abroad to a film school. Things have opened up now, I think a lot of Indian kids have access to global education, which is great, but back in my day, it wasn't really that easy to go to a film school abroad unless you were a really, really rich kid. So, for me, AD was a great way to learn the technicalities of film-making. I was always very conscious of the mental burnout that could happen if you keep AD-ing, and I knew I was never going to be AD-ing beyond a point in my career.

It's well-established that Zoya and you write great women characters. But I think you also write some of the best male characters that I have seen in Bollywood. Is it a conscious effort to develop well-rounded characters?

See, obviously, we're conscious about that. It does happen that sometimes when you are writing, your characters get sacrificed to the plot. But yes, I think instinctively, both of us look at the world in a certain way. One, it's about how you look at the world and two, it is about how you write characters. It's interesting what you said about some people writing women badly or some people writing men badly, but honestly, as a writer, you can't choose to write a character well or not depending on their gender. I think if you write women badly, chances are that you write men badly as well. Having said that, it is possible that as a writer, you might have a slightly lopsided view, a sexist view, a patriarchal view, or a sympathetic view. But within that, it's still your capability of writing good, rounded characters that shines through. Your worldview is what matters at the end of the day.

When you are writing, it's very hard for you to disguise yourself. I think writers who have an interest in psychology or people-watching have a slight advantage, you know. Like, I have a huge interest in people-watching. If you leave me alone in a restaurant, chances are that I will just watch people. It's something that I have been doing for years. At some point, of course, you become conscious that a particular person you're watching could become a character or could form shades of a particular character of yours.

There have been times when I have taken notes watching random people at a café or a restaurant or anywhere outside. But now since I have been people-watching and writing for so long, it's sort of become a natural process for me. I sometimes meet an interesting person and think about how he or she could become a delicious character. It's not that I am stalking people or judging them, but it's what they are telling me about human life and experience that matters. Similarly, newspapers inform my characters a lot. So, it's the people you surround yourself with, what you are reading, what you are watching – all of that comes into shaping your worldview and characters.

Zoya and I have become like a well-oiled machine so if we don't have a character rounded, it sticks out sorely. You don't want your characters to be a trope or a half-baked and hollow version of something you see or hear. I think that's where the craft comes in. There are certain things that we talk about every character. We set a universe for a person – what they want, what they are running from, what they are trying to achieve, what their problem is, and what the solution to their problem could be. All of that is putting it simply, but honestly, a lot of it is just common sense.

For instance, Farhan's character in *Zindagi Na Milegi Dobara*. We were very conscious that we were trying to make a very commercial, theatrical film so we had to set up three friends. We wanted each of them to be different, and we wanted each of them to have complete character arcs of their own. I think Farhan's character had some flaws, some negative things like he slept with his best friend's girlfriend. Meeting the absent father kind of makes him understand himself better and accept his flaws. The flaws of that character were that he was a little selfish, and a little insensitive. You know, that's how people are. Nobody is without a flaw, and that's something we look at while creating characters. Creating flaws in your characters is endearing, and it also gives you a sense of a real person.

You and Zoya have formed a long and formidable writing partnership that has lasted for so many years which is rare. Can you talk about that in terms of how it works and if there are any creative differences?

As I said earlier, we just met, became friends, and started writing together. The writing partnership started organically, and maybe that's why it's worked. Had we planned it too much, it may not have. Even today, when we are not just writing partners but also run Tiger Baby together, I don't think either of us has told the other person, 'I'll always write with you.' It has all just happened. Somewhere we did feel that we had a strong writing partnership, and we took it to the next level by starting Tiger Baby, which is our own production house. And yes, along the way, we have collaborated with other writers as well. Especially when we did our shows *Dahaad* and *Made in Heaven*, we collaborated with tons of writers. Even on feature film scripts like *Kho Gaye Hum Kahan*, we collaborated with Arjun Singh. On *Superboys of Malegaon*, Zoya and I have kind of just acted as mentors, but we were there with Varun (Grover) every step of the way. We didn't write the film, therefore he has the sole writing credit but we were very involved in the process.

About creative differences between Zoya and me, they happen all the time. When we were writing *Zindagi Na Milegi Dobara*, we were fighting so much and so loudly in Zoya's house that the neighbours called her mother to ask her if everything was all right. It was obviously not a personal fight, but we had a different point of view on something about the script if I recall it right. Also, I think before *Zindagi Na Milegi Dobara*, we had only written *Talaash* and one short film together, so it was still in the early days of our working together. Now, I think, we've also matured from that point, we've become wiser. Back then, we used to think everything needed to be sorted out at that very moment. Now, because we've done it so many times over, we have realized there is no point arguing. A good idea lives and two or three days after the disagreement, it becomes apparent what the right way to go is. The not-so-good ideas die a natural death. So, I think an important part of the writing process is also having the patience to allow things like this to happen.

I think Zoya and I have similar values, we have similar worldviews, but we are also very different people. We have had very different experiences in life. I went to boarding school at all those three places I told you about, my parents lived on a farm in Assam whereas Zoya's parents lived in Bombay, and she is very much a city kid in that sense. But I don't think we would have had that level of writing ability that we bring to the table had we been very similar people. If you have two people, they better be two minds and not one mind. There is no point in just being a yea-sayer. And the fact that we operate this way creates the synergy between us.

Many writer-directors in Bollywood, after they taste success, don't write much themselves. However, I have heard that both you and Zoya are very much involved with all the writing that goes out of your company even today. Is that true?

Yes, it is true. We do spend a lot of our time writing even today. And we also spend a lot of our time sitting on some Tiger Baby projects that neither of us is directing. I think that is because the script is your blueprint. And if your blueprint goes wrong, everything else is sure to go wrong. I do believe that writing is the most important part of the process of film-making because if a good idea is written badly and gets lost in that, nothing else can revive it. But I have seen many well-written ideas that are not done justice because of the budget or whatever else still making an impact because something is charming about them that has gone through. I am not saying that writing is the only thing. Of course, the director and all the technicians who work on a film have their expertise and calibre, and I'm not putting any of that down. But I do think that the number one is the script. The best director, the best DOP (Director of Photography), and the best technical crew can't fix a bad script.

We do many, many rounds of iterations of our scripts. I think that's the real secret of good screenplay writing. You are not some robotic machine that you are going to blurt out a brilliant script in one go and in the first draft itself. I mean, of course, I have heard stories like that from Zoya's father (Javed Akhtar). He sometimes tells us, 'What are you girls writing for so long? Draft number twenty-five, really?' Because he and Salim (Khan) Sahib, once they spoke about a story, would just write a dialogue draft, and maybe on the set, they would make some changes if need be. Most of their work happened that way. But I think beyond those two people, I have not seen anybody else who has the potential to write like that. And to me, the secret of what you said about rounded characters and stuff like that is layering. Zoya and I do a minimum of ten drafts on every script. A lot of times, the number is way higher. After writing a few drafts, we also give it out to some friends and writers for an opinion or feedback. At this point, I would mostly give it to writers because they have the best feedback. They know how to approach the problem. Other people sense the problem but are usually not able to articulate it or offer a solution. So, till we get a reaction that we are happy with, we keep doing more and more iterations of the script.

***Made in Heaven* has some of the most layered characters on Indian OTT. Can you run me through the journey of writing and creating the show?**

Well, we kind of started it when Netflix and Amazon were coming to India. For a lot of people at the time, it was an extension of TV. But for us, it was a very exciting new platform. The first thing that Netflix commissioned in India was Anurag's (Kashyap) *Scared Games*. And similarly, for Amazon, we were one of the first partnerships in India. So, for us, it was very exciting to do something which was long format. The good thing is that it is a limited long format. It's not like we are talking of a hundred episodes or something like that. We are talking of eight or ten episodes.

Zoya was very keen to do something around Indian weddings. It started with her talking about doing something that shows the opulence of India with the backdrop of weddings, but then we get into the cracks. That's how we zeroed in on wedding planners as central characters. Then we talked about a lot of characters, followed by a lot of arguments but then eventually these two – the two protagonists you see in the show – sat well because we thought it was interesting to have one character who has a divorce going on and the other can't even get married, and these two are in the business of organizing grand weddings. You know, the main characters had their own graphs but we also had the opportunity to get into Indian families and into the other issues that marriage throws up in a patriarchal society like ours. So, it was just a lot of talking between Zoya and me. We do a lot of talking before we write anything. So, most of this show, in a way, is just a product of our talking a lot about the idea.

How did you conceive *Dahaad* and how much of show writing, in your opinion, is about creating the world?

Creating a world is honestly something you have to do even if you are creating a five-minute film, a one- or two-hour-long film, or an eight-episode show. But I think the advantage of long-form writing is the amount of time you have to create and play with your characters, your plot, you know. You have to create the right hooks at the end of each episode and all that. Just because they love episode one, may not mean that they will love episode three, for instance. So, I think each form comes with its own challenges.

As viewers, Zoya and I consume things across the spectrum. So, if you see our work, it doesn't stick to one genre as such. In terms of how I came up with *Dahaad*, well, I am obsessed with crime. I watch all crime shows and even those YouTube channels with crime documentaries. That's how obsessed I am with crime. So, while we were making *Made in Heaven*, *Dahaad* was the other idea that we were trying to develop. It's based on many serial killers and there was also a case very similar to it that happened in India. So, initially, we had toyed with the idea of going and getting rights for that story but then we realized that wasn't what we wanted to do. Everybody knows about the famous serial killers and their stories. So, *Dahaad* was more about kind of going a little deeper, and we saw this as a way of looking at Indian society in a very different way than *Made in Heaven*. In *Dahaad*, you are looking at issues like caste and patriarchy from a serial killer's standpoint and looking at our world that is enabling certain things.

Can you tell me how *Zindagi Na Milegi Dobara* was developed?

So, Zoya's first film, *Luck by Chance*, was an ensemble piece, and when it finished, she said, 'I am done with these ensemble pieces with so many people and now I am just gonna go, put three guys in a car and go on a holiday and I am going to shoot it.' I think at that point, she said it as a joke, but eventually, the idea stuck with her, and then she decided to do that film. We talked about the idea and the layers of characters, and the plot points just fell into place. Spain just happened to be the country that seemed to have all the things the script needed, and that's how we chose Spain.

How did *Gully Boy* happen? What attracted you to this world of underground rap?

While Zoya was editing *Dil Dhadakne Do*, a common friend and editor, Anand Subaya, showed Zoya a video of Naezy and Divine. So, she sent me the video and told me that it was a very exciting world and we should talk about it. We contacted a whole lot of guys like Naezy, Divine, and a bunch of other guys as well and heard their stories. So, *Gully Boy* kind of came from there.

Honeymoon Travels and _Talaash_ did not do as well as some of your other work. If given a chance, would you go back and change something about them?

Honeymoon Travels, for what it's worth, considering the times it was made in, did do well. It was an alternative film, made on a very low budget, and it not only recovered its cost but also made a little something for everybody involved. Some people watch it today and tell me that they love the film. That, to me, is a success. You know, it's very hard to put down if I could have done a better job in retrospect because I feel that about all my films. You want to change something every time. *Talaash*, again, was made on a low budget, and it made much more than what we spent on it. So, I think, commercially, you have to look at what was spent on the film to analyse what it made. It's always budget vs. the profit. I know that there is a hundred-crore club going on but just because a film made 100 crores, doesn't mean it was a hit because you might have spent 120 crores making it. This is what people don't understand about the commerce of films.

Tell me some of the films and film-makers who have influenced you in different phases of life.

Well, that's an exhausting list. But just to name a few, as a kid, there was a lot of Salim-Javed that was an influence. All of Mr Bachchan's work as well – I am obsessed with him. Then Spielberg. *ET* was a big influence. When I discovered world cinema, Pedro Almodovar, Wong Kar-wai, and all the classics have been huge influences. And then, to be honest, the list of influences changes almost every year. There is so much amazing stuff happening around the world. You see that, and you love some of it. The only time in my life when I have felt jealous of a film, thinking I wish I had come up with this idea, was after watching *The Sixth Sense*. I love *Mad Men* as well along with many other shows. When I watch a film or a show, I watch it as an audience and not as a creator. I think that's what allows me to absorb the pieces better.

When you turn eighty and look back at your career, what would you like to feel?

I'd like to feel that I made more good films than bad films. That's what I want to feel.

TWENTY-ONE

Ruchi Narain

I met Ruchi Narain at her office in Khar. It was lunchtime and she offered me some pav bhaji as we discussed a few common acquaintances before we jumped into the conversation.

Ruchi Narain is the writer of *Hazaaron Khwaishein Aisi* and the writer-director of *Guilty* among other films. She is well-read, very intelligent, and spoke with me with great clarity of thought.

Did you begin writing as a child and what was your childhood like?

Well, I never wrote anything in my childhood. In fact, I had a sort of a nomadic childhood, mostly away from India. I lived outside, like a lot in the Middle East, Muscat, Dubai, and Doha. Also, sometime in Sri Lanka. Then for a couple of years in Mussoorie. I also went to many schools, but I didn't know where I actually belonged back then. I have done British American schools, ICSE schools, and schools of all kinds. You develop a different way of thinking growing up this way. However, having said that, we as a family were always connected to India culturally.

I have a huge family, an extended family, and we are essentially Dilliwalas. My family has been in Delhi since before Shahjahan perhaps. Both my parents are from there. So, in school, we would have two to three months off for vacation. One month, we would be in Delhi and meet the whole extended family, and one month, we would be with my bua (aunt) in Goa. Therefore, we were very connected to India and its culture even when I did not stay here as a child. We lived in those big houses with a big family whenever in India. Lots of cousins and a lot of fun! We always had a blast amongst us. Some thirty-odd cousins coming together, can you imagine? Including school and college, I have been to twelve different educational institutions. I was a very good student. I always topped every school I went to. So, growing up, there was never really pressure on me to choose my calling or that one thing I needed to do in life. I was always made to believe by everyone around me, mainly by my teachers, that I would be good at whatever I chose to do. You know, my physics teacher wanted me to be a physicist; my math teacher wanted me to be a mathematician, and so on. Strangely, my weakest subject was the English language and English literature where I had a B+ grade. So, I never really thought about being creative. And films were very, very far away from my world. Especially in the Middle East, where I spent the bulk of my early years, we never went to the cinema. There was no culture of going to the cinema. And even if we watched some films, they would never be Hindi movies. We saw American films and Hollywood films. And they were just movies for me. I didn't know who made them and how or anything like that.

Then I went to a boarding school called Woodstock in Mussoorie and with my grades, I assumed I was going to Princeton or somewhere like that in the west to study further. But my parents insisted that I must study in India because they wanted me to have a connection with India and to understand the country. Initially, I was upset but since I had to choose a place in India to study, I chose Bombay over Delhi because my family was in Delhi. That's how I made it to St. Xavier's. I didn't know anybody in Bombay and stayed in a hostel on Marine Drive. I fell in love with Bombay. Bombay really took me in. The way this city embraces you is beyond words. This city also makes you feel like you can do whatever you want.

I'll tell you, it sounds stupid, but when I came to Bombay and was studying history at St. Xavier's, Shyam Benegal came over one day to give a talk at college, and at that point, I didn't know who he was! But before the talk, we saw his film *Ankur* and I remember a scene where a character throws a stone and I felt like that stone hit me. It was eye-opening for me. I was like, oh my god, when you make a film, you can say so many things without spelling them out, you know. People are into it because they understand it, and connect with it. There was my realization! After the movie was played, Shyam Benegal talked to us and that was the first time I realized that films are not made by themselves but some people make them. Before that, I was a regular movie watcher who only thought of the actors I saw on screen. After that day, I started thinking that it would be cool to make a film.

After college, I was dying to make some constructive use of my time. I was interested in working on documentary films. So, I caught hold of a directory and started cold-calling people. I called up IDPA (Indian Documentary Producers Association) and because I had an accent, the receptionist connected me to the president of the IDPA. Can you imagine? I was only a fresh graduate who was looking for an internship. But here I was, on the phone directly with Aruna Raje. She was such a kind and generous person that she dictated the numbers of twelve directors to me on that phone call. And she also told me to tell the directors that she had sent me. And she hadn't even met me! That's how helpful she was. I went through that list but none of them at the time was doing a documentary.

The last number on that list was Gopi Desai's. When I called the office, the person who picked up the phone told me that Gopi was away for three months and asked me what I was looking for. After hearing my sob story, the person asked me, 'Is that Ruchi Narain?' I was surprised because nobody knew me. It turned out that this person was someone who knew me from Xavier's. He said, 'I am Nikkhil Advani.' Nikkhil asked me if he could introduce me to Sudhir Mishra who, he said, had made a film called *Dharavi*. I was excited. Nikkhil made me meet Sudhir Mishra and Renu Saluja. I knew of Renu Saluja because she was a big-shot editor at the time. Everyone wanted to work with her.

Sudhir took one look at me and perhaps thought, 'Girl!' So, he asked me if I would handle costumes for his next project. I had no idea about costumes but I knew it wouldn't take me too long to figure it out. So, I started working with Sudhir. You must understand that we are talking about twenty-five years ago and unlike today, there were no girls in the crew back then. I was almost always the only girl on a project. At that time, computers were new and I told everyone that I was a computer expert. That's how I moved from costumes to AD and writing. Because I had started typing the scripts on the computer. I remember, one day, a senior writer had come down to our office and he asked me, 'Oh, you like writing?' I said yes. He laughed and said, 'So what do they call female writers? Writerni?' I said, 'No, writer.' When I look back, I think, it was a bizarre time. Nobody wanted to give women any money to do anything. It's still difficult but at that time, it was impossible to find funding. Today, things have changed for the better. And especially with OTT, it is amazing.

I worked with Sudhir as an assistant director on one of his projects. After that, Renu Saluja asked me if I would assist her and it was a huge honour but I realized that the only part of the film-making process that I was yet to understand well was writing. So, I politely refused. At the time, Saurabh (Shukla) was writing a film called *Sarhad* for Sudhir Mishra, a partition story which never got made. I approached him and asked if I could type the script out for him. He was more than happy. Literally, I had zero creative contribution to that script but by sitting with Saurabh every day and discussing scenes, I understood the process. I started seeing myself as a writer as well.

Tell me about the journey of *Hazaaron Khwaishein Aisi*, which remains one of the better Hindi films of the post-*Satya* world. Tell me about writing it. And writing the many-layered character of Geeta played by Chitrangada Singh.

The story of *Hazaaron Khwaishein Aisi* started with a conversation between Sudhir Mishra and Shiv Subramaniam, who unfortunately passed away recently. Shiv was a highly well-read, educated, gentle, and generous person. He always saw himself primarily as an actor but I thought he was a better writer than an actor. Shiv was sort of a reluctant writer so most of the work I did as a young writer was thanks to Shiv. Because people would go to Shiv asking him to write something and Shiv would direct them to me.

Two incidents sparked off *Hazaaron Khwaishein Aisi*. One was the fact that Sudhir had assisted and worked with the generation of film-makers who believed in idealism like Saeed Akhtar Mirza, Ketan Mehta, and Kundan Shah. So, he always wanted to make a film about the idealism of that generation. And the other thing is that Sudhir and Shiv also started talking about how the wild west of Bihar is. Sudhir's grandfather had been the chief minister of Madhya Pradesh. So, he had a lot of those stories already. One of those incidents was about some guys in a small-town police station who couldn't find a cop there. So, they assumed that the Adivasi villagers had killed the cop. The guys went and brutalized the village. They burnt their houses, raped the women, and beat up the men. And then the cop who they thought was killed staggered back to the village. It was found that he had gone to some relative's wedding and was lying drunk somewhere in the village. So, Sudhir was talking about this bizarreness. He also wanted to make a film about that.

If you remember, there is a scene in *Hazaaron Khwaishein Aisi*, in the third act, which is an allusion to this incident when Geeta gets raped. That is actually how the story and the writing process started. And then they kept talking and started talking about Delhi University and all that. They couldn't understand how to write the girl's character. And they thought, 'Let's get Ruchi because she is a girl!' So Geeta's character brought me into the film as a writer but, of course, you can't write just one character in a film.

I was a very enthusiastic young writer. I got involved in the whole scriptwriting itself. Also, since I did not grow up on Hindi films, I was not trying to break any rules because quite frankly, I didn't know any. And because I was a history student, I was quite into the project. I remember I had so many arguments with Sudhir. For instance, the film was in English because we were getting French funding. But I was like, it would make no sense for the Bihari villagers to be speaking in English. Or even in Hindi. Because they should be talking in Bhojpuri. I told Sudhir that nobody in India was going to watch this film anyway. So, for an international audience, what difference would it make as they were going to watch it with subtitles anyway? And that's why in the film, although most of it is in English, you have Telugu, Punjabi, Bhojpuri, Hindi, besides English, depending on which characters are speaking. In those days, nobody did it. We were the first people who did it.

I feel because I was so new, I was able to disregard and fight the prevalent wisdom. I was twenty-four when I started writing *Hazaaron Khwaishein Aisi*. Though it took around nine years to get released. Meanwhile, I also did my TV serial *Talaash*, which I was initially writing but eventually also directed. At the same time, I even started writing *Calcutta Mail*, which was made and released before *Hazaaron Khwaishein Aisi*. *Hazaaron Khwaishein Aisi* was made on a shoestring budget. And most of the people except for Sudhir were newcomers. It was Shiney's (Ahuja) first film. It was Chitrangada Singh's first film as well. Kay Kay had done *Paanch* before that but it was unreleased. And he had done *Last Train to Mahakali*. So he wasn't that well-known back then. Though everyone in Aaram Nagar knew that he was a good actor. Along with writing it, I was an assistant director on the film. In those days, there were no casting directors. So, the ADs would do the casting. Between Swanand (Kirkire) and I, we cast the whole film.

Why do you want to make a cinema?

I think cinema is a medium that allows me to use all my abilities and allows me to express myself in the best way possible. It allows me to say what I think in a non-pedantic way … in fact in a very human way. That's why I love it. You'd be surprised but I am not a fan girl. I don't call myself a cinema lover or anything like that. I mean, of course, I love watching movies but that's not the reason why I make movies. I make movies because they allow me to share what I want to. And that's the only reason why I make movies.

You hit it quite young, at twenty-four. But I am sure it was not always a rosy ride. Tell me about the struggles you have had to face.

You feel I hit it early. But *Hazaaron Khwaishein Aisi* was another level of struggle. There was no money in it and we wrote it for six years. Then three or four months shooting it. We had to wait for another three years for the film to get a release. And before a film is out, there is always uncertainty looming over your head. High-pressure, high-anxiety stuff. Also, my film *Guilty* worked very well on Netflix. I know it because everyone reached out to me. Even some international guys reached out to me. But then the film I made with Chitrangada and Shiney, *Kal*, did not do too well. Even *Calcutta Mail* was not a success. Besides, along the way, I have had scripts stolen from me. One, I fought for and lost the battle. So, these things keep going on for a writer.

The only learning you can take is you have to pick yourself up and move on. You can't really prevent all the problems beyond a point. Because if the other person has decency, you could still fight with them and win. But if the person is too self-absorbed, you can't do much. Unless of course, you take them to court. But I didn't want to fight a legal battle. It takes too much out of you. That's why you only learn and move on. As a rule, today, lots of people send me scripts. But I always tell everyone that unless it's registered, I don't want to read it. Nowadays, people do support writers. Writers may have agents and all that. In my day, there was no such thing. Now, if something untoward happens to me, I think I'll be able to fight it better.

What's the advice you would offer to young, aspiring film writers?

My only advice to a writer is to write. Write as much as possible, get it registered, and contact people directly. Everyone is on Instagram, and everyone's contacts are out there, especially those who run companies. I think this world is far more accessible than it ever was. Basically, you have to try everything to get in. Once that is done, you make other contacts and build a network. I would say, get onto a set or get into an office. You may not get paid for three months as an intern but it's okay. If people like you, and you are someone who they need and want, you will get work. Some people say that you need to network and go to parties and all that. But your biggest networking is in the office or on the project you are working on. Because on the next job, these are the people who are going to recommend you. I genuinely believe that your sincerity and eagerness are going to supersede any technical expertise you may have. The first thing is to be good at your job. There is no alternative to that. Whatever myths people like to perpetuate such as writing is in the blood, acting is in the blood and all, are wrong. These are all skills that can be learnt. Keep working on your skills and keep building on them.

Is screenwriting a science or an art?

According to me, science is an art. Unless you can think artistically or creatively in science, there is no science. Even in Hollywood, where there are film schools and an establishment of film, they don't teach you to write a formula. They teach you different *fundas* (methods). And the number of *fundas* there are should tell you that there is no one way of writing a film script. You should do what works for you. I, for instance, really work from my life experience. I wasn't around in the 1970s but I worked on characters in *Hazaaron Khwaishein Aisi* from my life experience. The world, the politics are what I have seen in my life. The people I know. And the rest is research. I think people undervalue research in terms of writing. You need to get the world right. And then you should write from emotional experience. That's my way of going about it.

Who are your favourite film-makers and what are your favourite films across the world?

I read William Goldman, his lessons, his books, and his experiences in screenwriting. I learn from him. Sometimes I feel he is helping me to write. Not necessarily his instructions but his experience for sure. Two films are my go-to pieces whenever I work on anything or if ever I am stuck. One is *Chinatown* written by Robert Towne and Roman Polanski. That, for me, is an ideal film. The other film that I learned from as a director as well as a writer, in fact, for every aspect of film, is *The Godfather*. I study *The Godfather* and *The Godfather 2* for anything that I am working on. Whatever questions I may have or points that I have to tackle in my mind, even though it's a totally different film, I try and watch *The Godfather* and understand how they did something and learn from there. Sometimes I even understand how to use sound in a particular way on my project. So, *Chinatown* and *The Godfather* are my mummy and daddy of cinema, who help me learn and get out of difficult situations if ever I am stuck in some. I grew up watching a lot of American television. But you know, I won't call those shows my influences. I don't think I have any influence as such. I really operate from a very experiential universe, which is also why my work is a little different.

Any film or show you wish you had made?

Well, I think I would have made anything I see differently. But if you insist, I wish I had made *A Suitable Boy*.

If somebody gave you 100 crore rupees, what kind of film would you make?

I mean, there is a film I am writing right now. I would do that. And you know, 100 crores is not that much. I need more. Because there are multiple things I am working on and everything requires money though we know how to work on a budget.

TWENTY-TWO

Sai Paranjpye

Sai Paranjpye is a pioneering voice of the 1980s parallel cinema that has influenced a generation of film-makers. She has written and directed films such as *Chashme Buddoor*, *Sparsh*, and *Katha* among others. Her wit, intelligence, and optimism are apparent in not only her films but also in the way she spoke with me.

I met Sai Paranjpye for breakfast at a South Indian coffee house in Juhu. And when we realized that there was too much noise there for me to be able to record the conversation, she said, 'I don't usually call people home but you seem to be a decent enough chap so we could continue the rest at my house.' At her house, we continued the conversation which kept alternating between English and Marathi, over some fresh tea made by her house help.

The stories from her life were fascinating, her command over both English and Marathi was phenomenal, and the sharpness of her mind blew me away.

How did you grow up to be a writer and a film-maker?

My childhood was a dream. It was spectacular. I had extreme privilege and at the same time extreme strictness. I was the only child and my mother, too, was the only child of her parents. My parents were divorced. My father was Russian. My mother studied at Cambridge. She was an extraordinary woman just like her father. My grandfather topped the mathematics exam in Cambridge and he was the first Indian to do so. He was a major celebrity in India and he was particularly revered in his own city which was Pune. My mother, on the other hand, was an enigma for people in Pune. They couldn't figure her out. She was a rebel.

I was an outcome of her marriage to a Russian, which was unheard of at the time. First, her marrying a Russian was sensational, and then her divorcing him was even more sensational. After the divorce, she brought me back to Pune, when I was just two years old. Thereafter, my mother and my grandfather brought me up. And I really could not ask for a better upbringing. My mother was extremely strict. I can't remember a single day when I didn't get soundly thrashed. In fact, if any child in our locality misbehaved, their parents would tell them, 'Hey, do you want to get thrashed like Sai?' My ears would burn listening to all this. I would get so humiliated. So that was one aspect of my mother. On the other hand, she spoilt me silly. I could ask for the moon and I would get it. Here was this brilliant woman, who was a Cambridge scholar, and spoke Russian and French, among other languages. She worked no job here and she focussed her entire energy on bringing up her child, which was me. Now, it can be very taxing to grow up in an environment like that.

You'd be surprised that I learnt horse riding when I was a child. My mother sent me to painting classes as well. I would go to Mr Gondhalekar, who was a very senior artist and had spent some years in Paris. Then, believe it or not, she made me join a classical music tuition as well. The famous Mirashi Buwa, who eventually won a Sangeet Natak Akademi award, would come every day at 7 a.m. to teach me. We never went beyond Raag Asawari, I remember. Because I couldn't sing to save my soul. Eventually, Buwa mustered up the courage to tell my mother, 'Shakuntalabai, Sai doesn't have an iota of musical talent so please do not force her.' That's when my singing stopped, mercifully. This shows the height of my mother's ambition for me. On top of this, every day, she insisted that I write

Sanskrit shlokas. Even now, I know about a hundred Sanskrit shlokas by heart.

We were of an atheist background. my grandfather went to Cambridge and became a rationalist and my mother was an atheist too. So although there were no deities in our house, I was made to learn all the stotras as well – Ravan Stotra, Ganga Stotra, you name it! Learning those around the age of seven gave me a firm base for the languages that I was to learn later on. Whether I spoke Marathi, English, Hindi, or French, that early practice of Sanskrit helped me a lot to pick up languages, not mispronounce words, and articulate myself. My grandfather was a much gentler person than my mother. He never had crazy ambitions for me. However, he was quite disappointed when he learnt that I had no mathematical genes in me. I couldn't pass algebra or geometry properly. But then he came to terms with it and he realized that I had something else. I had a talent for writing. He would tell me tales by Grimm and from *Arabian Nights*.

My grandfather and I used to go for a walk in the morning along the canal – there was a lovely canal in Pune in those days. Alas, it's no more. What you call Canal Street today used to be a long canal back in the day. So, my grandfather used to tell me stories on these walks. When I was in school, I was an average student academically. But I used to always be involved in elocution competitions and writing and directing plays. When I was eight years old, my grandfather was appointed as the Indian High Commissioner to Australia. So, my mother and I moved in with him. I spent four glorious years in Australia where I saw magnificent plays and film productions and I read a lot of books by writers from the world over. And the world opened to me!

My mother used to read me stories to put me to sleep. One day, she told me she was bored of telling stories every day and asked me to tell her one. I said okay. And I just made up a story and told her. She realized that it wasn't a story she had told me. Then she asked me to tell her another story and I did. I was eight years old at the time. That's when she realized that I may have a talent for stories. That was my doom! From that day onwards, I had to write four pages every day. I had to write an essay or a story or anything. But four pages were compulsory and then my mother would give me marks. This was the kind of discipline I grew up with. From that day onwards, till today, I have never stopped writing.

Tell me a little bit about your work before you got into films.

My major working span was in Delhi. I was one of the first six television producers in India. It's an achievement I am really proud of. The five others were Habib Tanvir, Kumar Vasudevan, A. Pratap, Shama Zaidi, and Swadesh Kumar. Initially, I was quite a flop but then I gradually started getting a hold of the medium. It widened my vision. I have done some of my best work on television. My film *Chashme Buddoor* was first a teleplay called *Dhuan Dhuan*. *Sparsh* was first a teleplay called *Raina Beeti Jaye*. I did teleplays, women's programmes, children's programmes, art reviews, quizzes, and VIP interviews – I did so many things for television, and dare I say, I was quite good at it. Then my first documentary won an award in Tehran, which was a major thing for me and it got me excited.

Was it very difficult for you to cut through the male-dominated world of cinema back in the 1980s?

A recent article in a Marathi newspaper said that women entered cinema in India in the 1980s referring to me. While it is true in some sense, mind you, technically there have been women directors before me. There was Bhanumati in the south. Then there was a Bengali woman whose name I can't recall at this moment. Then there was Shobhna Samarth and four-five others. However, unfortunately, none of them made an impact. None of them was really talked about. So, when I made *Sparsh* in the year 1980, it made quite a noise. It won three National Awards – Best Screenplay, Best Actor (Naseeruddin Shah), and Best Hindi Film. Plus, it travelled to sixteen film festivals across the world. It also was a commercial success. Not to say that it was a runaway hit but it did do well. Suddenly, I was the flavour of the month.

Things are very different nowadays when women are working in every aspect of films. Even some technicians are women. In my days, I was more or less the only woman on the set or in the entire crew. And I was the director. But I never paraded it around. I never behaved like 'Hey, I am a woman and this is something great' or anything like that. I was always thoroughly respectful to my team and my fellow technicians. You have your pluses and minuses. I am not a very good technical person. As far as imagination goes, nobody can hold a candle to me. Weaving stories, understanding characters, and having a sense of the narrative were my strengths. But if you ask me what lens should be used for a particular shot, I may not have the best answer. So, I leaned heavily on my fellow technicians. I used to tell them, 'Look, this is what I want this shot to look like and please figure it out for me.' This way, my crew members felt challenged and loved working with me. They never felt like this woman was showing off or something like that. So, I gained the respect of people. And in some cases, I used to say, 'Hey, I am stuck with this. Please help me out.' So, looking at a woman in that situation, many men would help me.

Men can be very gullible, you know. Women know how to handle them. So rather than feeling disadvantaged as a woman, I'd say, on the contrary, I enjoyed so many advantages of it. I am telling you, because I was a woman, I could go to any village for a shoot or any work on a project and I would be welcomed by those people. If a male director or typically filmy people went there, the villagers would throw them out. But the doors of those huts would open for me. I used to walk in, chat with the woman of the house, sometimes by complimenting the smell of the food she was making, for example, and eventually get what I wanted. Those guys would think, 'Who is this fair woman doing something with films!' They would be excited to see me. At another level, the doors of the ministers were always open for me. I used to get appointments or interviews in no time. Whereas many of my poor men colleagues would take years to get them. I used the fact that I was a woman to the hilt.

Of course, there is a downside to this as well. For example, I don't know now if it was because I was a woman or because I didn't understand money, but I never really made too much money. I think it's got to do with my upbringing. People in my house would only talk about education and knowledge. Nobody spoke about money. My mother never asked me what my salary was when I got my first job. It was disrespectful to talk about money. And that worked heavily against me in the years to come. People who used to be my fourth assistants at some point are now better off than me. And it's good for them, of course, and I am happy for them really. They did the hard work and they were savvy, they knew the business and they didn't stick to only what they believed in. I, on the other hand, was only concerned with the work I wanted to do. And I don't regret it at all. Today, I am a name. Some people respect me and my work. And I have gained a lot of love from my fans. So, I am very happy about that. Yes, of course, sometimes one tends to think – 'Wish I had a bigger car or a bigger house!' but those are fleeting thoughts. I am certainly happy with what I have done and achieved.

Do you think the gender of a writer or a maker influences their work? If yes, how so?

Yes, I do think it makes a little bit of a difference. Not to say that people like Gulzar or lots of other men haven't made sensitive films. But, by and large, you see the output of women directors and you see a certain sensitivity. You see Prema Karanth's *Phaniyamma*. It's a story of a woman who refuses to get shaven when she becomes a widow. Such a beautiful film, that is. No man, I think, would make that film. Or a film like *36 Chowringhee Lane* by Aparna Sen. Such a lyrical film. I don't think a man would make a film like that. Or even my own film *Sparsh*. I think it had a lot of feminine aspects to it. However, having said that, *Chashme Buddoor*, I think, is a film that even a man could have made. So, it's a difficult thing to answer positively. Also, I can't recount a single film by a woman film-maker that is about random violence or terror and stuff like that. But many men have made that kind of film. I think women are more concerned with social aspects, family bonds, and things like that instead of violence.

After your first film *Sparsh*, you made what's perhaps your most popular film, the light-hearted comedy – *Chashme Buddoor*. Did you always want to be a multi-genre film-maker or it just happened that way?

I don't think I sat down and calculated it like that. People ask me how I choose my subjects. I say I don't. My subjects choose me. Something just hits me suddenly and I start writing it. Like *Chakachak*, my children's film, for example. It's a very fun film about cleanliness. One day, I came back home from somewhere and I was cribbing how people spit on the road and how there is so much dirt on the streets. My daughter said, 'Stop this cribbing, ma. Because when you do, you make life difficult for everyone around you.' She asked me why I didn't do something about the problem. At first, I thought, what can I do to stop people from spitting on the road but then she told me I was a film-maker and there must be something I could do. And I thought, well, I could actually do something. I immediately wrote *Chakachak* and I think it was great fun.

Sparsh also came from an experience I had while visiting a school for the blind. *Chashme Buddoor* was a film that did not come from a particular incident in my life. At that time, I used to think, 'What's with the youth today? They are just smoking their days away, doing nothing, chasing girls and stuff like that.' And then this thing sort of shaped up. Initially, in the teleplay version of the film that I had made earlier, all three characters smoked and all were no-gooders. I must give credit to my producer Gul Anand who told me I can't have all the characters cut out of the same cloth. At least one has to be hero-material. I thought, well, I am a writer. I could switch it around. That's how Farooq Shaikh's very adorable character shaped up and it worked beautifully for the film. Farooq did justice to it.

When I did, *Katha,* I sent the script to Farooq and Naseer. Both thought they were going to play the other guy. When I told Farooq the character I wanted him to play, he said, 'Sai, I just did *Chashme Buddoor*. People think of me as a nice, lovable guy.' I said, '*Farooq, zindagi bhar wahi karoge kya?*' (Farooq, will you do the same thing all your life?) And then Naseer told me, 'You've forgotten what a smart chap I am. Nobody will accept me as an idiot.' I said, 'Then what the hell are you an actor for? Don't you want a challenge? Are you a poster boy or what?' I gave them a long spiel. Later, both of them told me they were very glad they did the roles they did because they were so challenging and fun to do. Naseer is so sweet in that film!

What's the governing force behind the kind of stories you have chosen to tell?

I do my work to make people happy. I feel that we, in India, have such a tough life to bear. So, call it escapism, call it what you like, but if I can make people feel good, albeit for a little while, I will have achieved what I want to. This feeling has always been at the back of my mind. And I am a positive person. I always see the glass half full. I try to see the sunny side of things. For example, in *Disha*, Raghubir Yadav believes that once a man comes to Bombay, he will never go back but in the end, his brother, Om Puri, finds water in the village and he does go back to the village. In the same film, Nana Patekar has a shattering experience because his wife falls prey to a powerful man in the village but he decides to stay on.

What was special about the 1980s that a whole bunch of independent film-makers, such as yourself, started working at the same time?

Well, that's an interesting question because it's difficult to pinpoint why all of us happened at the same time. Yes, some of us would meet occasionally. We also had one attempt at having an organizing committee of the so-called good film-makers. We met at Ken Rathod's place, who made just one or two films, but he was a part of it. Then there was Mani Kaul, there was Saeed Akhtar Mirza, there was Kumar Shahani, then Virendra Saini, who was my cameraman, and then Basu Chatterjee came. There were about ten to twelve of us. But nothing happened to it eventually. We just had one solitary meeting and that's it. There was no regular give and take among us. We did bond though.

To answer your question about why it happened only in the 1980s is that at that time, gradually, all of us individually had realized that something had to be done, something needed to be changed. Also, when you see someone do some good work, you get charged and even you want to create something. There was mutual admiration among us and we enjoyed each other's work. So that could be one of the things. But having said that, a lot of it was coincidence as well.

How do you define success as a writer and a film-maker?

Why must one define anything? Success sweeps over you. It's a nice feeling. You feel the warmth of it. If someone you don't know walks up to you on the street and tells you that they and their family enjoyed one of your films, it feels so good. It's a feeling that lasts the whole day. You think all this trouble was worth it. That to me is success. I would assume that for every creative person, to be appreciated is an award in itself. And when I say appreciated, I don't just mean people telling you, 'Wow, very good, very good.' It also includes someone telling you, 'Hey, what a trashy film, you've made!'

I have been told that too. Not so much about my films. But I have been soundly criticized for one or two of my plays. But even in that, you feel good that the other person cares about your work. The person is so dismally disappointed because he expects something from you. That feels good. I remember, one of my plays called *Mogara Phoolala*, which I feel is very good, but at that time it was criticized because it had a little bit of sexual play in it. At one of the play's shows, in Pune, a guy walked up to me and told me that he had come down from Montreal the day before and came to watch my play and he was thoroughly disappointed with the play. He said, 'How could you write a play like that? This is just not done.' The reason for his disappointment was that he was expecting me to write goody-goody stuff. And a woman writing about a subject like that, especially at that time, was not easy to digest.

How do you define failure as a writer and a film-maker?

Would it be unacceptable if I said, I haven't tasted too much failure, except for some of the stuff I told you about? I accept failure if I know the reason why a play, a film, or a telefilm failed. If I don't find out the reason or if I am not convinced about it, it becomes a bitter pill to swallow.

As a writer, how does your work in theatre talk to your work in cinema?

See, all this works at a subconscious level. For instance, when I am writing a play, I know that I can't have a thousand-horse army marching in on stage. So, you know what you're doing. But all said and done, the relationships or the material that you're working with remain the same. And that material is human beings. I am writing about mother-daughter relationships or father-son relationships. I am constantly interested in human beings and I love watching and understanding them. That's why till very recently, I used to take the bus now and then. You see so much of human life there. People who you normally would not meet. So many fascinating incidents to look at, to observe.

Do you think we have progressed or regressed in terms of quality in Hindi cinema?

Technically, the quality has improved. In terms of stories, well, very frankly, I don't see a lot of Hindi cinemas. Because when I do, I am usually disappointed. So, I try to save myself from disappointment and not watch much of it. But then I also wonder if my disappointment is coming from the fact that I am not making films anymore. Is it a sour grapes situation? I don't know. Of course, some of the new films are pretty good. I'd start with *Lagaan*. I thought it was a splendid film. Then I liked *Chak De India*. Then there was a film that Naseer did, *A Wednesday*, I thought that was a very powerful film. I like that. I saw another film recently that really moved me. It was called *Jalsa*. Wonderful story. When I watch something like that, I think well, cinema is still alive.

Who have been your influences in cinema?

My favourite film-maker of all time is Federico Fellini. I love his sense of the comic and caricatures. Somewhere, I have always felt beholden to him. I am fascinated, really, by him. In Indian cinema, Satyajit Ray, to name the obvious. In Ray's films, I particularly like the comic part. No one talks of Satyajit Ray's comic sense. But what a fabulous comic sense he has! I remember some parts of *Shatranj Ke Khiladi* and they still make me laugh. You watch his characterization and you think, what a man is this! He was a major, major influence. Another film-maker I love very much is Tarun Majumdar. In one of his films is a delightful incident that is still very dear to me.

What do you think is your greatest creative accomplishment?

Disha. In my opinion, it is an all-round success. From script to acting, to editing, to the ambience it creates, to the effect it has, everything about *Disha* is of a certain quality. My most popular film, however, without a doubt, is *Chashme Buddoor*. It was a runaway success. Also, *Chakachak* reached a lot of people. Especially schoolchildren. It's quite popular among them. Then I think my last feature film, *Saaz*, which I made in 1997, is something I am happy with as well.

Is there something you wanted to make but couldn't for some reason?

Yes, I have got two or three unmade scripts. One of them, to be frank, I think, if it was made it would have been a milestone in Indian entertainment cinema. It's called *Xapai*. Xapai means grandfather in Portuguese. The film is set in Goa. An old man is about to celebrate his ninetieth birthday and all his younger family members are coming back to attend it from different parts of the world. And they also have a vested interest in the property. It's a black comedy, filled with humour. I wrote it ten years ago. But unfortunately, could never get finance for this.

When I was a nobody, when I made *Sparsh* and *Katha*, it was okay to knock on doors for money to make films. Today, I am not going to do that. I still think, if I can make *Xapai*, it would be wonderful. There is another story about an eminent man called Mashelkar, who won India its patent for turmeric. Mashelkar read the script and said, 'Sai, this would be your gift to the nation.' He, too, tried but we just haven't been able to make that film. Most studio people are so narrow-minded that you tell them about Ayurveda and turmeric and all of that, they flatly refuse. They are only interested in clubs and rape scenes and all that. They are just not ready to listen to stories like this.

A hundred years from now, if there's one thing you're remembered as what would you like it to be?

A happy film-maker.

TWENTY-THREE

Sanjay Chhel

Sanjay Chhel is the writer of some of the 1990s films such as *Yes Boss*, *Daud*, and *Rangeela* among others. I met him at his house one evening where we ventured into his thirty-odd years in the film industry over a cup of piping hot tea.

The brand of humour he was so famous for in the 1990s was apparent in the way he spoke and he came across as someone who believed in his ideas and backed himself to tell his truth in the most honest way possible.

What was your childhood like?

My father was into theatre. He did a lot of plays. Gujarati plays, Marathi plays. And also worked on some films – Hindi, Marathi, a few Odia, and Haryanvi films as well. So, there was always an atmosphere at home which favoured the arts. There were often scripts lying around at home which I would pick up and read. Besides, my mother was a professor of Gujarati and Sanskrit. So, I think my sense of language as well as my fondness for it came from there. Also, I think I was lucky that I studied in a very good school, Lions Juhu High School in Vile Parle. The school encouraged a lot of extracurricular activities and a lot of famous people have studied in that school including Paresh Rawal. The drama competition back in school was a big thing. Around twenty classes, including sections, used to compete with each other. So, we used to write our own plays and perform, and the teachers used to help and guide us too. I was good at writing essays too and I became famous in my school as a writer. So, at that time, I developed the illusion that I was the next Tagore!

Then I studied engineering at Bhagubhai Polytechnique because my mother wanted me to have a secure job as she had seen the uncertainty of this business through my father's career. But by the time I was in college, I had started writing all sorts of plays, many one-act plays. I had also begun to get some of my short stories published in some Gujarati as well as Hindi literary magazines like *Hans*.

How did the film industry happen?

After finishing college I started assisting Ramesh Talwar on some of his projects. Then I was working with Ashutosh Gowariker, who at the time was struggling as an actor but deep down always wanted to become a director. Eventually, I also happened to write his first film. Luckily, when I got out of college, the Indian economy had started opening up in the early 1990s. Star TV and Zee TV had come in with big plans and they all needed writers. So I started assisting Aziz Mirza, Saeed Mirza, Kundan Shah. Aziz had formed a new team for his show *Naya Nukkad Part 2* and I got to be on it as a writer. I wrote several episodes of that show. From there, I got an opportunity to write the TV show *Filmi Chakkar*. It featured Satish Shah and became a huge hit. It was a mad comedy.

At the time, the world was not scrutinized so minutely by social media as it is today. So, we could do a satire on anything on earth from the government to Amitabh Bachchan and it was all taken exactly as it was written – in good spirit. At the time, I also wanted to be a lyricist. I met everybody from Pancham-da (R.D. Burman) to Anu Malik but unfortunately did not find work as a lyricist. After I wrote *Rangeela* for Ramu and then *Yes Boss* with Aziz Mirza, I kept getting screenplay and writing work regularly. *Rangeela*, as you know, was a big hit. As was *Yes Boss*. In fact, I wrote *Yes Boss* before *Rangeela* but the latter was released before the former!

All through this, I shared a constant relationship with TV. Whenever I needed money, I'd write for TV. TV paid handsomely and much more frequently. In those days, cinema used to be a five-year scheme. These days it's a two-year scheme. Films took forever to get made, some never got made. Sometimes, I already knew that a film I was writing would never get released. But I still went ahead and wrote those purely because it was fun writing them.

Tell me about the process of writing one of the most defining films of the 1990s, *Rangeela*. How did you get to work on it?

As I said, I was also trying to become a lyricist in those days. So, one day, I took some songs I had written and met Ramu (Ram Gopal Varma). His Hindi wasn't very good at the time and he didn't like my songs. He had given me a tune from the south to write to. After he rejected my work, I told him casually, '*Lagta hai aapko Hindi poetry ki itni samajh nahi hai.*' (Seems like you don't quite have an understanding of Hindi poetry.) A few days later, he called me. He said, 'You talk interesting stuff. Come and meet me again.' That's when he offered me to write dialogues for *Rangeela*. I was fortunate that my friend Neeraj (Vora) was my co-writer. Ramu's brief to us was the one-line idea he had. He was very clear in his mind about what he wanted.

We had a fabulous time working on the film and it was made in about six to seven months from the time we started writing the script. At the time, Ramu used to come down from Hyderabad to work on the film. He had a flat in Mumbai but he still was living in Hyderabad. Another great part of *Rangeela* was Aamir (Khan). Aamir gave dignity to the character of Munna. Till then, nobody had seen Aamir in a role like that but the way he played it was amazing. I think instead of him, if any other actor had done it, he may have still managed to play a *tapori* well but I can't imagine anybody else making the character as lovable as Aamir did. Aamir spoke the *bambaiyya* dialect of Munna beautifully. Ramu, of course, was a great technician and at the time, he was at his peak. He gave me a lot of freedom. While growing up, I had seen a lot of rangeela people on the streets of Bombay and I am very glad I could write some of my life experience into the character and the film.

I remember there was a debate about the climax that we had written. Ramu and I favoured the climax that you see in the film. Aamir and Neeraj favoured another climax. But we ended up convincing them, the film happened and it worked. A.R. Rahman's music was a character in the film. It was his first Hindi feature and I had seen the film without the background music before. Once his background score was added, the film went to another level. It looked much faster and much more engaging. I still think *Rangeela* is one of Rahman's best works.

Tell me about *Yes Boss* and working with Aziz Mirza and Shah Rukh Khan.

Yes Boss is one of those films I enjoyed working on the most. Aziz Mirza had told me an idea for a character he had in mind. We then developed it from there. *Yes Boss* took about two years to finish. Shah Rukh's stardom had already begun by then but it was still before *Dilwale Dulhania Le Jayenge*. In fact, *DDLJ* came out while we were in the process of making *Yes Boss*. That took Shah Rukh to an unattainable level of success. I have great respect for Aziz Mirza. I have worked with him a lot even after *Yes Boss*. He had an eye for raw talent. He was the one who spotted Shah Rukh Khan as well at the time of *Circus*. I met Shah Rukh during *Circus*. I used to go to the sets because of some of my friends. So, Shah Rukh already knew me when we started working on *Yes Boss*. He was one of the most compassionate and cooperative people to work with. I got to learn a lot from him – his command over the language, his reading, and his life experience were sensational. Whatever we wrote, he performed those lines brilliantly. It added another dimension to the writing. *Yes*

Boss is so dear to me because if you hear the dialogues even today, there is a sense of softness about them. Also, a sense of subtlety, depth, and humour.

Sanjay Dutt was Uma Parvati and Urmila Matondkar was Daya Shankar in *Daud*. Tell me how you guys managed to make a mad film like that in 1997. Also, the iconic '*Mere Pitaji Bahut Bade Shikari The*' scene.

Daud was all-out madness, yes. It was a crazy trip we were on when we wrote that film. It so happened that Ramu was very happy with my work in *Rangeela*, and *Daud* was to be his next film. He asked me to write it and asked me to go madder this time. The Uma Parvati and Daya Shankar bit was my idea. I knew Ramu would allow it because he loved madness too. We could go ahead and make a film like that because those were days when there wasn't as much scrutiny of films as there is today. People knew how to have fun with films. I think too much scrutiny or analysis of any film would make it worse. It's like a bottle of perfume. If you open it too often, it will lose its fragrance. So, in the days of *Daud*, we just did what we felt like. Ramu and I were free and riding high on the success of *Rangeela*. So even the producers gave us a lot of freedom to do what we wanted.

Sanjay Dutt had just come back from jail and was raring to get back to films. Urmila, after *Rangeela*, was a big star and oozing confidence. All the energy was right for us, as a group, to go unabashed. *Daud* did well at the box office but did not do as well as we expected it to. I think it was a film ahead of its time. A funny incident about *Daud* is that in those days there were not as many TV channels. Our promos were running on Zee TV and Aaj Tak. In the promo, there was a high-pitched sound in the background that went something like 'Daaaaaauuuuud'. Now, to some people, it sounded like Dawood, and a rumour was spread that this film is about Dawood (Ibrahim), and for a little while there was some scare amongst us if we would get threats.

About the '*Mere Pitaji Bahut Bade Shikari The*' scene, some people love it and some people hate it. There is no in-between. Neeraj (Vora) was our co-writer on *Rangeela*, and Ramu said let's call him to play Chacko in *Daud*. Chacko was a character we wrote on the spot as was the case with that scene. I still think it should have been shot with multiple cameras instead of a single take. I think the appeal of that scene would have been even greater. The best part about *Daud* is that Ramu had given me a vague idea as a brief that a couple is on the run. The rest of it was developed by us through writing and discussions. The screenplay was more or less ready but the film evolved while we wrote the dialogue. There are so many scenes, like the Chacko one, that we wrote after the shooting had already begun. We used to shoot some things and then write some more and then shoot more. In a journey like that, there is a sense of discovery. You don't know where you are going, you may go wrong but then you might even reach a place you never imagined. *Daud* was an unplanned journey. I am not saying I am against the discipline that hard-bound scripts bring. They have their own place as well. But not all hard-bound scripts ensure a good film either, right? If you have an insurance policy, it doesn't mean you will never die.

How do you look at lyric writing differently?

Honestly, I don't. I have written around thirty songs so far. I think the dialogues I write very often become the take-off point for the lyrics. Initially, I didn't get much songwriting work but when I made my own film, *Khubsoorat*, who would have stopped me? So I wrote songs for that film. Then I even wrote '*Nikamma Kiya Iss Dil Ne*', which became a super hit. Then Himesh became a friend and I wrote many songs for him. '*Mohabbat Hai Mirchi*' was a big hit amongst them. I also wrote the title track for David Dhawan and Salman Khan's *Partner*.

Out of screenplay, dialogues and songs, what do you think is the most challenging to write?

I think dialogue writing is the toughest skill in Hindi cinema. Because dialogue very often fills the holes in the script. Also, dialogues get noticed a lot more because they are spoken. A bad line of dialogue will prick everyone in the ear and a good one will make people celebrate you. Screenplay, on the other hand, is a tedious job. It's also the one that takes the longest time of the three.

I have learnt many lessons in writing both these by working with David and Ramu. Also learnt a lot from Aziz Mirza. When I wrote for David, the pace of the film was different compared to when I wrote for Ramu. David is an excellent editor as well. He edits brilliantly on the paper itself. He knows when to end a scene and has a knack for comedy.

If you ask me, lyric writing is a lot of fun because compared to scripts, it takes much less time and you get paid much quicker as well. Music meetings are a lot of fun too. You get many ideas from those. I am lucky that I worked with a lot of music directors like Jatin-Lalit, Anu (Malik), and Himesh (Reshammiya).

How was a writer's life different in the 1990s? Tell me a little bit about that time.

You are making me feel old now. Well, makers are more disciplined today than before. So, there is a sense of structure and I'd say less chaos. But with that, I feel what today's film-writing lacks the most is spontaneity. Too many people have a say and even after the film is out, everyone on social media is a critic. This overtly critical world is not necessarily good for writing and writers because you never know what could be taken wrongly and held against you. Today, there are very few people writing films but too many people writing about films.

I also think that when we used to work in the 1990s, we used to work with big people. And I mean big in stature, work experience as well as age. So, there was always a lot to learn from. Today, with corporates in the film industry, several people from their teams have a say as well. And not all of them may have the experience of film-writing or film-making. Some of them are marketing people who are today working for a film production studio and might tomorrow move to a cold drink company. Do you think they would be as passionate and knowledgeable about films? They have brought in so many rulebooks and structures today that film-making has become like defusing a bomb: Should we cut the red wire or the green one?

Do you feel out of place in the era of OTT?

No, I don't feel out of place career-wise. I do get offers and I have been working at my own pace. I am working on an OTT show which I can't tell you more about at the moment. But I don't feel out of place even in the sense of the content that is made. Because I have always been in touch with world cinema since the 1990s. It has become popular only now. Having said that, I don't think Indian web series have really impressed me so far. There were a few like the Season 1 of *Panchayat* which are good but overall, if you ask me, I think most Indian shows are the same story.

Plus, everyone is writing only crime and mindless crime. Now, what used to be Bombay-based crime stories in our times are happening in some villages in UP. But the stories are the same. I am all for creative liberty but I think some shows are so random that a person travels to Baluchistan or Karachi as if he's going from Borivali to Kandivali. Another thing I notice is that a lot of actors are trying to do what they call natural acting but let me tell you there is no greater cinematic torture than to watch a bad actor attempting serious acting.

What is your creative purpose? Apart from livelihood, what do you write for?

I have always thought that I wanted to make feel-good films. Of course, over the years, your thinking changes. A man often thinks of different ways of committing suicide throughout his lifetime. So, I have thought of different ideas too. Some worked, some didn't. But I think the process of film-making itself is something I enjoy the most. To continue doing that is my ultimate creative purpose. I may be a writer, a director and a lot else but before all that, I am a cinema lover.

Who are you early influences?

Billy Wilder, Francis Ford Coppola, Woody Allen in Hollywood. In India, I love Hrishi-da (Hrishikesh Mukherjee). I think he has a fascinating range. I love Gulzar Sahib too. People know him for his songs or as a director but I think Gulzar is the best dialogue writer ever in the Hindi film industry. I think Gulzar Sahib brought in a new language of dialogue in films. There are many scenes where he subtly writes poetic dialogue. There is a dreaminess about his dialogue writing that, to me, remains unmatched. *Aandhi* and *Mausam* are all examples of this. Even *Namak Haraam*, which was a commercial film, is elevated a lot by his writing. And one can't forget *Maachis* either!

Then of course, right from my college days, I have been an admirer of Kundan Shah. His *Jaane Bhi Do Yaaro* is a kind of comedy that the country wasn't ready for at that time but is now a cult. Even *Kabhi Haan Kabhi Naa* is charming. I am fortunate that I got to work with Kundan Shah myself.

When you look back on the last thirty years of your career, what do you see as your best work?

I like *Yes Boss* a lot. Then *Daud* and *Phir Bhi Dil Hai Hindustani*. I like the dialogues I wrote in *Partner* a lot as well. Then a children's film I had written for Santosh Sivan called *Halo* is a piece I am proud of. I think I have never not enjoyed writing any film that I have written. In thirty years, there are some lessons too. Like, for instance, the last film I wrote and directed, *Patel Ki Punjabi Shaadi* which starred Paresh Rawal and Rishi Kapoor, took seven years to get released. And by the time it got out, I thought it had become a little dated. Sometimes I think I shouldn't have written and directed it. But some things are in your control and some others are not. But honestly, there is nothing that I look back on that makes me feel embarrassed.

What's the advice you would offer to young writers who want to break into films?

I think the process of writing is a discussion that would take many days. But as a piece of practical advice, I'd say, listen to your heart but don't be too choosy either. Instead of thinking too much about what to do, just do. At the end of the day, the film industry is a bit of a gamble. No one can ever tell you with certainty that a particular film would work or not. So keep doing projects. Another thing is that don't be stuck to just one group of people. Only if you are working with different people and companies, can you survive for twenty-thirty years. Also, try and be on the sets. If there are changes on the spot, do them yourself. A writer should think of his scene like his own child. And without becoming too nosy, try to be involved in the editing process as well. A writer needs to understand every aspect of film-making to hone his skill. And the obvious last thing is to read as much as one could. Read about current affairs, and books, and watch the latest plays too.

If your life were a film, which one would it be?

I think one of the Woody Allen films in which the protagonist is a bit mad.

TWENTY-FOUR

Satyanshu Singh

Ihave known of Satyanshu through his younger brother Devanshu, whom I have known for a while through advertising and common friends. This was my first meeting with Satyanshu. We met at WTF in Versova which is one of Bollywood's favourite hangouts. Satyanshu is dedicated and amazingly methodical about his craft. He knows every word of what he is talking about and has a measured approach to films.

He co-wrote the film *Chintu Ka Birthday* with his brother Devanshu and wrote the famous poem from *Udaan*, 'Pata Nahi *Joote Kahan Utare The*'. As a parallel career, he also teaches screenplay writing.

How much of your early life in Bihar comes into your work?

The first feature film that I wrote and directed, *Chintu Ka Birthday*, is set in Iraq with Bihari characters. A lot of quirks, dialect-related nuances, mannerisms, the family equation, and the warmth and idiosyncrasies that I observed while growing up in the small town of Munger in Bihar comes into the film. A lot of Biharis loved the portrayal of Biharis in the film. This is obviously great because, over the years, there has been a great deal of stereotypes associated with Bihar and Biharis. The film, in a way, challenges that. After this film, many of my projects have a connection with Bihar. Initially, I thought that maybe I am limiting myself, but then, because of my lived experience of Bihar, the richness, and the nuances that I am able to bring, or just the ease with which it allows me to write, I don't mind this anymore.

Tell me about those wonderful poems from *Udaan*. Did you write them for the character?

I have written three poems for *Udaan*, and each has its own story. '*Joote Kahan Utare The*' is the most favourite of all the poems I have written in life. I wrote this in flat three to four minutes when I was graduating from AFMC (Armed Forces Medical College), Pune. I was making a feature film for my batchmates and planned a poem for the climax. This is the one I wrote. When I shared this poem with Vikramaditya Motwane, he loved it. So that poem was not written for the film but I am so glad that that poem was my first work for the screen.

The second poem is the one Rohan recites to his father on his uncle's insistence. The script had some themes mentioned here. But I decided to write something different. I was new in Mumbai. I was supposed to meet Vikram in Anurag Kashyap's office in Aaram Nagar one evening. I reached a little early and while waiting I discovered the Rocky Beach of Versova, right next to the road. It was a wonderful feeling to discover this beach hidden behind the buildings. It was quite dark. So, I just sat on the rocks. There were people singing and playing a guitar and they were drinking and it was a nice atmosphere out there. But I could not see beyond the waves crashing at the shore. The sea was dark and it merged in the darkness of the night sky. So that is when the first lines of this poem came to me, '*Jo leheron se aage nazar dekh paati, toh tum jaan lete main kya sochta hoon.*' (If the eyes could go beyond the waves, you would understand what I mean.) I wrote this poem with my father in mind, because I was going through my own struggles. I had given up my job as a doctor in the army to make films. This wasn't received well by my family. That poem is a reaction to my people, my family members and my parents back home. It was perfect, because it's also Rohan's reaction to his father.

The third poem is 'Chandu ki Cycle'. It was already mentioned in the script that Rohan recites a poem for his brother Arjun, about a young boy and a cycle. I gave a name to the boy and created a story around him.

What was the journey of your short film *Tamaash* and did you expect acclaim from it?

Tamaash is a very, very special film for Devanshu (Singh) and me because of many reasons. The film single-handedly changed our lives. Of course, while we were making the film, the idea was to only make a decent short film, to practise the craft, and to showcase our work as directors. I think it was on the last day of the shoot when our DOP (Director of Photography) Sahir Raza casually asked if we would send the film to festivals. Until then, this was not something I had thought.

The second incident that I remember is that after the shoot was done, I came back to my hotel room in Srinagar and I was taking a shower, and at that moment, I felt for the first time that I was a director. It was a new feeling. I had never seen myself that way until that day. So, you see, we were not expecting much from *Tamaash*. But, of course, we had worked very hard on it. And a lot of people from Mumbai and Kashmir had helped us. We owe our success to all these people. Eventually, the film brought us a lot of awards and cash prizes. Most importantly, it won us a National Award. Our parents came to Delhi to attend the ceremony. My father was finally very proud of us and we resumed talking because of this film. I went back to my hometown after seven years. It was like the first chapter of our life in Bombay ended well with this film. So, of course, it's very special to us.

***Chintu Ka Birthday* took twelve years to be made if I am not wrong. Did you start seeing the original script differently over the years and make changes during the process?**

So, the first draft of *Chintu Ka Birthday* was written when I was twenty-three, in medical college, and my brother was twenty-two. And, although it was received very well by whoever read the script, I remember that after a couple of years, and after two or three drafts, we started feeling that the script was not very good. Then, almost four years after it was written, the script was revived again. And it was finally five years after writing the first draft that the script reached a stage where we were very happy with it.

But then, of course, the film wasn't made for another five years. So, we kept improving it. And the final draft that was shot was, hence, written over ten years. I must underline the fact that although the script was ready to be made in five years, the further work that we put in over the next five years elevated the script. And in fact, the shooting script that we made over the last three months before the shoot had some of the most beautiful moments in the film. However, there are many things in the final film that were present in the very first draft of *Chintu Ka Birthday*, including the song situation where Chintu's mom sings followed by the blast, the opening shot of the cake, the Garden of Eden animation that starts the film, and the final scene when Nani talks about Raktbeej. Many of the key moments never changed. The number of characters did not change. That's because the setting is so limited – it's just one house and just a few hours over one day. So, one has already cut down several possibilities. The script kept evolving, but many, many things were present since the first draft.

Did it become easier to do the kind of work you want to do after *Chintu Ka Birthday*?

Actually, the kind of work that we want to do is a question we are still trying to answer because Devanshu and I don't see ourselves doing just one kind of film. If you ask me, what my kind of film is, I am not very sure. But yeah, *Chintu Ka Birthday* is a good representation of the kind of work we want to do. And the film, of course, has given us credibility and the industry takes us seriously. But as of now, we are just grappling with different story ideas, and we are doing different kinds of projects. And we are still trying to figure out things.

How easy or difficult is it for a young writer to find work in Hindi cinema according to you? Any advice you would like to give them?

I have a very clear answer to this question. If you want to be a classical musician, you will not expect to work for money until you have put in ten to fifteen years of solid practice. That's the bare minimum. If you want to be a doctor who is hired by good hospitals or who has a reputation, you would put in ten to fifteen years of education and practice. If you want to be a sportsperson who makes a living through sports, you would spend many, many years trying to become a skilful sportsperson. And there are many careers like these. If you want to be a credible lawyer, you want to be a credible politician, you want to be a painter, you want to be a dancer, an architect, a scientist – you spend a minimum of one-and-a-half decades training yourself.

So, the advice that I have for young writers is that you prepare yourself to go through this fifteen-year-long training. If you are expecting anything to work out sooner than that, sure, you may, but don't feel entitled to a response from the industry. If you work hard for fifteen years, you will definitely be noticed by the industry. I think the biggest mantra for success here is longevity. If you stay in the race, you will win. Most people quit. And if you quit, obviously, you will lose. So if you stay in the race, you keep writing for fifteen years. And you will be noticed by the industry. I also feel that you should write your first feature film as soon as possible. Don't wait for any education. Don't wait for anything. Just write your first feature film.

Meanwhile, also keep educating yourself through screenwriting courses, school or workshops, YouTube videos, or books, but don't wait to write your first feature. Then write your second feature. And then the third. And keep writing for fifteen years. I also think that you should not quit your job. You should always have a way to sustain yourself. If you're a lawyer, if you have a corporate job, don't quit it. Make time to write irrespective of your job. And try to write films across different genres. Because when you make someone read your script while judging the script, they are mostly judging you too. They may not be interested in producing that script. But they will be interested in hiring you as a writer. So initially, the first few scripts that you write, try to write across different genres.

I started with examples of sportspersons and artists and musicians and doctors, because I really, really disapprove of the entitlement that a lot of writers have. Having written a few short films, or having written a few sketches, or a few short stories or magazine articles, they expect to get work in the industry. That's a very, very wrong approach to have. Write long-form. Write features. Write web series and pilot episodes. And just keep doing this one after another. Keep improving your work for many, many years. This is the only way to reach anywhere.

Do you think screenwriting can be taught? What has your experience of teaching been like and why did you decide to do it?

I most definitely think that screenwriting can be taught. Now whether you take a course or read the books and material available and teach it to yourself is a choice. But 100 per cent, screenwriting must be learnt. Unlike poetry or, say, music, screenwriting is not an instinctive art. It involves a lot of method and craft and there is so much to learn about how it interacts with various other aspects of a film.

I started teaching screenwriting because when I started learning screenwriting on my own, I was amazed by the craft, the science behind it, and the different tools and techniques that people have already discovered. I just wanted to share it with people. It also helped me master the concepts. I realized that I was good at it. In any case, as you wait for your films to be made, you do things to sustain yourself. You either become an ad film-maker or you write for others. I realized that this is something that I like to do and it has proved to be very profitable to me. I am very thankful to the hundreds and thousands of students who have paid money to attend my lectures. And it has become a wonderful parallel earning option for me. Of course, as I kept teaching, teaching itself as a craft has revealed a lot of nuances and joys to me. Teaching has also helped me connect with hundreds of people from across the world. So, I would like to keep doing this all my life.

How useful do you think are script labs for writers? Tell me about your journey of heading the AIB lab.

The biggest advantage of being noticed at a script lab is just that – of being noticed, of getting a stamp of approval that out of hundreds of entries, you made it to the top few. Script labs also bring you face-to-face with mentors, which is great because, as I maintain, when people read a script, they are also interested in the writer, irrespective of the script. At First Draft, we create different kinds of courses. We did six-month residency courses for screenwriters, we keep doing one-day workshops, and presently, I'm doing a two-year fellowship for directors. So, that is very different from a script lab.

A script lab generally has limited commitment, but what we do at First Draft, apart from workshops, is long-term courses using which we train screenwriters and directors. Of course, the experience has been wonderful. First Draft has always been received very well and enthusiastically by aspiring screenwriters and directors and I have met some wonderful talent and made some amazing friends in the process. I intend to keep bringing different versions of First Draft so that more and more aspiring writers and directors can get opportunities to learn and to enter the film industry and then reach out to the right kind of people who can enable them to tell their stories.

Was cinema always your first choice of medium as a writer? Did you start writing films because you wanted to direct films?

I think I developed a love for cinema very early in my life. By the time I was fourteen, I was already interested in how the medium is used to tell stories. So, cinema as a storytelling medium has fascinated me all my life. Of course, the craft of screenwriting is something that I discovered late. I wanted to make films, but I couldn't afford a camera or a laptop. So, I started writing because writing doesn't require anything except paper and pen. I eventually realized that screenwriting for me is a ritual, which I need to do. I have been doing it for about fifteen-sixteen years. I think, another ten years and I'll be good at it.

What are your favourite films and who are your favourite film-makers across the world?

Of course, my love for *Lagaan* is now quite well-known. So, it looks like *Lagaan* is my favourite film of all time. But, you know, this is something I realized very late. I think others made me realize that *Lagaan* is my favourite film. My favourite film-maker of all time is Krzysztof Kieslowski, the great Polish master. I especially idolize him because of how late he bloomed. The last five years of his life were when he did his best work. So, all his life, he kept improving, until he reached that stage. I don't see myself as a film-maker who starts great. I think I will eventually learn and grow and become a competent film-maker. And that's why Krzysztof Kieslowski is my favourite.

Among the film-makers who are currently working, Richard Linklater is my absolute favourite, mostly because of his tone, how he deals with relationships, his use of perception of time, and also because of his independent spirit. It's so inspiring to see him repeatedly make films that are small and contained.

How much creative control or say does a screenwriter actually have in a film?

I think creative control is not the right objective when it comes to films, even for a director. It's good to have a certain creative freedom. But to have absolute authorship – cinema is not that medium. You can write a blog or you can tweet or you can write a novel. So, I think creative collaboration is what writers should look for. Writers should look at the value and the opportunities collaboration brings, the wonderful scope of creating something special with the help of other great artists around you. But that doesn't mean you are not responsible for what you write. There is a lot of responsibility that a film writer has to fulfil. Screenwriters who understand this easily and sooner than others tend to thrive well. But those screenwriters who are extremely possessive of their creative control may have a tough time in the industry.

If you had 100 crore rupees, what kind of film would you make?

If I had 100 crores, I would not make one film. I would actually make ten to twelve films using this money, and the budgets of these films would range from twenty-five lakhs to two crores. Because of many reasons, but most importantly, I don't take money for granted. The chances of breaking even are high if you make more films than one. The idea should be to earn that money back so that you can keep making films. Also, personally, I would not direct more than one or two. I would produce all the films, and I would invite wonderful writers and directors to come and share this money. So that different people get the opportunity to tell their stories, that would create a community and that would enable a lot of people to fulfil their dreams. It will also enable a lot of technicians and actors and generate so much employment. Cinema is a very expensive form of human expression and we cannot take money for granted. So perhaps this is not the most artistic or romantic way of answering this question. But when it comes to cinema, you have to have a pragmatic approach.

Apart from earning a livelihood, is there a reason why you write?

I'm very clear about why I write. I write not because I'm great at it. I write because it's a ritual. It's like if I keep writing, after twenty-five years of writing, I will perhaps become a good writer. So, I write because this is the only way for you to learn writing to solve the mysteries of the story and to learn this craft. And since it's a ritual, I don't really write to make money. Making money through writing is a dangerous proposition. It may force you to be insecure, it may force you to unnecessarily compromise on your work. So, I would rather make money through other means and keep writing every day not to make money but as a ritual. I don't think I write to prove a point. I don't think I write to earn fame. I think I write only to master the craft. I'm very sure about that.

Do you think Hindi cinema is an industry averse to critical analysis?

I think whatever I say, however I answer this question, I will create trouble for myself. I think, in general, human beings are averse to criticism. We Indians are very averse to criticism. So yes, Hindi cinema is an industry averse to critical analysis. But the problem is bigger than that. There are very few critics who are equipped to have that kind of knowledge or understanding of the medium, just as there are a lot of people who call themselves screenwriters and directors without having any understanding of that. So, I feel that all of us film-makers, directors, writers, as well as critics have to take this collective responsibility of first trying to learn.

I'm using the pronoun 'we' very consciously and I'm very clear-headed when I say this: I need to work on my craft and all our fellow film-makers need to work on their craft and all our critics need to work on their craft. And once that is there, we will understand the importance of criticism. I don't see that happening anytime soon. But that's what should ideally be the case.

If you had only up to three words to describe yourself, what would they be?

Three words will be tough, and tricky. But a 'film buff' is what I would like to call myself. Everything else is just a projection of that. Nothing is bigger than that. I want to celebrate films. I want to write, direct, watch, and support cinema and film-makers.

TWENTY-FIVE

Saurabh Shukla

Saurabh Shukla is a celebrated actor, a film and theatre director, an avid reader, a table tennis player, and several other things, but my conversation with him tried to explore the screenwriter in him who has written films such as *Dil Pe Mat Le Yaar!!*, *Calcutta Mail*, *Raat Gayi, Baat Gayi?* among others, has co-written *Satya*, which is probably the most iconic Hindi film in at least the last thirty years if not longer.

I met him over a Zoom call on a Sunday morning when we had a leisurely conversation as he recounted his three-decade-long journey in Hindi cinema. Saurabh Shukla was only my second interview in this series, and the first with someone I had never met before. Special thanks to him for agreeing to do this because had he turned me down then, I may not have been able to see this book happen.

How did it all begin for you as a writer?

Let me begin by telling you why I became a writer. I was in Delhi and movies aren't something that the city offers you. So, I joined the theatre. And more than acting, I was interested in directing a play. I found that it was difficult for me to understand others' work. Because stage-writing or screenwriting are specific kinds of writing. They're not as fluid as novels and stories and poetry. I told myself that I must make something that I understand. So, the need for writing came up. I wrote my first play, and my journey as a writer began. Then I started reading more too. Acting happened by the way. People liked my acting and I started liking myself because of that. One day, Shekhar (Kapur) called me for *Bandit Queen* and I moved to Bombay. There began my journey as an actor as well!

Let's talk about the film that changed my perception of cinema as a schoolboy – *Satya*. Could you walk me through the journey of writing it while you also played the iconic Kallu Mama?

By the time I came to Bombay, people started knowing me as an actor but only a few people such as Shekhar Kapur and Sudhir (Mishra) knew that I write as well. Honestly, writing is a rather tedious process for me. And writing for others becomes even more difficult. Because film-writing is not like writing a novel where you are sitting alone, ideating with yourself. Film is a director's medium and although you may have your own ideas, you're working towards the director's vision. At the time, I wasn't keen on becoming a 'writer, writer'.

One day, Ram Gopal Varma called me and asked me to meet him to write his next film. He was a very big and respected director and I was working out ways in my head how to say no to him. But when I met Ram Gopal Varma, he offered me a role in the film and told me the character. I loved the character and I thought it to be a great opportunity for me as an actor. After that, he said, he wanted me to be one of the writers on the film as well. I didn't want to let go of the acting opportunity so I nodded a reluctant yes to co-writing the film as well.

Anurag (Kashyap) was at that point working with Ramu as an assistant. So, they had been working on the script – the idea, the characters, the world, etc. I got involved in the process and Anurag and I became co-writers. *Satya* was a bound script the two of us wrote and then it was rewritten at the time of making it. Because the actors improvised a lot. A lot of things that weren't in the script found their way in because of the actors. I always say there are more than four writers in *Satya*: Anurag and I (who are officially credited), Ram Gopal Varma, of course, who directed the film, and then the actors. It was very early in my career and I learnt a lot of things about screenwriting in that film. It was an enriching experience.

Many films are co-written. How does the process of co-writing happen?

There are two or three ways of going about co-writing and I have done it all. When Rajat (Kapoor), for example, brings me a script, I sit with it and improvise it and then we meet and thrash out what's working and what's not. That's one way where the writers are working in isolation initially and then they exchange ideas and arrive at the final script. The other way, which is more fun, is when the writers meet every day and ideate together. It's like a party because you become friends with your co-writers and you're meeting over coffee, chatting about whatever is happening in the world, and also working on the script. I personally like this process very much.

In fact, *Satya* was written this way. Anurag and I would meet and chat. Then Ramu sent us to his beautiful farmhouse in Hyderabad, which was all paid for. We got to fly there, there were caretakers and a lot of food too. In the evenings, we would open a bottle and have a party. It was a great experience early in my career.

You started writing at NSD (National School of Drama) and even before that. How did that start?

There are two writers who influenced me a lot when I started reading plays. One is Arthur Miller whose play, *All My Sons*, blew me away when I first read it. It put me in a conflict about one of the characters – whether he is good or bad, whether he deserves my sympathy or anguish. That play really inspired me. Then another writer, a landmark figure in Hindi playwriting, Mohan Rakesh, influenced me a lot. Mohan Rakesh has written three plays. The first of his plays that I read was *Aadhe Adhure*, which was a contemporary play. The other two plays are historical. One is about Buddha and the other one is about Kalidasa. I am most drawn to stories of my time. So *Aadhe Adhure* fascinated me a lot. It was set in the modern world and it had no ornamental dialogue. It was simple everyday writing as if the play is not written at all but it is happening for real. My quest is to write scripts where people are left confused if this guy is actually writing it or just saying it. I like to keep things simple and natural.

Screenwriting is a sort of mysterious territory for a lot of people, even writers. Do you think so too?

Yes, screenwriting is both mysterious and magical. But so is poetry. For a poet, though, poetry is not mysterious because they practice it. Similarly, screenwriters, those who know the craft, know how to go about it. The mystery unfolds when you spend time on it.

Could you speak a little about the craft of screenwriting and how it is different from other forms of writing?

In a novel, say, one writes, 'I entered the room and it was gloomy,' it's up to the reader to interpret how exactly it was gloomy. Was it a gloomy afternoon, evening or night? And gloomy as in how gloomy? In screenwriting, however, that's not the case because you will have a scene to see, an actor to look at, and a lot changes with that. I think the most interesting part of screenwriting is to be able to hold attention to the script despite there being so many other elements at play. Another thing is, I have often seen many screenwriters get furious when someone changes their lines. I personally believe, in screenwriting, words are not at all important. Yes, they are there and they mean something. But I don't think that words alone carry meaning. I believe, on the contrary, that meaning makes you choose the words. Meaning changes completely with the context of the scene. Say, one says, 'Let's die together.' But in a scene, for all you know, it may even mean a marriage proposal.

I have heard that in the 1990s it was more like the 'Wild West' for writers in cinema. How has a writer's life, especially a writer without connections, changed from then to now in the age of OTT?

There's a saying in French which means, 'The more it changes, the more it remains the same.' For a young writer, who does not have a tangible piece to prove their ability, it is still as difficult to get people to believe them and find work. And that's because film is an expensive activity. The smallest film that you could make today would cost nothing less than a crore and a half. The moment that kind of money comes into play, most people find it difficult to risk it with a total newcomer. And that hasn't changed since the time I came to Bombay.

Now, the writing part of it back then was different in that the makers in the early 1990s and even in the '80s or late '70s wanted to have a mixed bag of emotions in every story. They wanted to make you laugh, cry, everything. So, if one went with, let's say, an intense, dark story, chances were that it would be rejected back then because it had only one colour. When I started in the 1990s, I met a lot of people who said that in the seventh to the tenth minute of a film, you should have the first song. At that point, you couldn't imagine a hit film without many songs. Music was such an integral part of our culture. And films would be two-and-a-half to three hours long those days. So, in a way, you needed songs to hold attention for that long.

I came in at a time when this had just begun to change. We had to fight for our ideas and stories. I remember there was a time when Vijay Krishna Acharya (director of *Dhoom 3*) and I were roommates and Tigmanshu Dhulia and many other writer-directors were frequent visitors. After seeing that nobody was accepting our ideas, we came up with a new strategy. We'd go to producers and say that this script is inspired by a Polish film. At that time, the producers did not watch much international cinema and they would think, okay, something like this is already made so they could try it too. Such was the importance of tried-and-tested work that an original idea had to be sold in the garb of a stolen one! From there, things have definitely changed. Now the same people ask me, 'Saurabh-ji, please give me something original like you generally think of.'

With OTT, the industry is a lot more open to ideas and experimentation in terms of what to say and different ways of saying it. For instance, now you can make a fully dark film and could still run with it.

For all this time, until very recently, when people made formulaic films, they usually said that this is what the Indian audience wants. Do you think it's fair to blame the audience for that long an era of monotony in cinema?

No, not at all. I think the reason for that kind of film was lethargy. Human beings are lethargic by nature and the people who ran the show just wanted to let whatever was happening carry on. They didn't care enough to change or experiment. In fact, if you look at my father's time, we had great stories in cinema. There were films like *Guide*, *Bambai Ka Babu*, *Pyaasa*, *Sujata*, all of Bimal Roy's films, a film called *Sharda*, *Jaagte Raho* and they were all commercially viable films. Imagine, *Bambai Ka Babu* has a man falling in love with his own sister, *Sharda* is the story of a man who goes away for a while and realizes that his father, a widower, has remarried and the person he has married, not aware of his son's relationship, is the son's beloved. Now, we might say that these are brave stories for that time. But the fact is that these are brave stories of our time, not theirs. Till the 1960s and the mid-1970s, these kinds of stories were regularly getting made. They were regularly breaking paths at that time.

Then what happened post the mid-'70s that it all changed?

Well, I have a long theory on that. I am no historian but I have my take. Movies are largely an unorganized sector. Now, sometime in the '70s, the import of gold in India was legalized. This made the underworld go crazy. Smuggling of gold was the underworld's main source of income. The underworld got very rich and accumulated a lot of black money. They needed an avenue to make it white and they found the movies. With this, the underworld started becoming the financier of many movies. It slowly started assuming control over every aspect of the film including the story. Imagine trying to sell a socialist story to an underworld don! The dons wanted stories they could relate to or enjoy. Hence you had mad love stories or films glorifying characters that don't give a damn about the law.

The aesthetics of storytelling in cinema as well as that of the whole of cinema itself started being controlled by people who had a very different aesthetic. They favoured stories that showcased their aspirations and bravado. The audience had no control over the stories. But they wanted to watch films every Sunday with their family. If these were the only options they had, so be it, they'd still watch them. And because of this those kinds of films became hits and super-hits. And people in the industry then started saying that this is exactly what the audience wants. In reality, the Indian audience has been very sharp, understanding, and accepting. All that we need to ensure is not to bore them. If you tell a great story in a boring way, that won't do.

A film-maker whose film is creating great conversation and controversy, recently said, 'I am not just a film-maker. I have an agenda.' Where do you stand on this? Do you have an agenda as well?

In a way, everyone has an agenda. I want to tell my stories and that's my agenda. I want to write what I personally believe in. Now, there's another thing called political agenda. I don't necessarily want to make political comments but what a lot of people speak is not really what they mean. Beware … what every person speaks may not be what they actually mean. I am not saying who and what is right or wrong. I'm just saying the receiver has to be evolved enough.

As a writer, what's your most creatively satisfying experience thus far?

I believe my best piece is yet to be written. The journey is not over. Having said that, I don't think I am a prolific writer. I write because I have to write. It's as simple as that. Writing fills my day. I remember, during my low patch, writing kept me occupied. In those days, I may have been out of work but was never free because I always had something to do, I had to write.

TWENTY-SIX

Shakun Batra

Shakun Batra is considered the blue-eyed boy of Dharma Productions. He has been attempting to challenge the norm at the heart of traditional and mainstream Bollywood by writing and directing films like *Ek Main Aur Ekk Tu*, *Kapoor & Sons*, and, as I write this, the creatively ambitious film *Gehraiyaan*.

I met Shakun on a bright, sunny, and humid afternoon at a vegan café in Pali Naka called Greenr where over our conversation he offered me some vegan chocolates – which I tried for the first time and enjoyed – along with coffee.

Would it be fair to say that you are a photographer-turned-film-maker who started writing because he couldn't find writers?

Yes, I did photography and I was quite into it. I wouldn't say I was earning much money from it but my first love was visual imagery. From there, I became a cameraman – I went to film school to become a cameraman. Then I came back to Bombay and I started assisting directors. That's when I realized that I enjoy watching directors on set. The directors were the ones who were more in control. They were in control of where to put the camera and the performances and pretty much everything on set. That's when I realized that I hadn't given attention to screenwriting in school. I had to start learning again and that's how screenwriting began for me.

Film is something that I have to learn every day. I watch something every day and I watch it from the lens of learning screenwriting. I think in screenwriting, learning is endless – I mean so is any learning – but screenwriting is a particularly vast discipline that involves craft and so many nuances and different permutations and combinations that the learning never ends. After making every film, I feel that I am sure of my direction but less sure of my screenwriting. Writing is never something that you can be sure of. Directing is interpreting something that is on the page whereas writing is not interpretation, it is creation. And I think in the world of film, screenwriting is the real creation.

A film is supposed to be a director's medium. Would you agree that writing is, at best, a supporting act in the world of films?

I think Spielberg said it best, 'If it's not on the page, it won't be on the stage.' I feel that you can never say, 'I am such a great director that I will make a below-average script great.' That's not going to happen. It's a myth that a great director can save a bad script. Nobody can save a bad script – not an actor, not a director, not anyone. I think why it's called a director's medium is that it needs orchestration – you need to control about fifty-sixty different functions while making a film. And writing would not make it to the screen without that person. That's where I think direction started getting more credit on a film. A writer could do a beautiful job sitting in his room but unless somebody says that he is going to walk into this jungle and control these beasts, it won't materialize. I think that's where directors deservedly started getting more credit.

But having said that, none of it could work without solid writing. Now I see that the times are changing and you can see that most creators or showrunners in OTT shows are the writers. Over the years, we have somehow balanced it off in the sense that great writers now can be equally well-known as directors. Maybe it doesn't make sense to compare apples to oranges but we have realized that maybe orange is as rare a commodity as apples are.

After Salim-Javed, there has never been any writer who is well-known outside of the film industry, among the general public. No one says, 'Let's go watch a film because it is written by a particular person.' Why is that?

I think one reason is that all the good writers are now directing. Look at Farhan (Akhtar) or Zoya (Akhtar). Also, another reason may be that we have not had a Salim-Javed in a long time. We lack that kind of a strong writerly voice. Salim-Javed fought for their work and visibility. I don't know if we have a writer like that any longer who can command that place in the industry. With the emergence of OTT, we have realized that a show cannot be sustained on direction, and writing has become more important than ever. You see a Sudip Sharma or Raj and DK – they are commanding the respect they deserve. But I do agree that most writers' fame so to say is limited to the industry and hasn't transcended into the general audience and I hope that changes.

How did studying at film school add to your knowledge of cinema?

I went to film school and made a terrible film and that was the wake-up call for me. I think contrary to a medical or engineering course, film-making is not something that you learn much of at school. Just because you went to film school doesn't mean you can make a film. That's rubbish. Film school may be a great place to find out how it is done but you still need to find your voice to make a film. Recently I met two kids from Indore and they were phenomenal. They learnt most of what they know from YouTube including editing, how to shoot, storytelling, etc. So, I think training, going forward, is going to be more and more an accessible thing and it won't require big names or infrastructure. Now you can literally shoot a film on your phone. I, for one, trained myself as a writer online. I don't think I learnt anything that I know about screenwriting at film school.

How do you choose your themes?

Theme to me is something that I am curious about and how I explore the questions in my mind in a narrative. For instance, in *Gehraiyaan*, I am trying to explore the past and how a past trauma plays into your choices. Infidelity is the plot and the past is the theme. I was coming out of an experience where I was questioning if anything was in my control, if the choices I was making were really mine or just an effect of the experience. So, I wondered how I could explore that in the next story I would write. What I try to give my characters is what I am feeling in my own life. I have learnt that the easiest way of letting something lose control over you is by putting it on film. You explore it in a film and it lets go of you. It's a funny thing, you know. People who are making films just to earn money are letting go of a terrific opportunity because making a film is the most therapeutic profession that exists. Writing for me is a one-time chance to put your crisis into something and let go of it.

Could you walk me through the process of writing *Gehraiyaan*?

I always wanted to explore infidelity because I have seen it in my house and up close and it is something that has had a strong impact on me while growing up. And as I grew older, I started seeing it from different lenses. I started seeing it from the man's point of view, the woman's point of view, the other woman's point of view. I was interested in finding a darker romance and infidelity within a family. And then as I said, I was always interested in the idea of my past defining me. So, while writing it, I said, what if this character was dealing with something in life where her past is defining her choices? She is trying to run away from her past but she finds herself exactly where her past was.

Gehraiyaan could have been a fully off-beat, arthouse film and suddenly you have Deepika Padukone doing this. How do you straddle the line between arthouse and mainstream?

I have always been fascinated by directors who have successfully straddled the line between mainstream and independent cinema. Like Alexander Payne, Wes Anderson, Woody Allen, or Billy Wilder who was a studio director with a very strong individual voice. I liked what they were doing because it didn't feel like assembly-line production. It's not a formula story where this happens and then that happens, they are trying to tell a very personal story but they are doing it with mainstream stars. I always wanted to do a bit of that. Plus, I know that actors are looking for meatier parts. Even they want a character that they could just run with and put themselves out there.

Having said that, sometimes, I wonder how it would be if *Gehraiyaan* was a really small film because the moment stars come in, people view it a certain way. I think people thought it would be a relationship film where all will be happy and nice in the end. I think I should have done better in preparing the audience for the film. I should have tonally prepared the audience better even in terms of the marketing of the film.

The truth is that I always want to be the bridge between mainstream and independent. I don't see myself doing anything that doesn't have my voice but at the same time, I don't see myself sitting with a three-person crew in some small town, wondering how I am going to finish this film and put it out there. I have such huge admiration for people who have made films with such difficulties, people as Achal Mishra or the way Chaitanya Tamhane made his first film *Court*. These guys just went out on a limb to make what they wanted to. They didn't care about who was going to watch this film or who was going to watch this actor, they had a voice and they did it. I think that's the part where I got corrupted. I started as an AD right away. Excel Entertainment to start with, then with Aamir Khan Productions and then with Dharma. I saw the set-up around me and I got very comfortable with the set-up. But I still admire independent voices a lot.

How do you successfully pitch these complex stories to mainstream production houses that usually don't sanction that kind?

Look, I may tell you about past and death and infidelity while I am speaking to you. But when I am pitching, I don't talk about any of this. I pitch mainstream. For instance, in the case of *Kapoor & Sons*, I told Karan (Johar) that I hadn't seen this dysfunctional Indian family on screen for a very long time and I was going to make a film where there's going to be a very funny granddad at the centre of it all – he is going to be a laugh riot and we're going to have this strange, unconventional brother relationship that we haven't seen for a while and I want to do an antithesis to the Barjatyas. I want to show an Indian family opposite of that of a family in a Barjatya film. That is what got Karan excited.

If you can work within a certain budget, you can make these things happen. I am not playing with a budget of 100 crores. I am playing with a budget where they know they can recover this money. And I never scare the producer or the actor off by telling them what's the deep thing that is playing on my mind – it's in my mind and I can figure that out on the edit as well. But the idea is to pitch people something that will excite not just you but also them. And once you win their trust, show them footage that keeps the excitement going. I see a lot of young people coming in and they are not open to conversation. They are more about 'this is who I am and this is how it's going to be', which may fly if you're a visionary and the producer wants to invest in you but for the most part, a producer wants you to listen to them as well. I think it's only fair to think about the producer who is investing in you.

For me, I have my producer's interest in mind but I don't have their voice in mind.. The voice is mine. They need to support my voice. And I think that in some way, I have been fortunate that my producers haven't made me fight for my voice.

Where do we compare in terms of the quality of cinema with Korea, Iran, Hong Kong, Europe, and America? Do you think we are, as an industry, people with rather low creative ambition?

Listen, I hate to say this and by no means am I saying that this applies to everyone in our industry but I think that, for a large part, we have managed to be okay with mediocrity. I think we have celebrated mediocrity for a long time. We have celebrated a mediocre film doing 200 crores. I know there are people now who are trying to push boundaries but largely that is how we have been. I do hope, however, that as younger people come into play, we will have more and more people who are trying to push the envelope.

We don't have an A24 that is supporting independent voices. I don't think we need to be in jail like the Iranian film-makers to make good films. I just think we need more and more of our independent voices to break through in such big ways that it inspires younger people to be like them and not like mediocre film-makers. I think so much of our industry thrives on assembly-line production that the next person thinks, 'Why should I put my head into this and attempt something original when I can just easily follow and do the same thing?' I think that's what needs to change.

I think there are people like Shoojit Sircar and Vishal Bhardwaj or even a Zoya (Akhtar) or Farhan (Akhtar). If more and more great stuff comes from these people who have done very good work, the younger people might be inspired to do work like that. For instance, I wanted to come into the industry after watching *Dil Chahta Hai*. So, we need more and more films like that.

I also have a lot of hope from people like Chaitanya Tamhane. I think all of us including Chaitanya, myself, Sudip (Sharma), Abhishek (Chaubey), Guneet (Monga), and Vishal-ji (Bhardwaj) are waiting for that one project to cross over to the West and get real worldwide recognition. I think our system is designed for India-safe. And if your film is India-safe, it is definitely not crossing over to the West because an India-safe film is already a mediocre film. What Guneet has managed to do so well is that she has broken out of the system. She is running her own ecosystem now, working with American and French producers. She has managed to not sustain this system. I think there is a need for an alternative system that has the resources and the funding to back film-makers who are not doing India-safe. In the US, for instance, there is an A24, the studio that funded Jordan Peele and many other exciting independent films including *Hereditary*. But we don't have anything like that yet.

What are the kinds of films and film-makers that have influenced you over the years?

I know it has become quite controversial to say his name now but I'd be a hypocrite if I don't. My biggest influence would be Woody Allen. His films are ingrained in my psyche. Then there is Billy Wilder and Wes Anderson – these are the people from the US. Asghar Farhadi has a huge place in my mind now. He has managed to work on narratives that are so complex and sophisticated and his structuring is so subtle that he works on a very nuanced level of cinema. That, for me, is very, very special. Then right now, I am loving Ruben Ostlund, the guy who made *Triangle of Sadness*.

Would you have done anything differently in any of your films?

I don't think I have ever been satisfied with any of my films once I finished them. I always want to change this and that though I don't live so much in my head about the things I could have done. I tell myself that I have learnt and I'll do things differently the next time.

Say, if you were to make *Gehraiyaan* in another country, say in the US, would it be exactly the same with a different star cast?

Well, I don't think the story would change significantly because it's a different country but the treatment would change. The songs may not end up being where they are. I think we were a little scared that Deepika's character would be judged by the larger audiences in India. Maybe it would have been more unbridled in another country. Even in terms of *Kapoor & Sons*, we took a call to not reveal Fawad's sexuality right away because there was a fear of people judging him. So, we let people live with the character for some time, develop a liking for him, and then reveal that he is gay. So, if you are asking if I am confined to India while making films in India, in some ways, the answer is yes.

TWENTY-SEVEN

Shivam Nair

Shivam Nair came to Bombay in the 1980s and has spent over forty years in the industry. He has seen generations of film people and worked through and adapted himself to different eras of the industry. He has directed and been involved in the writing of films such as *Maharathi* and shows such as *Special OPS* and *Mukhbir: The Story of a Spy*.

We met for lunch at 1 BHK, a beautiful restaurant in Oshiwara, which is a walk away from his office. And after our meeting, he did take a walk.

From Kerala to Bihar to Bombay, what was your childhood like?

I was born in a nondescript village in Kerala, which didn't even have electricity earlier. I have seen electricity arrive there. We lived in a joint family. In my fifth standard, my father and our family moved to Bihar. This was the first turning point in my life. Around us were only two-three families from Kerala. I had passed the fifth standard back in Kerala but had to join the same standard in Bihar because I did not follow Hindi. Everybody else spoke only in Hindi and since I did not understand it at all, the local kids bullied me a lot in my initial days in Bihar. Then it became a matter of survival. After settling down in the new environment for a couple of years, to escape bullying, I somehow befriended a couple of notorious kids in school. They were goons. That's when my life took a sort of wild turn. I started bunking school and got into all sorts of fights and quarrels that one is not supposed to in school. It was in stark contrast with my days in Kerala which were cultured and simple whereas my initial days in Bihar were rowdy and rough.

I consider myself extremely lucky that I started playing cricket soon – I even played at the district level eventually. Otherwise, nothing would have stopped me from becoming a criminal. All those guys from my school in Bihar eventually became criminals. Now, in this wildlife of my teenage, outside of cricket, I developed another interest which was cinema. These two things kept me away from the path of crime.

After the tenth standard, somehow cricket took a back seat and cinema took precedence in the then unruly vehicle of my life. But what was cinema? I kept wondering. And how could I get into it? I had heard of Satyajit Ray and Mrinal Sen and of other film-makers in Calcutta. So, one day, I thought I'd just go to Calcutta and work with them without thinking of the practical probability of it happening. It so happened that one of my cousins had started working a job at the Bank of India. One day, he had to go to Calcutta to meet his boss. I told him I wanted to roam around the city and would like to accompany him. It was on the train that I told him my real intention of going to Calcutta.

After his meeting with the boss was over, I announced with the confidence of youth, 'I want to meet Satyajit Ray!' His bosses didn't know what to say. But one of them finally showed me his house and said, 'This is his house, see it and go back.' But I was pretty sure I wanted to meet him and I entered the house. My acquaintance was so afraid that he only stayed on the staircase. He was behaving as if we were there to commit a crime. But I rang the doorbell. For the first few minutes, nobody opened the door. But I kept trying. Then, one of Ray's housekeepers arrived. It was such a tall door that the guy was standing on a stool when he opened it. I told him with great confidence that I was there to meet Ray. He asked me to wait. After some time, he asked me to walk into a room. There was the great Satyajit Ray in his study! I was amazed to see him but at the same time, I told him that I wanted to assist him and learn film-making. He never made eye contact with me. He asked me what I had studied and then told me to take the FTII exam and learn film-making from there. But I insisted on learning from him and then he said nothing.

After a silence, his house-help came back and asked me to leave. I don't remember the exact year but this was the time when Ray was working on *Sadgati*. I went out the door with a strange feeling. Such a big guy had rejected me upfront, I thought. I told my cousin that Ray spoke to me very well but in reality, I was not feeling good. Now I was all the more convinced that I had to get into films and prove myself. From there, my by-then Bihari mind found a way to reach Mrinal Sen. Mrinal Sen spoke to me politely and told me he wouldn't mind my working with him but he explained his financial situation and said that he and his family were not in a situation to afford to pay me anything. Now, there was no way I could have survived in Calcutta without money. At that point, I wasn't even a graduate. Saddened, I went back to Bihar. But as soon as I took my final-year exams, without waiting for the results, I ventured out of home on another journey. This time, to Bombay, which was going to define my life.

What was your first impression of Bombay in the 1980s? How was the city different then especially in the eyes of a young writer, and film-maker?

I arrived in Bombay in 1981. Initially, Bombay looked like a dream to me. Everything looked big and surreal. Bombay is one city that lets you achieve what you want to – I can totally vouch for this notion. It doesn't let you be lazy or slow down, it facilitates your journey. When I came here to work in films, Bombay for me was mostly Juhu and Bandra because that's where the biggies of the industry lived. In the first film that I got to be an assistant on, the chief assistant used to tell me to get paan and cigarettes. I felt humiliated. Most people in the unit in those days weren't educated. People waited for years to assist big directors. There was a lot of lobbying back then and I found it difficult to enter. I assisted on many films that never got made. And I was finding my way. Then, fortunately, TV happened.

You've worked extensively in TV. Tell me what it did for you.

Without TV, I may not have been able to survive in Bombay in the 1980s. As I said, the '80s was a tricky time for a youngster like me to break into films. TV gave me and many others the work and the money that we were desperately looking for. I think TV's contribution is huge even in some of our journeys as a film-maker. Look, if you are an exceptional talent, if you're brilliant, you'd break through anyhow. But TV was a platform where average people could find work. Average talent needs the experience to get polished. And it's very difficult for average talent to get transformed and make it big.

TV in India became big with Doordarshan in the 1980s. However, its revolutionary moment came in the 1990s when private channels joined the trade. There came a point in the 1990s when some of them started the episodic format – *Rishtey*, *Saturday Suspense*, and *Star Bestsellers* were all platforms for us to tell stories that were about forty-five minutes long. Along with me, Imtiaz (Ali), Vishal (Bhardwaj), and Anurag (Kashyap) found amazing opportunities there to express ourselves. All of us put in a great amount of hard work, without caring about money to prove ourselves. We were all outsiders so we would be there for each other. There was a healthy jealousy amongst us as well and we would support each other's work. At that time there was nothing called a creative head in channels and stuff like that. This allowed us to explore our aspect of film-making.

When did you start writing seriously?

I think pretty late. It took me too long to realize that it was all about the story. I spent many years finding my way from one film project to another and TV. In those days, there were no books, and no internet available. There was no source really to even develop the feeling of wanting to learn writing. I got to hone my craft – I edited, assisted, and directed. But writing was elusive to me. I think it was (Sriram) Raghavan, in the early 1990s, who was the first person to show me the importance of writing. He had studied at FTII and was exposed to world cinema. He introduced me to that world and also made me realize the importance of scripts. I edited his documentary, *Raman Raghav*. Then I wrote *Ranga Billa* and also worked on *Auto Narayan*. But it still took me longer to realize that craft is important and necessary but writing is the only place where your voice could come through. It's the story that makes a film truly yours. Some people have insight at an early age and some take longer to discover it. But one must discover oneself in the practice of film-making and it can only happen through stories.

Do you think writing a role for a particular star is a good approach? Have you ever done that?

No, I have never done that. Maybe the big directors who are friends with stars have done that. But I never was in a circle like that. So even if I wanted to write a character for let's say, Aamir Khan, I really doubt if he would ever do it. I also believed in the story and would also look to cast the right actor for the story. Stars could be big or small but stories are not big or small. Stories are stories.

You've worked on four serial-killer documentaries. Could you talk about those films? How did this genre start appealing to you?

It all started with Sriram Raghavan. He first started working on *Raman Raghav*, in which I was involved as an EP as well as the editor. That's the time he introduced me to the works of Scorsese and the like. I told Anurag (Kashyap) about Scorsese and his work, and look, today, Anurag has even met Martin Scorsese! That's been his journey. Coming back to Sriram, he introduced me to many films and film-makers across the world. I started enjoying it. After *Raman Raghav*, I worked on *Ranga Billa*, *Auto Narayan*, and *Feroz Daruwala* in different capacities. Those days, everything I was doing on film involved murder and crime. And people around were interested in that too. But slowly, I wanted to move away from that and go back to my roots. Yes, I did a lot of thrillers after that too. Spy thrillers that I worked on later are also a similar genre.

You waited twenty-five years after coming to Bombay to direct your first feature film *Ahista Ahista*. Was it a choice?

No, I couldn't break in earlier. That's the straight truth. Just never got a chance. You know, the first feature film I wanted to make was called *Informer*. It was written by Anurag (Kashyap). This must be somewhere around 1994-96. Anurag had written *Auto Narayan*, the serial-killer documentary I had directed. And he also wrote *Informer* which I thought I'd make into a feature film. We tried a lot to make it happen. Anurag and I met Subhash Ghai, Pooja Bhatt, and many potential people who could produce it. But nobody did. The film never got made. I still have that script.

I went back to TV and told myself that this is what is helping me survive and I should stick to it. Many years later in the mid-2000s, Imtiaz had a script and he wanted to direct it as his first film but his conversation didn't work out with the producers for some reason. Now the script was ready and he and Anurag insisted I direct it. That's how *Ahista Ahista* happened in 2006 and it worked out very well for me. Had the two of them not pushed me, I would have never made it because, at the time, I still wanted *Informer* to be my first film.

How did the process of making *Maharathi* unfold?

Maharathi was adapted from a novel by James Hadley Chase called *There's Always a Price Tag*. The script was written by Uttam Gada originally for a Gujarati play. Initially, Vikram Bhatt was supposed to direct the film. But just before he was to start the first shooting schedule, something happened and he decided not to. Then he called me asking me if I'd be interested in doing it. The cast was ready and I was enticed by the idea of working with actors like Paresh bhai (Rawal), Naseeruddin Shah, Om Puri, and Boman Irani. I was thinking in my gut that the story had to be rewritten more cinematically. The story and screenplay were all good but I was constantly feeling that it might look like a play, because of one location and the way it was written. I told Paresh bhai about this but somehow that did not work out. Paresh bhai still tells me he should have listened to me.

Was there a time of frustration in your life as a writer?

Frustration that comes from not getting to do what I want to has always been present. I think for many years I kept working on projects that came my way. Somebody had the material, I had only limited ways of handling it and stuff like that. Till very recently, that's the way I went about it, and often found it difficult to convince producers and financiers to let me do what I wanted to. Although I think I consciously changed this approach very recently. On the OTT show I am doing, my approach is different. I have now decided not to work on anything where the idea doesn't appeal to me.

You are working rigorously on OTT. Do you perceive the medium to be transformational?

OTT has allowed me and everyone else to explore stories that were impossible to be told before. In OTT, writing is the hero; the story is the hero. Also, you don't have to be afraid of a Friday release any longer and crumble under the huge financial expectations of producers as it happens in films. Another thing that OTT has allowed us to do is to understand and learn more about characters. It allows us to get into layers that were unthinkable before. On the show I am working on, I am involved in the conception of every character and every aspect of the story.

The Malayalam film industry is doing very well. Have you ever thought of making a film there?

That industry is doing well but in the smaller pie that it is, the competition is quite tough there as well. Another thing about me is that although I know the language, I don't think I belong to that world. I have never lived there after the first five years of my life. I know many writers from the Malayalam film industry. Their strength is that they are rooted in their reality and the everyday life that they experience. Some successful writers live in villages even today, drink at the same bars, do the same gossip, take a bus to Kochi for a meeting, and back to their village. This rootedness is one of the main reasons for those kinds of stories to come up there. But I don't live that life in Kerala so it may be difficult for me to create those nuances on film.

Do you think the Hindi film industry is creatively much less ambitious and rather averse to experimentation than it could be? If so, why?

The reason for the why is layered. This industry believes in formula-based film-making. If a particular genre becomes successful, everyone tries to jump in and make the same kind of cinema. Secondly, everyone here wants a cut of the money. It's a chain of people from producers to distributors who have had their own lobbies who dominate the final product. Plus, the kind of money that rides on Hindi films can be stupendous. Hence as an industry, people here are averse to experimentation, and good stories and good writers often suffer.

Who are your favourite films and film-makers?

The first film that influenced me a lot, when I was in Bihar, was Shyam Benegal's *Junoon*. The film didn't work at all in Bihar and ran only for three days. But I was fortunate to watch it. It impacted me a lot and transported me into another world. Earlier in my life, I loved Guru Dutt's films a lot. Then Raj Kapoor's initial films – *Awaara*, *Shree 420*, etc. As I said, I discovered international cinema much later in life. Martin Scorsese is my favourite. I might even go on to say that *Goodfellas* is my favourite film of all time. That storytelling is fantastic. I have also been a huge fan of Akira Kurosawa. His lensing, blocking, his craft of film-making are marvellous.

What are your favourite OTT shows?

Honestly, I don't think India has reached anywhere in the OTT world yet. We are like the kids who hope to grow up and become good people one day. OTT surely has a lot of opportunities. I think in the next five to seven years, a lot of good stuff might come out of India and a lot of new writers may get a chance. Young people are watching Spanish and Israeli shows and that is bound to influence them as audiences as well as writers and creative people. But let me tell you, as of now, nobody is watching Indian shows outside of India. What we are doing on OTT is using a lot of swear words and a lot of regional lingos. But using authentic lingo is not thinking of original ideas. I think we lack character understanding on a deeper level and a sense of originality and plot. Internationally, I like *Breaking Bad* and *Narcos* a lot. But I don't think I have seen as many shows yet as I would have liked to.

In the over four decades that you have spent in the industry, is there anything you have done or not done that you'd do differently in retrospect?

Definitely. Most importantly, I would rather have discovered earlier in life that my purpose of being here is to tell stories. I drifted and floated around a bit too much. I would change that given a chance. I spent a lot of time on marriage, kids, friends, partying, drinking, and all other worldly indulgences. But I did not discover myself enough. I lacked focus and kept drifting. I realized this at the age of fifty-eight. If I were to get 300 more years to live, I might end up with more wisdom.

TWENTY-EIGHT

Sita Menon

Sita Menon has been a long-time collaborator of Raj & DK. She is the writer of films such as *99*, *Shor in the City*, *Go Goa Gone*, and shows such as *Farzi* among others.

I met her on a Zoom call for the conversation, which started with her childhood in Bandra East before venturing into topics like cricket, journalism, and, of course, her body of work. All through the conversation, I observed that she was naturally funny and although she is a woman of few words, she made for a captivating conversation.

Why did you become a writer?

I am actually a journalist's daughter. My dad was an editor with the *Economic Times*. So, I grew up in a colony called Patrakar, which is exclusively a colony for journalists. It's a very innovative concept that the Maharashtra government had come up with back then. Patrakar is located in Bandra East. It's right next to Sahitya Sahwas, which is a colony exclusively for writers and literary figures. This entire neighbourhood is full of a certain kind of people that impacted my childhood. There is Kala Nagar, which is a colony for artists, then there is Sahitya Sahwas next to it, and then Patrakar next to that. In the vicinity is also a colony for architects. It used to be a very peaceful, leafy neighbourhood. So, I have grown up around writers all through my childhood. The only catch was that my dad did not want me to become a journalist. He thought, back in the day, that this was no field for a woman. But I always wanted to become one. I had no interest in science and mathematics. I felt more comfortable expressing myself with prose and poetry than expressing myself through science and mathematics. At that point, I had huge clashes with my dad.

In my tenth standard, I got exactly 75 per cent which was not good enough for science or even for commerce but they were good enough for literature. After college, I became a journalist and I was a journalist for about fifteen-sixteen years going through *TOI* (*Times of India*), some digital media, etc. I did a lot of lifestyle and movies. I also worked with *Femina* for a long time. When I was in Xavier's, I happened to reach out to Raj & DK for an interview. In those days, Indian-American film-makers were just about booming. They had just come out with a short feature called *Shaadi.com* or *Matrimonial. com* and I interviewed them. We hit it off well. The feature eventually was done and dusted but our conversation continued.

They asked me if I wanted to take a look at a feature film script that they had just written. I said, 'Sure, why not!' I had zero experience in cinema at that point. I didn't even think of getting into films. I just looked at the script as a friend. That film was called *Flavours*. It was their first full-length feature film. It was based on their diaspora experience of living in America. I was involved in the production and the post-production of that film and I got hands-on into the process.

After that, Raj & DK quit their software jobs in America and moved to India. Then we started jamming about this film, which eventually became *99*. That kind of kick-started my career in films. I had a job then and I continued working a job for ten years after I met them. After *99*, *Shor in the City* happened and then *Go Goa Gone* happened. My last job was at Star India and in the last two years at my job, I had not written a word of film. So, at that point, I started thinking if I should take a leap of faith and follow films full-time. I was very middle-class and job security mattered a lot to me so it was a tough choice back then. But I am glad that I made it. I don't want to call it coincidence. I don't believe in coincidence but it all just happened without any such plan.

You have written films and now with *Farzi*, you have transitioned into the longer format space on OTT. How difficult has that transition been as a writer?

Actually, for me, it was extremely organic. I don't find the longer format a challenge at all. I'll tell you why. I love diving into characters and exploring several aspects of them. And a feature film does not give me that space. I love exploring each character fully and getting into the details and nuances of everything.

The difference between film writing and show writing is essentially that in a feature film, you have to tell your story in about two hours so it's about how concisely you can tell your story, whereas in a show you have two plus three or four hours so you can get into a character's childhood, his beliefs and many other themes. So, it's a mindset shift that you have to make.

Do you think screenwriting can be taught in a school or must it be learnt on the job?

I think a film school will make it easier for you in terms of understanding the fundamentals of a story and its structure. Self-taught is a much harder way, which I took. It can get extremely frustrating. I remember *99* and *Shor in the City*, where I had not done the full stories. It was a case of proper collaboration. I was new and raw to the world of writing a film. I had no clue about the story flow, the beats, or the giant screenplay. I had no idea what to make of a screenplay for a very long time. I just kept honing it. I wasn't very good at it when I started, which is why I relied heavily on Raj & DK when it came to the actual screenplay writing of it. But somewhere along the way, as I kept practising the craft, that switch happened and I think I figured it out. That is not to say that it becomes easy eventually. Writing is never easy. But somewhere along the way, it stops being daunting. You develop a feeling that you can handle it.

You have collaborated so often with Raj & DK. What is it like to work with them daily?

First of all, I have been extremely fortunate in this aspect. Not a day goes by when I am not grateful for the fact that I have collaborators and friends like Raj & DK and I started off with them. They made the journey easier for me. I did not have to struggle in the sense of figuring my way out with many producers and directors in the sense of making them take a look at my work. It was always the three of us who were excited about a story, we wrote it, we collaborated with a producer, and then made the film. It has always been like that.

Similarly, with OTT, on *Farzi*, we followed pretty much the same pattern of work except that on *Farzi*, we had a writers' room and had Suman Kumar, the writer of *Family Man*, on board as well. But even with Suman, he is a friend. All of us go back a long way. We started as friends and then became people who worked together. So, luckily, unlike what you might find in some other writers' rooms, we never had to deal with the clashes and the interpersonal struggles while working together.

As for the process, I am not a talker or a discusser. So, I go into my hole and write and I send it to them. And then it is put to discussion. That's how we work. On the other hand, Raj & DK are great talkers. Their ideas come when they talk. But my ideas don't come when I talk. In fact, no idea comes to me when I talk. So, I always go and write and figure things out on paper.

The other part of collaboration is when you have to collaborate with directors on shows and the MBAs in the OTT teams. How does that turn out for a writer?

Collaboration is always going to be part of this profession. Let's take the example of *Citadel India*. It's a mammoth global franchise. You are answerable not only to Amazon India – the heads of which will be IITians and MBAs, who are very sharp and savvy business heads, and to the creative heads at Amazon India. You are also answerable to Amazon US and to the Russo brothers, who created this entire universe. You are answerable to the global showrunner, who is another entity. They all bring their different opinions on what works and what doesn't work and their creativity to the table.

All of them on *Citadel India* have been extremely cognizant of the fact that we are creators and writers and successful at that in our own right. So, there's a whole lot of healthy respect going there. Of course, they may have points of view that are at odds with ours. No creativity process can exist without that. But at the same time, we all believe that conversations can solve anything. Now, let's say from a budget point of view, the business head might come down and ask us to stick to a certain budget because there is so much at stake with shows like these. It's up to us to tell the story most effectively with what we have without bankrupting anyone. So yes, these things are not always easy but that's how they go and that's probably one of the things that make the process more interesting as well. There will be a pull and push at both ends but, in the end, if logic and creativity prevail, I have nothing to complain about.

Do you think that gender plays a role in screenwriting?

Of course, it does. To give you a very basic example, Raj & DK are men. They bring in the male perspective beautifully. I am a woman. I bring in the female perspective. I balance it out. *Farzi*, for example, is a very male-dominated space. The only prominent female characters are Raashi, the Megha character; Regina Cassandra, who plays Rekha, Michael's wife; and then there is Kubbra Sait, the Saira character. So, the only real estate that could be explored fully was the Megha character. Megha, in many ways, is my baby and I am extremely proud of how and what she turned out to be in the show. She's a woman in her own right who is in a completely male-dominated world. But she knows very well how to be herself in a world like that and how to deal with the male ego. A lot of my personal experience went into that character.

Similarly, with the Rekha character, which did not have much screen-time, I would like to believe that whatever screen-time she had, she was explored well. I believe that each character needs to be explored to its highest potential in whatever screen-time it may have. So, yes, gender does play a role. Especially while working with Raj & DK because we have been a team like this for years and we divide our responsibilities accordingly. I have never worked with other teams so I can't say how it works there.

Having said that, fundamentally, I believe that if you are a writer, you need to be able to write masculine, feminine, neuter, all genders well. You need to be versatile as a writer. Not just in terms of gender but also in terms of genre. Tomorrow, if I am asked to write sci-fi, I would have no clue but I can at least start with research. So, yes, I also believe that if you are a woman, it certainly doesn't mean that you cannot write a male character. That has never made sense to me.

Your first film, *99*, was a truly independent film at the time it came out. Could you run me through the journey of writing it?

Every Indian has two great loves – films and cricket. All three of us were huge fans of cricket. Or at least of the cricket that was going on in those times. It's not that our love for the game has waned now but we probably just don't have the time to follow the influx of matches that are happening these days. My dad was a Ranji player as well. He played for Punjab. He wasn't a very famous cricketer, but he instilled in all his children a great love for cricket. And, as I said, Raj & DK are huge fans of cricket as well.

The story of *99* started when Raj came up with the idea that the year 1999 was a watershed event in cricket. Sachin Tendulkar got out a few times on ninety-nine and we thought what if we were all stuck on ninety-nine, without ever making a 100? We took that as a metaphor for life. Also, the match-fixing allegations against some of the players had surfaced and the whole world of betting and bookies was out in the public eye. The Boman Irani character is into betting. So, *99* was this huge homage to cricket. We were great fans of Guy Ritchie and his films like *Snatch* and *Lock, Stock and*

Two Smoking Barrels. Crime comedy was a huge thing for us and we were very excited about exploring this genre. Also, both Raj & DK are genuinely funny people and they don't like to explore a story without any humour. To me as well, handling serious subjects in a light-hearted manner comes naturally. So, it's easy for all of us to sync up that way.

Go Goa Gone is a film that divided people and assumed a cult status. There are people who love the film and others who dislike it. What's the story of writing it?

It originally started as a slacker comedy. I'd say, it still is a slacker comedy. Later, people started calling it zombie comedy. But it is a story of three slackers who hate their jobs and whose only source of great happiness is going to Goa and attending this rave party and getting drunk out of their minds. That's how the idea began. We thought what if they woke up the day after the rave party and realized that the whole world around them had turned into zombies? That turned the whole thing around. Now, again, all of us are huge fans of zombie comedy. So, once this zombie angle got in, it made a whole lot of sense to explore it from that angle.

Writing *Go Goa Gone* was a mad ride. And a fun fact is when we wrote that film, we had never smoked up or indulged in any substances. That's when research came into play. People told us that there are substances that give you a high and substances that give you a low – I didn't even know of these things.

After 99 and before Go Goa Gone, you wrote Shor in the City. Do you sit down and decide consciously that you want to explore different genres?

I would say yes. It comes from a space of exploring yourself fully in the creative space. We have been curious to explore every possible genre there is to explore. The common thread across all our work has been humour. *Shor in the City* was a homage to Bombay and was in many ways my baby because it was a culmination of three-four news articles about Bombay. It was gritty, grounded, and earthy overall. And yes, after that came *Go Goa Gone* so we wanted to explore different genres and I think we are still trying to do that.

Now, coming to the piece that everyone is talking about – *Farzi*. You started your career with independent cinema made on shoestring budgets and have evolved into mammoth projects like *Farzi*. Does the transition from shoestring to huge budgets affect the storytelling?

Well, if I have to be honest, there is a film called *A Gentleman*, which we did and which had a good budget. It had many stakeholders and we probably took too many opinions and at the end of it, we thought we could have made a much better film with that material than what it turned out to be. It was a huge learning for us. Because of the way the film turned out, we had to go back to our very basic production budgets for our next work. I think we did get carried away with the demands of the commercial market at that time and realized that it wasn't the best way to go about our work. That project did a lot to reorient ourselves and go back to proper storytelling.

When it came to *Farzi*, which is much more recent, we had learnt our lessons and we knew how to handle big-budget shows. *Farzi* was originally Raj & DK's idea. They wanted to make a film on counterfeiting. And this was many, many years ago. When we first came up with the story, it was supposed to be a film and the story was nothing like this. It was about a policeman who discovers fake currency notes in a mithai box and we had a whole story built around the policeman. But slowly, the story started evolving with time. We then put in the actual artist, who became Sunny (Shahid Kapoor's character) in *Farzi*. There is a line he says, '*Ek din main itna paisa banaunga ki paison ki izzat hi na karun.*' (One day I'll earn so much money that money won't matter to me.) That's his character arc, his core angst. Thank God, the feature film did not get made, and thank God, we got to explore this world in long-format storytelling because today, I don't see it working as well as a feature film. I am very glad that we got to explore this world at a storytelling pace that we like and that it deserves.

Have you ever thought of working on projects that Raj & DK aren't involved in?

I have tried and it's not that I am tied to Raj & DK. But it's just that we are friends and we have worked together on so many projects for so long that there is a connection and we always discuss work. Even on projects that I was not involved in, like *Family Man* or *Stree*, we did have some discussions. They do consult me and I do offer my point of view. And similarly, I am working on a feature film just by myself and I do discuss it with them. Yes, I have had offers to work on projects from outside and I have tried and failed. Maybe, the wavelengths don't match, or maybe something else. I have tried many, many times but it just hasn't happened yet except for this film that I am writing by myself.

At a systemic level, what would you like to change to improve the lives of writers in the industry?

It's very simple. Just bring along pay parity about the project. And although things have improved a lot, there is still a long way to go. You know, the other day, I was watching a *Film Companion* interview with all these film-makers – Karan (Johar), Zoya (Akhtar) and others. And Karan said something very right. He said, 'It's just been the norm and nobody questioned it.' Technicians and writers have been paid poorly for years and nobody bothered about it. Now, they have started to up their prices, and more power to them because it's only fair. After all, a project begins with a writer. There is no story without a writer. No matter how popular the actor or the actress is, it begins here at the writer's table. So why would you not have a basic parity? Nobody is demanding something they don't deserve. But fifteen crores (for actors) vs five lakhs (for writers) is a huge gap. That's disparity staring at our faces. Some people are cognizant of this and are beginning to effect this change. But there are studios who still ask, 'Why would you pay so much to a writer?' That has to change. There is no other way.

What are the films and shows that have influenced you?

I can't even begin because there are lots of them. There is Quentin Tarantino, there is Krzysztof Kieslowski. I am influenced hugely by world cinema. There is Wong Kar-wai, there is Lars Von Trier, there is Guy Ritchie. Then Greta Gerwig, Phoebe Waller-Bridge, Noah Baumbach, David Lynch and it doesn't stop. I could go on. And, of course, Aaron Sorkin, where writing is concerned.

In the OTT space, I love *Succession*, *The White Lotus*, *The Newsroom*, *The Wire* and so many more.

Name a show in the world that you wish you had written.

Succession. Or *Fleabag*.

TWENTY-NINE

Sudip Sharma

Sudip Sharma is the writer-creator of what to me is one of the best OTT shows made in India till today – *Paatal Lok*. He has also written films such as *Udta Punjab*, *NH10* and *Sonchiriya* among others. Sudip Sharma's work tends to explore the dark realities of authentically Indian worlds and it does that with an eye for nuance which is rare in the space of modern Hindi cinema and rarer in the Indian OTT space. I admire Sudip's work not only because it's often moving and disturbing in parts but also because of its consistency in quality.

I met Sudip over a Zoom call as he was in Delhi, shooting for *Kohra*, when we did this exercise.

In what way does a screenwriter contribute to society?

I think everyone contributes to society in their own way. Even a person who drives a bus contributes to society. So, in that sense, there is a role that a screenwriter plays in society. It is also commensurate with the kind of role that art plays in society. At the end of the day, a screenwriter is a storyteller. And stories are what shape cultural narratives. Even the Ramayana and the Mahabharata are stories and have contributed to society in their own way. But I don't think we should put the cart before the horse and forget the most important responsibility that lies with the screenwriter. The most important allegiance that a screenwriter has is to himself and his stories. Your first responsibility as a screenwriter is to ensure that you can tell the story that you have chosen to tell.

How are the life and the challenges of a modern screenwriter different from those of a screenwriter from the past?

I think there is a lot more respect for screenwriting now, so in that sense, it is easier. If you look at it, apart from Salim Sahab and Javed Sahab, no screenwriter has been celebrated in India. Songwriters are always more popular in India, even dialogue writers. But I don't think too many people in the industry even understand the role of a screenwriter – the fact that he really is the architect of the film, the fact that he is the one laying down the grounds. Some of the blame for that lies with us screenwriters as well because we didn't give them the kind of confidence or the material that would make them sit up and think, 'Hey, this guy is building a world through his words or he is building a story block by block.' It's not really the director who is telling the story first. It's the screenwriter who is telling the story first and then it's the director who is building on it.

Because of all these historical reasons, the screenwriter's contribution hasn't been emphasized enough in India but things have improved now. When I started writing, about eighteen–twenty years ago, screenwriting was opening up as a topic of discussion. I think *Satya* was the film that made people sit up and take notice of the writing of it. *Satya* was in 1998; it took us about a hundred years to get there. Maybe it happened with *Bandit Queen* a little before that. It started in the late 1990s and then in the early noughties, some of the work that Vishal (Bhardwaj) did or people like Anurag (Kashyap) or Jaideep Sahni did, brought a sort of a healthy discussion around screenwriting.

One way of showing respect to a profession is by showing money. It's only in the last five years or so that money has come into screenwriting. In contrast with the time when I had written scripts for free, written scripts for food or an incredibly low amount of money. And now when you see even young screenwriters walking in and demanding their fair share, it's great. In terms of the challenges, there is so much work happening right now that keeping the quality intact could be a task, especially under the pressure to submit work sooner than it should be submitted. Another challenge of today is how to tell a story that you want to and in the way you really want to or how not to fall into the rut of writing another nationalist drama, which seems to be the flavour of the decade, or do you go against the grain and tell a story which is appealing to you as a person?

Many people have the opinion that film is a director's medium and writing is a supporting act. Do you agree with that?

This deserves a more nuanced look. To begin with, yes, it is partly true that film is a director's medium. But then we are talking about film. If you look at long-form storytelling, if you look at OTT shows or TV even, it is a writer's medium. And yes, film may be a director's medium but how do we know of Aaron Sorkin or Charlie Kaufman or Salim-Javed? So many writers have made a mark. If you do great work and if your work pushes through these notions we may have about screenwriting, you can make a mark. Creating a film out of nothing is a great privilege as well as a great responsibility. When there was nothing, as a writer you created something. Everyone comes in the process after you. In fact, the film itself comes into existence after the writer comes on board. That makes you more than a supporting role. You are a mother. The child may grow up and find a girlfriend or find many girlfriends later but a writer is the mother of a film.

Now, with huge corporate houses commissioning films and shows, is there too much interference in the creative process of a writer?

If you have worked a bit and your work has earned some respect, they let you be. I am working on my third series right now and more or less they let me be. Yes, they will tell me what they think of what I have written or what we have shot but if you give them strong, rational arguments, they let you be. At the same time, we must understand that when someone is investing crores and crores of rupees in a project, they are going to ask you a few questions and you have to know how to answer them and navigate around those. I wouldn't belittle the point of view of a platform because they are just doing their job and as a screenwriter, when you fight it out or stick to what you believe in, you are doing your job.

How easy do you think it is for a young writer without a proven track record to approach OTTs or get something made?

You have to write a great spec script that doesn't cost anything and pitch it around, you know. I mean, honestly, I didn't start with a proven track record. I'll tell you when Navdeep (Singh) and I were pitching *NH10*, on spec, there was no producer and no money. So, we pitched it around and then it reached producers and eventually, it reached Anushka (Sharma) and got made.

I would say it is easier to be a twenty-five-year-old screenwriter with no proven record than a twenty-five-year-old cinematographer with no proven record. Because as a screenwriter, I can write a script at home and someone reads it and says, 'Wow, I want to make it.' Also, now some agencies get young writers on board and pitch their work for a percentage. And the only thing they ask for is a spec script. You know, most of the time, when writers say that no one is reading my script, trust me there is always someone reading the first page. Till today, when a script comes to me, I always read the first page and then decide if I want to read further or not. You can tell, on one page, whether the person knows how to write or not. If you don't know how to construct a scene or how to write dialogue well, trust me, nobody is going to be interested. The fact is that the world doesn't owe you anything.

NH10 was critically acclaimed. Could you run me through the journey of its writing?

The idea came from Navdeep. At that point, both of us were interested in the class structure that exists in society. In fact, I am interested in that even today. At that time, it was more fascinating for me because I was trying to understand my own privileges, the man-woman divide or the rural-urban divide in the country. I was also interested in what hot money or instant money had done to Gurgaon. I have spent about five years in Delhi and Navdeep is from Delhi. So, initially, it was about understanding what was going on and then it became an idea about a woman in peril and the place of a woman in society. At that point, there was also a lot of anger inside me, the frustration that came with trying to pitch scripts for ten years and thinking that nobody was reading them. So, we were two angry men wanting to tell a story about a woman. The film does have a male gaze and beyond a point, I can't help it but we were trying to tell the story with some amount of empathy at least, even if not from the deepest understanding.

You have collaborated with Abhishek Chaubey on two films – Udta Punjab and Sonchiriya. Can you explain the working relationship between a writer and a director using that example?

A writer-director relationship is a lot like dating. You meet a lot of people and then you finally hit it off with someone. And it's also a very intimate relationship. You end up spending so much time with each other, you end up sharing so many of your ideas and thoughts. Yes, it involves a lot of fights as well but I think the two people need to have a similar worldview at least.

So, yes, Chaubey happened to read *NH10* and he pitched an idea to me and *Udta Punjab* happened. We really enjoyed working together on *Udta Punjab* and wanted to do another film together. That's when *Sonchiriya* came along. We used to always tell each other that we should do three films together. Because the first is when you start understanding each other, the second is when you really get each other, and the equation is great and the third is when the fallout starts as you have outgrown each other. So, we still have a third film pending and I hope we come around with something soon.

Udta Punjab isn't a script that one would normally expect stars to be part of. How did you manage to attract them to what could be called a rather dark script for the Bollywood mainstream?

It's funny because I didn't write either *NH10* or *Udta Punjab* with a star in mind. I was always writing the film I wanted to see. Honestly, I had no interest in taking it to a star. Till today, I have no interest in taking anything to a star. It's always about writing the script first and then thinking about who fits the role best. I'll be very happy if it's a great actor. That's all I require. At the same time, you can't underestimate the power that a star brings to a film. Also, I was quite lucky to have the stars because, as you rightly said, these are not the kind of films that they normally do. But for some reason they did. I am no judge of my own work but my friend Avinash (Arun) tells me that the reason why my work has attracted stars and some amount of mainstream appreciation as well is that although it is pretty intense, there is a larger viewpoint that is at play, which people connect with.

Your biggest success so far, *Paatal Lok*, is based on Tarun Tejpal's book, *The Story of My Assassins*, but despite buying the rights, the book is not credited in the show. Could you walk me through the journey of creating the show?

Yes, it is loosely based on the book. The idea started from the book. However, I was very clear that only certain sections of the book excited me. Basically, I like the take of the book – the class divide, the caste divide, and the regional and religious divide. That is what I found very interesting. But I thought that the author had written the book that he wanted to write and I was going to write the show that I wanted to write. That's what I have always done – I draw from all sorts of sources but eventually, I want to tell my own story. Why the author was not credited is entirely the studio's decision because I don't decide on the credits at all.

For me, *Paatal Lok* is about a lot of things and it also tries to explore some questions that I was grappling with such as who we are as a country and where we are headed. The character of Hathiram gives us an insight into the different worlds that I was trying to explore, the three worlds as we called them in the show: Swarg lok, Dharti Lok, and Paatal Lok.

The second season of *Paatal Lok* came out recently. Was it always planned that way?

I was always clear that there would only be one season of *Paatal Lok*. I was done in my head and to me, the story was complete. And I like the idea of complete stories. I don't like cliffhangers. It was only on the edit of the first season that I felt that I was not done with Hathiram. I sort of fell in love with the character of Hathiram Chaudhary and with the actor (Jaideep Ahlawat) who was playing it. It's that character who is purely the reason why I decided to do the second season. I took my time to find the story. The first story is over. I wanted to understand in the second season where he is now, where the people around him are now, and where he sees himself in relation to that. I would rather take my time than just do something hastily because the world wants me to do it.

Who are the film-makers that have influenced you?

As an artist, you are always indebted to the people who have influenced you. I have always loved films and so many film-makers have influenced me. Be it Martin Scorsese's work or the Coen brothers' work. Whenever I see a great film, it humbles me and I go 'How did it happen?' It fires me up or it makes me feel small by the magnitude of its achievement.

When I was growing up in the 1990s, when I was trying to form a cultural opinion of my own, *Bandit Queen* and *Satya* were huge influences. In shows, which are what I have been doing for the last four years now, I think *The Sopranos*, *The Wire*, and *Mad Men* are such outstanding achievements in terms of writing and film-making that they are a huge influence on my writing. I think these three shows are the greatest achievements in screenwriting over the last twenty years. They are just complete masterclasses and I keep watching them whenever I can. Forget how and when we will reach there but even in the West, there are rarely any shows that touch even the periphery that these three shows operate in.

Why do we lag behind many other countries in quality in terms of the longer format?

I think many other countries have had a long tradition of long-form storytelling and we don't. The *Sopranos* came out on HBO in 1999; *The Wire* came out in 2001; *The West Wing* was in the 1990s and Aaron Sorkin was writing it. So, they have had a twenty-thirty-year head start on us. Having said that, I think it's also because screenwriting is not considered an art form in India. We rarely paid attention to it at all. Our films have mostly been about song and dance or about who is the hero and who is the heroine. Just look at the conversations that happen around a film. For the last twenty-thirty years, when they were making *The Wire* and *The Sopranos*, we were discussing which item girl to put in our film. So, it's going to take a lot of time to come out of that and we have only begun five-six years ago. You know, the race is for us to catch up with. We need to work harder.

Among the shows that are out there in the world, can you name one show that you wish you had rather made?

I'll name two. *The Wire* and *The Sopranos*. And if I had made even one of them, I would never touch my laptop again or would never write a single word again. I'd happily retire.

THIRTY

Sumit Purohit

Sumit Purohit is the writer of the hugely popular show *Scam 1992* and is also one of the writers of India's first OTT show *Inside Edge* among other films and shows. He is one of the writers who looks at cinema as a visual medium as he comes from a sketching and design background. I met him at his house in Versova where we had a long and interesting conversation about his journey into the world of films, his upbringing in Uttarakhand, and writing *Scam 1992* as well as other pieces.

How did writing begin for you?

When I was in school, I used to write and I used to sketch a lot as well. But now when I look back, my sketches had a narrative, I was trying to communicate an idea through them. After my twelfth standard, I wanted to get into animation because I wanted to tell stories through animation. This was in Uttarakhand where I am originally from and where I grew up. I was not very serious about writing at that point, but I was writing a few plays. Then I was preparing for NID (National Institute of Design) but ended up getting admission to MSU (Maharaja Sayajirao University) in Baroda for their Fine Arts course. That's when I started realizing that I probably didn't have the skill for animation, and what I was actually enjoying was the narrative part of what I was doing. Baroda has a strong theatre presence. There were people around me who were involved with theatre and I started contributing to some of those plays, and I started writing.

After Baroda, I took up the film appreciation course at FTII. It's a one-month-long course. And that's where I discovered cinema. Till then I had only watched Bollywood and Hollywood cinema but at FTII, I discovered world cinema. I was very inspired by Abbas Kiarostami. I watched *Where Is the Friend's House* and loved it. The landscape of the Iranian villages, for me, was reminiscent of Uttarakhand. There's a similarity in the villages. So, I could immediately connect with that film. I even applied for the FTII course in direction but did not get through. After that, I went back to Baroda and kept working on some plays. Once, one of the plays I had worked on was being staged at IIT Bombay – at their college festival Mood Indigo. Luckily, my junior's mother had come down to watch that play and she came to know I was interested in films. She told me that one of her relatives was working on some telefilm in Bombay and she could put me in touch with him.

As things turned out, I came to Bombay and started assisting with a film. There, I met someone who said, 'Let's make a film.' So, I wrote a film that was set in my hometown, and one thing led to another. One thing I always maintain is that I don't think I am a writer; I am very specifically a screenplay writer. And there is a difference. If I call myself a writer, I would write books. I can write visually. I need to see the scene in my head before I write anything. I need visual stimulation to be able to write. Also, I believe, as a screenplay writer, you need to have some skills that are different from a writer. If you want to be a professional screenwriter, you need to know the software to write screenplays, you need to have a sense of the structure, and so on. There are certain skills you need to have as a screenwriter. I have seen some good new writers finding it difficult to see how some of their ideas could translate onto the screen. I am an editor as well. Somewhere that helps me as a screenplay writer. I think

Sudhir Mishra once tweeted, 'All writers should spend one year in the editing room.' I think he had a point there. You should definitely understand editing. I think editing is the only skill that is unique to film-making. No other art form has it.

I always thought the real hero of *Scam 1992* was its screenplay. Tell me all you can about the journey of writing *Scam 1992*.

I knew Hansal (Mehta). He had seen *Inside Edge* and had liked it. So, one day, he asked me to meet him, which I did. He told me the idea; he told me about the book he wanted to adapt. Now, the only memory of Harshad Mehta I had was back in my hometown, when all of this was happening, people knew about Harshad Mehta. I remember people talking about him. In my town, issues from Bombay and other places are rarely discussed, or at least back then, they used to be rarely discussed. So, that was quite something. I remember people saying, 'Such a rich man has been put behind bars and he has to now make do with shoes in place of a pillow.' If you remember, there is a dialogue in the show, when Harshad comes back home from jail, his mother asks him, '*Beta, maine suna jail mein joote ko taqiya banake sona padta hai.*' (Son, I heard that people have to sleep on their shoes as a make-shift pillow in jail.) When people ask me, where I do the research from, I say my life experience is my research.

When I started writing the show, it was already greenlit by Applause Entertainment, who produced it. The book rights were bought and we had access to Sucheta Dalal and Debashis Basu, who helped me with the information. I was really interested in the story but the only problem was I had no idea how the stock market worked. So, I told Hansal that my friend Saurav (Dey), who I had met years ago at my FTII interview and had kept in touch with, would be a great co-writer on this. That's how he came on board. He is very good with research. We started reading the book and realized that it's not an easy book to adapt. Many concepts of commerce and the stock market are not easy to understand. That's when we thought we should also get into the story of how the book was written. Because along with Harshad Mehta, in a way, it's also the story of Sucheta

Dalal and Debashis Basu. We spent some time understanding it. You know, there are two kinds of research when it comes to writing. One is numbers and statistics, which is the easy part. What is difficult is the concept part of it. In the case of this show, what Harshad Mehta was talking to, say, a stock market guy, needed to be understood at a concept level, first by us and then by the audience.

For us to simplify those concepts for the layman, we needed to understand them well. That's when Sucheta also introduced us to some of the characters in Harshad Mehta's life at that point. Most of them didn't want to be on record and they just helped us with information. So, imagine, a lot of times they didn't allow us to record the conversation – we could just write and take notes. So, a lot of examples and metaphors in the dialogue of the show came from what they told us and how they told us what they told us. The fact is that *Scam 1992* is a very technical show and we had to get the facts right. But along with that, everyone we met had a Harshad Mehta story and those stories became seeds for some of the moments in the show and the dialogue.

How true was *Scam 1992* to the book and how true was the book to the real events that unfolded? Also, how committed should one be to the truth while adapting a book that is in a way an adaption of a real event?

Well, truth is important, but at the same time, you need to have your own politics. And for us, Harshad Mehta was not a hero. But where he rose from – his rags-to-riches story – was meant to make him feel like a hero to a lot of people. Even if you watch a show like *Narcos* which showcases a full-blown criminal, you do end up developing sympathy for the protagonist and somewhere you are rooting for him. So, we were aware that this was going to happen. You must know this when you start writing. To tackle this issue, we surrounded Harshad Mehta's character with people who keep telling him that what he is doing is not right. There are many such examples in the show – his brother, Sucheta, his friend who commits suicide. Now when it comes to the others, we live in a time when it's difficult to imagine journalists as heroes. But for us, Sucheta and Debashis were the heroes of this story. As far as accounts are concerned, some of them are fictionalized.

For instance, I never met Harshad Mehta and nobody really knows what the police did to him but I met someone who was once arrested for something and I know how the police treated him. So, I used some of that in Harshad's story to create those scenes. Another example is that someone told me that in those days, they used to fly business class to strike business deals. That's where the scene of Harshad flying business class comes from. Now, we know that R.K. Laxman worked at the *Times of India* at that time. So, we thought when a character enters the office, instead of meeting the receptionist, he bumps into R.K. Laxman. These incidents may not have happened exactly as we wrote them – there is no way to know – but you must retain the soul of the scenes and the events they stand for while you fictionalize them to make them interesting on screen. You know, Debashis and Sucheta were already married when this event took place but we played around a little bit with the timelines and posed their love story simultaneously unfolding while this event was taking place. You do these things to make your show as interesting as possible.

Inside Edge is in a totally different space compared to Scam 1992 and was made much before that. What was it like to work on it?

Inside Edge was the first Amazon Original in India. In fact, it was the first OTT show in India. It happened even before *Sacred Games*. Karan (Anshuman) and Ameya (Sarda) were already developing the show and then they needed more writers, so I came on board and so did some others. So, although we are all credited for separate episodes as writers – and I am credited for two episodes – in reality, it's hard to say who exactly wrote what. Because everyone contributed to everything. It's not like we were writing separately. I was around for the whole first season and I also edited some of the episodes.

At that time, the show-writing process for an OTT was not tried and tested. So, we were all jamming, changing, writing whatever we could. But even at that time, we made sure that we got our facts right. We got the cricket part right. We researched how match-fixing works, and how the bookies approach the players. We also followed some of the betting sites and understood how the odds are set. It was all pretty real. Even the way the show was shot was very different. In any other film or show, the cricket doesn't look like it does in *Inside Edge*. Because it was shot using sports cameras and not your regular cameras. The approach to the show was honest and I think that showed in the sense that the show was very well received.

Do you think you found your voice more in OTT than you did in film?

I don't think I have done enough work to think that. I have enjoyed writing my films a lot – some of them never got made. Writing *Bangistan* was one of the most fun experiences for me. Yes, *Scam 1992* was very special because we wrote it with complete freedom which Hansal gave us. We never knew it was going to be so big. We didn't even know if it was ever going to get made. We kept researching, found interesting stories within, and wrote them. It was a very organic process. We thought nobody was going to see this show beyond people from the share market or a small group of people in general. But yes, it all worked out well. If you call that finding my voice in OTT, maybe I have. But at the same time, I maintain that I have a lot more work to do to discover the answer to this question.

How important is money in the journey of a screenwriter?

Money is very important. Screenwriters deserve money because that's where the entire process of film-making begins. The actors, the producers, the crew, they all come on board after and because of the screenplay. So, writers definitely deserve good money. You cannot expect someone to write a big project and pay them like they'd pay you for an independent film. I think with OTT and the studios, it is becoming a little fairer for the writers than it was before. I would strongly suggest all screenwriters, even the young ones, to get an agent. I had an agent since long before *Scam 1992*. Writers tend to undervalue themselves. Agents help in negotiating contracts and take that load off us. And some agents are really good.

Now, I do not write unless there is a signing amount. There is a reason for that. If someone is paying you a signing amount, you know that they are serious about you as well as about the project. Of course, if there is someone I know very well and trust enough, I may not take a signing amount. But as a principle, now, I always take a signing amount. If you are working for a studio or a platform, it's very important to have a proper contract with strict timelines and the terms of the deal must be followed. The projects where you don't have these things in place, mostly go nowhere. I am telling you from experience that I have done such projects in the past and all of them remain unreleased to date, some of them didn't even go to the floor.

What are your influences in cinema and shows as a writer?

I think different films have influenced me at different points. I can name three films that have had a lasting impact on me at different stages of life. Looking back, the film that got me interested in film-making, at least the one that got me interested in the craft of film, was *Sholay*. I remember watching it on VHS back in the day and it stayed with me. In the scene where Thakur narrates his story of why he did not pick up the gun when Gabbar attacked, I went like, 'Wow, how did this even happen!' *Sholay* is a film I remember shot by shot. Other than that, it would be *Jurassic Park*. I read about the film before I watched it. There used to be this Hindi magazine called *Sarita* and I don't know why but they published a two-three-page-long article on *Jurassic Park*. That article made me watch the film and then I loved the film. The third film would be Abbas Kiarostami's *Close-Up*. It's a very big film for me and very different from anything I had ever seen before in my life. The first film I ever made, the first documentary, is in a way influenced by *Close-Up*. These are the three films that have been milestones in my journey into cinema.

Other than these, I am a very big David Lynch fan. What he achieves in the first season of *Twin Peaks* is nothing short of greatness.

I believe everyone should watch *Twin Peaks*. Also, I am a very big Tim Burton fan. I also have great respect for Guru Dutt's films and I grew up with Hrishikesh Mukherjee's films. Then of course I love Michael Haneke, Charlie Kaufman and several others. I love Scorsese and Vishal Bhardwaj as well. When I watched *Maqbool* for the first time, I was blown away. I won't say there is one influence that I have. I have different kinds of influences. And as I said earlier, anything that has a strong and unique visual appeal is what I love.

What do you seek from your journey as a writer?

That's a difficult question. I would say freedom. At the end of the day, you want to be free of the tangibles like box-office collection and how many people have seen your film; you just want to be able to write what you want. I believe that is what I seek. People in the industry say things like 'The audience likes this' or 'The audience won't like this'. I want to tell them that I want to meet this audience. I don't think anyone can ever predict what the audience is going to like. People think that OTT is going to change things and someone else is going to change things. But the fact is that some of our best work has happened on TV. Look at shows like *Malgudi Days* in the 1990s. They were not written by crunching numbers and wild predictions about the audience's behaviour. They were made with freedom and that's why they were so good.

THIRTY-ONE

Sumit Saxena

Sumit Saxena is the writer-director of the show *Kaalkoot* and the writer of films such as *Doctor G* and *Pyaar Ka Punchnama* among others. Sumit's interest in science and mathematics, his background of having worked in IT as a coder, and his predictions about AI (Artificial Intelligence) made way for quite an unusual conversation about writing. I met Sumit on a Zoom call as I had another meeting lined up that day.

Did you always want to be a writer?

I was born and raised in Lucknow. My family wasn't into literature as such except that my grandfather was interested in Urdu poetry. But it was my school group that was interested in fiction. We would read books and discuss them at length. I did start writing pretty early. I wrote my first play in the sixth standard. There was a story called 'Waseehat'. One day, my friend and I sat on the last bench in class and wrote an English adaptation of it. I kept writing in school, but it was only when I went to college, which was IIT Varanasi, did I start writing regularly. I went to IIT not because I wanted to get into a fancy institute or a fancy job at the end of it but because I was genuinely interested in physics and mathematics. I had some unanswered questions while I was growing up and thought the answers to them lay in science. But it was only after going to IIT that I realized that those answers may lie in art. If science could not answer a few of my questions, maybe fiction could.

Vijay Varma has performed and articulated some of those questions very well in a series called *Cheers*. It's probably one of his finest performances ever as well and both of us are very passionate about the series. One of the questions on my mind was 'How to live a life when you are least bothered?' or 'How to live in a fashion where internal turbulence is minimized?' I still haven't found answers to these questions. But there is a longer philosophical quest that I am on to find them. I have a theory of my own about this which I call The *HMS Beagle* Theory. Let me tell you a story.

In the nineteenth century, a guy got onto a ship called *HMS Beagle*, and with a small crew, he went from one island to another, sailing in difficult waters. He picked up animals, dissected them, and made drawings of their anatomy. About ten to fifteen years later, the guy came up with the theory of evolution. That guy was Charles Darwin. My theory is that by taking a dangerous journey, he added an inch to human consciousness and awareness. Without his theory, we would be a dumber race. And I feel that it would be good for every person to have their own *HMS Beagle* and have their own sea. If you have your own ship and your own sea, it's easier to live through life, and you might even end up discovering something that adds something to our knowledge as a race. I think the quest of life, at least of my life, is to find the truth. And the more truth you know, the less turbulent your life will be.

Being a writer with a keen interest in science, what's your take on the advent of AI in the field of creativity?

You know, I have never given up on my scientific pursuit. I still code and I am still trying to learn to code. I am trying to learn Python currently. I think with the advent of AI, every artist who wants to stay relevant will have to learn how to code. I am predicting this and, hopefully, it will be true in the next three to five years. We will be watching a film in a cinema hall that is written and made entirely by AI. Very soon, Netflix will have a separate section for films that are entirely generated by AI. That is inevitable.

Do you think AI taking over creativity is progress or regression for society?

I think it is progress. For you to be relevant as an artist in the world of AI, whether your art is text-based, visual-based, or music-based, you will have to be ferociously original. If you are truly original, you will be relevant. Because currently, what AI does is use precedence and adapt it in its own ways. It is not creating something original. In a world like that, if you are mediocre, you will die. AI will eat you up with the sheer speed at which it can function. And it's going to push the limits of all those people who intend to be original. And all this will happen in the near future. Then, as it is predicted when AGI (Artificial General Intelligence) comes in by 2029, it will be able to think on its own and start creating original ideas and films. One big fear I have with this is that whatever you can do, AGI will do it faster and better.

At this point, you would have no reward for creation. If there is no reward to be had, human intelligence might stop being curious and original. That would lead to a kind of intellectual laziness. If you allow me, let me float a radical idea. Look, the DNA is 4.5 billion years old. We physically evolved into what we are today throughout this time. Simultaneously our frontal lobe was being developed, and the language circuit in our brain got developed. We first mechanized physical labour. Then we mechanized the intellect using computers. Now, when AGI is up and running, we might need to change our own biology. We might need to change our own neurology. Imagine a person with four hands, for example. Would they not play the guitar better than someone with just two? I think this is the kind of stuff we will be getting into in the next 200 years or so. If you have heard of CRISPR – the DNA-altering technology – we are already moving in that direction.

Your most critically acclaimed film so far is *Doctor G*. Could you run me through the journey of writing and conceptualizing it?

Somen Mishra was working at Dharma. He is someone who is always on the lookout for new writers and great writing. He had these fifty-sixty pages that were written by two people – Saurabh Bharat and Vishal Wagh. And Anubhuti (Kashyap) was already in the project. I had a meeting with Somen and Anubhuti and they shared the idea with me that a man goes into the gynecological department, and in the process, he changes. I said, 'That's a great idea.' What was already on paper was a lot of research. What needed to be done with it was to create a coherent story. We needed to see the man evolving beat by beat and not in a one-directional way. I thought he needed to evolve one step forward and two steps back continuously throughout this film. And to ensure that it happens smoothly was my job on the project and I did that.

On the journey were Somen Mishra and Anubhuti Kashyap. Then Somen Mishra left that company and Anup Pandey got involved in it. The film was in cold storage for quite a while and suddenly, the project came back on the table one day. I wrote the first draft in 2017 and then the next one in 2021. I remember this incident when we were narrating the script to Vicky Kaushal (eventually Ayushmann Khurrana played that role) and he suggested that there is so much one step forward and two steps back happening but at some point, it should also be two steps forward. Only then does it become a real journey. I thought that was a valuable feedback. That's when it stops being a small arty film and looks at its heroism with more push to it.

From a film like *Doctor G*, allow me to move onto something in a totally different space – *Pyaar Ka Punchnama*. The film has its takers but is also criticized by some as being sexist. How much do you agree with that and what was the journey of writing it?

Let me tell you how I got the project. It was my first project. I had written a short film that Anurag (Kashyap) had read. He told me it is not a film, it is a play. I said, 'It breaks my heart but I think it is a film.' One-and-a-half years later, I made a thirty-minute short film out of the same script and showed it to him. Anurag said, 'Your scriptwriting is off and the performances aren't great.' But he also said, 'You proved me wrong. I didn't see a film in it but you saw it. And now I think, it is a film and not a play.' That gave me a lot of confidence. He also praised my dialogue writing and told me he would recommend me. Within a week I got a call from Luv Ranjan to write a film which was *Pyaar Ka Punchnama*.

The accusations of it being a sexist film are something I completely agree with. Today, if you ask me, I would always want my writing to reflect my politics and not someone else's. But back when *Pyaar Ka Punchnama* happened, I was just twenty-six or twenty-seven and I was working an IT job, trying to find my way as a writer. I was approached by Luv Ranjan for this project. He had a vision where he wanted to make a certain kind of film. He was inspired by Chris Rock's brand of standup comedy and wanted to make a film in that space. Luv Ranjan made us – my co-writer Vaibhav and me – see some of that work. Chris Rock at that point did some work that could be labelled as sexist. This was in 2009. It was even before Twitter existed, I think.

I immediately knew that this wasn't a film I would want to make myself ever. But it was the first time I was getting to see what it was like to be a professional writer. I intended to write it as funny as I could. During the process, I did suggest to Luv Ranjan that this could be a Woody Allen kind of film where the boys talk about what they go through in a relationship and the girls talk about what they go through. But Luv was very clear in his vision and wanted to make it the way he wanted to, which I think is fair because it was his idea and his vision.

Now, do I regret writing that film? Absolutely not. Would I want to write something like this again? Not at all. My job was to make the film funny and I did make it funny – at least as funny as I could. And I did bring life to the characters – at least, the male characters. And also, was it a success for me in my career? Hundred per cent. After that, I started receiving like seventeen phone calls a day from people who told me, 'Let's make a Delhi-based boys' flick' and all that. Of course, I didn't take any of those projects up.

What's the strangest feedback you have had to hear as a writer?

These days, I don't hear the strange things. Earlier in my career, I used to hear them a lot. But honestly, I used to zone out in all those meetings, which in retrospect was a good thing. So, I don't remember them. I don't remember them at all, to be honest.

How did you navigate rejections in the early part of your career?

I'll tell you something that I wish every young screenwriter would know. When I started, there were a lot of small production houses that were popping up. Across Versova and Andheri were production houses everywhere. And it took me a long time to know which one to go to with my work. Sometimes, we get rejected because we are trying to sell our script to the wrong person. It's the person who is wrong, not the story. And actually, it's not that difficult. If you write an email with a synopsis of your story to the right people, they will respond. Looking back, I think I was caught in a limbo of approaching the wrong people with my stories, working on the wrong ideas with the wrong people who had neither the capacity to make a film nor, very often, a real intention to do so. I tried to shake them up and make them want to make a film, which was not healthy. I think, after *Pyaar Ka Punchnama*, I should have gone to the right people with the right ideas and those ideas would have been entertained. If today I were to conduct a workshop for screenwriters about screenwriting, it would not be about how to write better; it would be about how to pitch their ideas better.

Well, let's say you don't know anyone. You don't know the heads of Junglee Pictures or Dharma or any production houses and studios. I think you could still approach a writer who would know them and writers usually help other writers. People send me material to read and I try and respond to them. It helps me discover new writers. In fact, I am looking for new writers so that I can set up writing rooms for a few projects. But to those who are young, I think reaching out to people and understanding how the system works is very important.

Where do you stand on the whole arthouse vs commercial debate?

You know, I love to watch *Ankhon Dekhi* time and again. If given a chance, I would love to write an *Ankhon Dekhi* even if I don't get paid for it. I wrote a film called *Geeli Pucchi* which is part of *Ajeeb Dastaans*. Without Netflix that film wouldn't have been made. It's a film I am very proud of and Neeraj Ghaywan did a really, really great job of directing it. So, if you ask me, I want an *Ankhon Dekhi* to exist and I want a *Masaan* to exist. As a creator, I love that.

I created a show called *Kaalkoot*. It's got Vijay Varma and Shweta Tripathi in it. I think it was something I was really looking forward to from an artistic point of view. So, do great ideas get rejected? Probably, yes. But I would say, you should keep coming up with them. Sooner or later, you will have your moment. And that journey is also the fun of it. There is a line from a Charles Bukowski poem: 'To do a dull thing with style is preferable to doing a dangerous thing without it. To do a dangerous thing with style is what I call art.'

This is a line I swear by. If you ask me who my heroes are, I'd say, Gillian Flynn, Aaron Sorkin, David Fincher, Christopher Nolan, Vince Gilligan. All these guys have been telling exceptionally complicated and profound stories. And they have done it with style. I find that heroic.

As a creator, when you say that your story is non-commercial, you are in other words saying that your story doesn't have an audience or has a limited audience. I find it truly heroic to say that I am going to tell you a very dangerous story to which, at least I believe, in my own delusion, that there is a huge audience.

The way we watch Korean films or Scandinavian shows, not too many people from those countries watch our work. Why do you think is the standard of Hindi films and shows not world-class?

I believe we can evoke and provoke people to develop an interest in original stories. I am not the right person to talk about the nature of pop culture or the reason for the success and the failure of films at the box office. I don't have that skill. I don't have a very good reading on it. There are people who have a great reading on it and they are successful. There is a similarity between politicians and successful film-makers. The ability to read the masses is what both these sets of people have. But unfortunately, I don't have the box-office reading.

***Geeli Pucchi* was released to huge critical acclaim. What was the journey of writing that film like?**

Neeraj (Ghaywan) had a five-page-long story for a very long time. One day, he shared it with me. I immediately had an idea of it. Neeraj's story was that of a Dalit woman who was a psychopath and who manipulated a Brahmin woman into taking her job. In that version of the story, the Dalit woman was not gay and her intention was conning the Brahmin woman into getting a child. My point to Neeraj was that we are going to represent a Dalit and we are showing her as a psychopath. I thought, right there, it's wrong. Because anyway we don't have enough representation of Dalits. Neeraj does come from the Dalit community and he can show that world with a lot of empathy and lived experience, so I told him not to show a Dalit as a psychopath. Secondly, conning an Indian woman into getting a child is not a big deal. That is the patriarchal setup that she lives in and she is eventually going to have a child.

If it were a woman who is working in New York or some such place, conning her would be a big deal from a story point of view. I told him that it would become a great con if the Dalit woman were in love with the girl she was going to con. Initially, Neeraj didn't agree with it, and I told him that I would write whatever he wanted me to write. I sat in his house for five days and wrote the film. I emailed him the story and told him that I was going to take a shower. When I went back, he felt betrayed because I had told him I'd write what he had asked me to but I ended up writing what I wanted to. But by now, he had gone through the emotional experience of reading the thirty-five pages that I had written and I went to him prepared with arguments for my point. Once I argued for my point and explained it to him, he bought it. That was a very good experience. I am so glad that Neeraj has such creative integrity that he bought my argument after seeing the merit in it.

About the film *Hamid*, there is a perception that the film-making did not do justice to the script. Do you agree?

Yes, I felt that way. But to be honest, *Hamid* was written by someone else. I am not the primary writer of the film. In fact, the film was already written when the Saregama people approached me. They said, 'Can you save the film?' They felt that there was something powerful in it but it had to be reworked. So, I reworked the script. But the original writer had a huge part in it and had done a fantastic job to a great degree. Now, the job was of the director to guide the writer to get over the line. But the director was failing to do so. So, the Saregama people told me that I don't have to speak to the director or the original writer. They asked me to just go and do my own thing and I did my own thing.

What is success to you as a writer?

I think writing a good story is about finding and then submitting yourself to the emotional truth of the story. There is another process which is very similar to this – the process of praying. The act of praying is submitting your being to a larger being and the act of writing is to submit your being to a story that is larger than you. That's why I think that stories are prayers that we make to other human beings. If you can move collective consciousness a little bit through your stories, you are successful. Just like Charles Darwin, as I said earlier, told us where we came from and changed our perception about who we are. I think if there is a greater number of *Doctor G*s and *Chhapaak*s in the world, we will become a little more evolved, a little less toxic, a little more inclusive. That is what I intend to do.

If in the last seven-eight years, I have dealt with masculinity and gender politics, in the next ten years, I intend to deal with the nature of intelligence, what is the emotional value of intelligence, and where it leaves us. There is another question that I am exploring which is 'What is the relationship between the nature of intelligence and the binary nature of gender?' I think there is a deep connection between the two. The only intelligent species that we have largely had a binary nature of gender. Does gender fluidity change our neurological architecture in a fashion that also changes our intelligence? That's going to be a big, big question in the years to come.

What are the films that have influenced you as a writer?

Back when I was growing up, we didn't have TV at home. It was in 2005 that my friend Siddharth Agarwal – the person on whom Vijay Varma's character in *Cheers* is based – introduced me to films. Here are the exact films that made me come to Bombay: The Arshad Warsi-starrer *Sehar*, Vishal Bhardwaj's *Maqbool*, Sudhir Mishra's *Hazaaron Khwaishein Aisi*, Anurag Kashyap's *Black Friday* and *Gulaal*, and then two films by Chandan Arora – *Main, Meri Patni Aur Woh* and *Main Madhuri Dixit Banna Chahti Hoon!*. I watched all these films while I was in college. At that time, *Gulaal* was just about eighty per cent made and I met Anurag accidentally in Delhi and he said, 'Let me show you a film which isn't released.' He showed me that film on DVD and I was blown away by Piyush Mishra's poetry and the overall madness in the film. I love *Gulaal*.

Then, when I was working my IT job, I used to watch two-three films every day. Films by Asghar Farhadi, Fatih Akin, the list goes on. There are film-makers whose names I don't remember who changed my life.

THIRTY-TWO

Swanand Kirkire

For a long time, I have been a fan of Swanand Kirkire's lyrics. I have hummed and listened to songs from *Barfi!* and *Khoya Khoya Chand* in different life situations, and if the song 'Bawra Mann' from *Hazaaron Khwaishein Aisi* did not steal your heart, you probably never had one.

Meeting Swanand was as much an interview as it was a fanboy moment. We met one afternoon at a café called Method on Chapel Road in Bandra, where every member of the staff seemed to know him very well.

A conversation with a lyricist of Swanand Kirkire's calibre is not just a conversation, it is music.

Tell me about your childhood and how and when songwriting began for you.

Not even in my wildest dreams as a child did I ever think that I'd be a songwriter or something like that. I come from a very middle-class family in Indore. My parents were working in a bank and simultaneously learning music. They were disciples of

Kumar Gandharva. But culturally in the city of Indore, nothing was happening that would produce a songwriter. There was no such environment. The only place was Pandit Kumar Gandharva's house where sometimes, if I got the window, I would get exposed to art.

The other thing was theatre. Everything that has happened in my life springs from theatre. It was because of theatre that I started reading things and getting attracted to literature, songs, etc. My uncle used to do theatre and so I sometimes would go there. But my parents wanted me to finish at least my graduation before I got into theatre full-time. At that time in Indore, there was nothing specific one would do in theatre. It was amateur theatre that we were involved in. Sometimes, I'd write, sometimes, direct, sometimes work on the lighting. Indore did not have the kind of college theatre that Bombay or Delhi had. Once a year, sometimes, for Ganesh Utsav, we would do a play. Maharashtra Rajya shows and competitions would happen in Bombay or Delhi and we would apply for that. Most of the theatre I was involved in at this time was Marathi.

Sometimes, we would have one show in Indore and one in Nagpur or Jalgaon. We were happy working-class people coming together to do theatre for fun. That's it. Also, cinema was a passion. I grew up in the 1970s and '80s, listening to film songs. My mother would show me plays and films. Gulzar was writing at the time. So, a lot of stuff that was happening was reaching me. I got to know about the National School of Drama (NSD). In a magazine, I happened to read an article about Ebrahim Alkazi, who was the director of NSD then. And it was written that it was because of him that people like Naseeruddin Shah and Om Puri and all these people became the actors they were. But at that time, I had no idea how to get to NSD. I was not very good at studies and I was failing everywhere else. I became a commerce graduate just for the sake of it. I am a person for whom no method has ever worked.

At one time, an NSD workshop happened in Indore. At the time, I was working in a bank as an ad-hoc worker. On daily wage. So, I left the job and joined the workshop. That was the first time when I met some serious actors who were talking about acting as a passion, acting as a science, and acting as a career option. I was hearing all this for the first time and getting fascinated by these ideas. It was also there that I heard some songs for the first time.

Ashish Vidyarthi was one of the people at the workshop and he sang us a few fascinating songs. They were from a play by a theatre group called Act One. The songs were written and composed by Piyush Mishra. We are talking about the year 1991. I thought those songs were as good as, if not better than, any film song I had heard. When I inquired how it all happens, people there told me that they write their plays and songs. That experience was mind-blowing for me. Then I asked Ashish if I could go with him to Delhi and join this group called Act One. Initially, he was hesitant but then he agreed. I fought with my parents and went to Delhi. I had an uncle who offered me his house to stay for a month or two.

I joined Act One, which was one vibrant theatre group in Delhi. M.K. Sharma was the director of the group and people like Ashish Vidyarthi, Manoj Bajpayee, Piyush Mishra, and Gajraj Rao were all part of the group. That was the first time when I saw Piyush Mishra in action. M.K. Sharma would ask him to write a song for a scene, he would go to a corner and come back with a song. Sometimes, the song would be '*Jab Sheher Hamara Sota Hai...*' (the one that was used in *Gulaal* many years later). That was one thing I was fascinated with. A man was doing this kind of writing in real-time. And it was top quality. It was not inferior to Gulzar Sahib's or Javed Akhtar Sahib's songs for films. In the group, people would even sing the songs, there used to be chorus singers as well. People used to talk about big Hollywood films and stars. It was a great environment to be in.

Later, people told me that if I did theatre in Delhi for too long, NSD wouldn't accept me. It had happened to people before. I went back to Indore and started working on a play that was written by Mahesh Elkunchwar. The original play was not a musical but we wanted to make it a musical. That's when I wrote songs for the first time. I think I wrote four songs. Another friend of mine from

Indore also wrote a few songs. We also wrote a few new scenes into the script and we did that play and people liked it. After that, I thought, okay, this is what I want to do in life. Later, I went to NSD and studied there. While I was there, I wrote a few songs for Waman Kendre and he loved them. One day, when Piyush Mishra was out, M.K. Sharma asked me to write a few songs for Act One. By that time, it was established in the circles that this boy could write songs.

I wrote a play which was on Bhagat Singh. In 1997, India's fiftieth year of independence, Manju Singh, who was making a TV show on Bhagat Singh, once happened to see my play and decided to hire me. For that, I moved to Bombay. It was a Doordarshan show called *Swaraj*, which I wrote. I was one of the lucky few who came to Bombay with a source of income already. Although, it's another story that the source vanished after a couple of months and I had to struggle to find work and survive for a year or two.

How similar or different are songwriting and poetry?

Poetry and songwriting are different for me. Poetry is something you write for yourself. Often, without even thinking what people would make of it. It's a very, very personal and pure art. But in songwriting, the most important thing is that it is meant to be heard. In poetry, there are occasions when sometimes you don't even want to share your work with anyone else. But songs are meant to be heard and appreciated by people. Also, they need to have a certain lyrical quality and they should be married to a certain kind of music – whatever kind of music it may be in each case. For instance, a 'Piya Piya' song may not work with rap music and a rap song may not work with 'Piya Piya' lyrics. Songwriting for Hindi films is a specific trade. A Hindi film song has a specific purpose to fulfil. The song needs to very often need to inform people about a character, the story as well as the opinion of the film-maker while evoking a certain kind of emotion. Sometimes, poetry can become a film song but not always.

Is there a process of writing a song, some kind of method of going about it?

Yes, everybody has an internal process that they follow. If you ask me, I always look for the most urgent need of the song in a particular situation. If I give you an example of the song '*Behti Hawa Sa Tha Woh*' from *3 Idiots*, the situation was that two friends were looking for an absconding friend and the song also had to introduce that missing friend. It was also a need for the script. I had read the script multiple times. The urgent need, for me, was what these friends think of the friend instead of getting into what the film-maker thinks of that friend. And that cracked the whole song for me. '*Hum aise the, woh waisa tha.*' (We were like this; he was like that.) That was the pattern I followed. '*Humko toh raahein thi chalati, woh khud apni raah banata…*' (We were led by the paths, he created his own path…) That's what establishes how the third friend, Rancho, is or was different from them.

Between writing to the tune and writing before it, what do you prefer?

When you start, you find it easy to write first and then let the tune get created. You imagine writing to the tune to be a tough task. But slowly, you learn the craft. Today, if you ask me, I am equally comfortable with both. Sometimes, while writing to the tune, you also discover another set of words and it can be very interesting. In our industry, of course, sometimes, we get to write before the tune but mostly, it is the tune that is composed before the song is written. In popular understanding in the industry, people get to tune more easily than lyrics. So, it can work both ways. Most people in my generation write to the tune.

Does a lot of life experience come into writing a song?

It's not possible to write anything that's completely devoid of life experience. No song is emotionless. Unless you have related it to your life, you cannot write a song. You always go back and think about what would you do or feel in the situation that the song is for. For instance, '*Chaar Kadam*', from the film *PK*, comes from one of my poems. Now I don't remember which life situation I had written that poem in but I was happy with the idea that life is just a moment. Can we spend this moment without knowing who we are? This was my idea. My poem was '*Bin bole, bin kahe sune, bas hathon mein hath dhare … chaar kadam bas chaar kadam, ek saanjh chaloge saath mere?*' (Without speaking, without hearing, just take my hand and let's take a few steps, just a few steps, would you walk this evening with me?) In the song, I modified it to: '*Bin kuch kahe, bin kuch sune, hathon mein hath liye … char kadam bass chaar kadam, chaldo na saath mere.*' (Without saying anything and without hearing anything, just a few steps, walk just a few steps with me.) And lines like '*rasmon ko rakh ke pare*' (keeping traditions and rituals aside) were additional lines.

Basically, this comes from my philosophy of life. I don't want to know your name, you don't want to know my name, and can still the purest form of love happen? Just for a moment? So that comes from my life. My thoughts come from my life so whether it is a song or even an advertising jingle I have written, it always has something to do with my own life experience and ideas.

Do you think writing to meter and, in turn, writing a song itself is an inborn talent that can't be learnt?

I am of the opinion that there is nothing in the world that you cannot learn if you spend enough time and hard work on it. Singing for instance or songwriting cannot be taught, yes. But it can be learnt. If you decide to learn it, you can. Music is all about awareness. It is about whether you are aware of the faculties that make you sense some frequencies. If you truly try, you can become aware of them.

Tell me about the process of writing one of my favourite songs in the world – '*Bawra Mann Dekhne Chala Ek Sapna*'.

To tell you the truth, the first line of that song was something I had thought of in a rickshaw, while I was humming something. I used to laugh at myself in those days when I was new to Bombay.

Where have I come from, what am I doing here, roaming around in local trains? So, the line '*Bawra Mann Dekhne Chala Ek Sapna*' was something on my mind. One of my friends heard it and told me it was beautiful. I didn't know if I was ever going to make someone else listen to it. But I knew it was good so I finished it pretty much in one draft, excluding a few basic edits later. It was more of a stream of consciousness that I wrote it in. This was written two to three years before the film *Hazaaron Khwaishein Aisi* was made. But in the film circuit and at parties, this song had already started doing the rounds. Two songs had become very popular in the filmi party circuit back then. It was this song and Kailash Kher's '*Allah Ke Bande*'. Both eventually got into films. I was assisting Sudhir Mishra on *Hazaaron Khwaishein Aisi* and Kay Kay Menon heard my song and told Sudhir Mishra to listen to it. He liked it and the song made it to the film. '*Bawra Mann*' became a success without any marketing or promotion. Because of some rights issues, it is still not available on any streaming platform.

Now, could you tell me about the journey of writing songs like '*Aashiyan*' and '*Saawali Si Raat*' for *Barfi!*?

I wrote three songs for *Barfi!*. The title track, '*Ala Barfi*', and the two you mentioned. Whenever an artist is made to feel comfortable and given freedom, magic happens. Anurag Basu, the director, said that he wanted my song. That's it. He made me feel safe and secure. Your state of mind reflects straightaway into your song. And *Barfi!* is a film where everyone feels secure and loved. The brief was 'Create song magic'. That's it.

In '*Ala Barfi*', I introduce the character. But in the other two, even that is not a need. '*Aashiyan*' is about their relationship. And since the characters were a little childlike in the last moment, I changed '*Itni si hasee*' to '*Itti si hasee*'. That change of one word creates all the magic. In '*Saawali Si Raat*', the line '*Khwabon ki razai mein baat ho teri meri*' comes from childhood. You must have spoken to someone under a blanket when you were young. It comes from all those things. But as I said, everything has to do with trust and safety.

The third project I want to talk to you about is the film *Khoya Khoya Chand*. Can you tell me about the journey of writing all its songs?

I think a lot has to do with Sudhir (Mishra). We had worked together earlier and had a rapport. It was a fun experience working on that film. *Khoya Khoya Chand* is a period film and I wanted to create a sense of that era through my lyrics. In those days, even a song situated in a club would be philosophical. For instance, Sahir sahib's '*Aage Bhi Jane Na Tu*' or '*Babuji Dheere Chalna*'. I wanted to write something big, you know, in terms of thought. Also, I decided to use words and images from that era like '*shama*', '*parvaana*', etc. which people no longer use or even understand today. I used a very different vocabulary for that film which I usually never use. A lot of Urdu-inspired shayari. For instance, '*Naye se dard ki firak mein talash mein udaas hai dil*'. I don't usually write like this but I had got into the world of Urdu poetry. Just like an actor prepares for a role, a songwriter, too, prepares for his role.

These days, some people are quite gung-ho about the concept of hook lines. Where do you stand on that?

In the search for hook lines, we have forgotten the meaning of songs. You tell me which songs are being appreciated today. People are not getting anything from this kind of song. It's not about good or bad. It's about trends. The industry always follows trends. And then there are trendsetters. They are the ones who take risks. They sometimes fail and nobody cares about them but once something that they do clicks, others start following the trend.

How's it for a songwriter to work with different music directors? How do they influence the lyrics you write?

My biggest collaborator is Shantanu Moitra followed by Amit Trivedi. Working with different music directors is like batting with different batsmen. You have to adapt to their style and pace. And learn on the job. Rigidity is an enemy of a writer; fluidity is their strength. Sometimes, a Bengali music director will come from some regional influences. Another time, a Gujarati composer will come from his own experience. For instance, the song '*Meethi Boliyan*' from the film *Kai Po Che!*. Amit Trivedi was humming something and the word '*boliyan*' was hidden in his humming itself, which I picked up. Shantanu is a very open man. He can even change the tune on the spot for the lyrics. He can add two to four, sometimes even eight lines to a song if the lyrics demand it.

Who are your favourite songwriters and what are your favourite songs or Hindi film albums?

There are many. And I love them all. But if you ask me who has inspired me the most, it started with Gulzar. Then Piyush Mishra, who was the first songwriter I ever saw in action. Then another person I have read very carefully is Shailendra. After that is a long list. Sahir Ludhianvi, Kaifi Azmi, Rajendra Krishan.

Among albums, I think *Pyaasa* and *Kaagaz Ke Phool* are vital. I love Gulzar Sahib's *Ijaazat*. His film *Mere Apne* features the song '*Koi Hota Jisko Apna*'. Then Shailendra Sahib's *Madhumati*. I love *Hum Dono* as an album. Sahir Sahib's '*Allah Tero Naam*' as well as '*Abhi Na Jao Chhod Kar*' are brilliant. Honestly, it's a long, long list and however many names I mention, I would miss out on something.

What's your favourite song that you have written?

Well, there are some songs I have enjoyed more than others or have satisfied me more. For instance, the title track of *Khoya Khoya Chand* is one such. Then a song from *Parineeta*, which is just about darkness, goes like this: '*Raat hamari toh chand ki saheli hai … kitne dino ke baad aayi woh akeli hai*'. I like '*Ala Barfi*' a lot. There was a song I had written for the film *Hunter* which I quite like. I also have some unsung songs which I like.

Can you name a few songs that you haven't written but wish you had?

Yes, there are songs like that, for sure. '*Mann kasturi re, jag dasturi re*' by Varun Grover. Then '*Abhi Na Jao Chhod Kar*' by Sahir Ludhianvi. There are many songs by Gulzar Sahib I love, like '*Beedi Jalai Le*', and wish I could write it. In fact, I think if someday I get to work with Vishal (Bhardwaj), it would be amazing. I have never worked with him. He works so well with Gulzar Sahib that you don't want to bother that pairing but somewhere, someday, I wish I could work with Vishal. Something of the calibre of *Omkara*. It is one of my favourite albums ever. You remember that song which Vishal has sung himself – '*O Sathi Re*'? What a song! '*Tere dohre badan se sil jaungi main … tu karvat lega, chhil jaungi main.*' Wow, what writing!

THIRTY-THREE

Vijay Maurya

I met Vijay Maurya in his office in Vile Parle one afternoon. He was so casual and calm that it felt like I was meeting someone I had known for a long time. In the conversation, I figured out that Vijay grew up in the same vicinity that I did, in Goregaon East, and that made us have some conversation off the topic as well.

Vijay Maurya has been around in the industry since the mid-1990s and is known for his dialogue, screenplay as well as for his acting. He has written several films and shows including dialogues for *Gully Boy*, for which he won the Filmfare Award.

What's the first thing you ever wrote in life?

Well, that must have been a really long time ago! I grew up around the Hindi language. Even at home, we used to speak a lot of Hindi. In my early days, I used to think that anything that rhymes is poetry. I used to write something that combined poetry and prose. Mostly stuff that would be full of what I thought was wrong with the world. I used to write about pollution, population, save-the-nature kind of stuff. Then college started. By mistake, I am a science graduate. In our college magazine, I wrote a piece called 'Nasoor'. This was the first time I saw my name in print. And it felt amazing. I used to read that piece over and over again. However, I didn't keep writing regularly after that. I used to lurk around backstage of my college plays, sometimes writing some lines about sun-moon, flowers, and stuff but I did not start writing seriously then.

How did you foray into writing as a career?

In my college days, I was motivated to do something of significance in life. After college, I did some odd jobs, at Citibank, then at a teakwood plantation company. I was just going with whatever was happening to me. I wasn't really myself in a marketing company, wearing a tie, selling Diners Cards, Mastercards, etc. Somehow, one day, a loose contact I made at my job, who had played character roles in some films, recommended I go to Prithvi Theatre after I told him about my interest in acting and theatre. At that time, I didn't even know what Prithvi Theatre was! One day in 1993, all alone, I went to Juhu beach and threw my tie and the sales brochures I used to carry into the sea and just showed up at Prithvi which is a walk away from the beach.

As soon as I entered the premises, I saw a slightly dejected guy, who had just had an earful from a director, sitting there. When he saw me, he said, 'Hi, I am Anurag Singh Kashyap.' I said, 'Hi, I am Vijay Maurya.' He asked me what I do. I said, 'Currently, nothing.' Then we got talking. He told me that there were workshops that were conducted at the Prithvi Theatre every Monday and anyone could join for free.

The following Monday, I dressed up, put on some perfume, and reached there. It felt like a market. I saw many people of my age, some talking to each other, some rehearsing some dialogue in various languages: Hindi, Marathi, Gujarati. And whatever they were speaking sounded great to me. Some were reading poetry, some prose. I loved the atmosphere.

Hidayat Sami and Inayat Sami, two students of the late Pandit Satyadev Dubey, were conducting the workshops. Dubey-ji was a concept for me. Everyone was talking about him with great respect. Having gone there from another world, at the time, I did not know who he was. But then I became a regular and started having a lot of fun there. I met Makarand Deshpande. People there were awakening the artist within themselves. That was the time when I developed a taste for words.

I read *Aadhe Adhure* by Mohan Rakesh, the writings of Tendulkar sahib (Vijay Tendulkar) or even Kalidasa for that matter. I began writing seriously. Some people used to ask me to write a one-minute-long monologue or dialogue or anything that they needed. Once I wrote something called *One Minute*. It was about what could happen in one minute. I wrote something like 'If your mother has slept with another man, who your father is could be decided in one minute.' I was trying to be an actor. But the director said, 'I don't know about your acting but we should talk if you have really written this!'

My family was completely okay with my doing this because there was always an artistic environment in my house. My father was into music, he used to sing Qawwalis and even played the tambourine. We still have that tambourine.

In the next couple of years, I met Vipul Amrutlal Shah, who eventually made the film *Aankhen*, and asked me if I would write a TV show for him. That's when I started writing *Ek Mahal Ho Sapno Ka*. I used to get 750 rupees per episode.

What are the qualities or experiences that make you the writer you are?

Primarily, observation. I always used to observe a lot. I still do. I grew up in a chawl in Goregaon, where you see a lot of different characters together. We used to celebrate all the festivals. Diwali, Rakshabandhan, Ganpati, and even Nagpanchami. We used to fly kites and play with marbles. The fights over tap water, carrying rent receipts to people, I have seen it all. Among so many different people were so many different dialects. So, I understood characters from an early age, the way different people talk, in different languages like Hindi, Marathi, and Gujarati.

Besides, I was always in the habit of speaking to people on the streets, rickshaw-wala, paan-walas. All this helped me a lot with character sketches and dialogue when I started writing professionally. In Hindi films, back in the day, a lot of the dialogue used to be presented and not how it is naturally spoken. I, however, because of my life experience, had a sense of natural dialogue.

From theatre, how did film writing begin?

I wrote a lot of television after *Ek Mahal Ho Sapno Ka*. I wrote many shows, some song-based shows, *Superhit Muqabla*, *Lux Kya Scene Hai*. Also, *Star Bestsellers*. Television involves a lot of writing and I could write for television very fast. I used to follow one thread of thought or one character and write countless scenes in very little time. That was the time when I was also looking for acting assignments. I acted in Anurag's (Kashyap) *Paanch* but it was never released. Same with *Black Friday*. I played a role in Imtiaz's (Ali) *Socha Na Tha*. I had a good role in Sudhir Mishra's *Tera Kya Hoga Johnny* but that didn't release either. A lot of acting work was happening but nothing was getting released. Those were extremely frustrating days. For about seven years, I had no work. Many of my actor friends quit the industry, someone lost his mind, someone set up a shop, someone joined production, and someone got married and picked up a job. But I didn't want to leave. That's not why I was here. That was the phase when I went back to writing. I used to pick up any writing work for survival.

I started writing advertising projects too. The good part of advertising is that you get paid well and usually on time. Unlike in Hindi films, it won't happen that today a place is a studio and the next day you go there, you find a saloon. Advertising was reliable work and helped me stay afloat. I worked closely with the director Rajesh Krishnan, who once gave me an Apple laptop instead of paying me for a job and introduced me to the world of the internet and email. This must have been around the early noughties.

Slowly, a lot of people started knowing what I wrote. The first feature film I ever wrote was *Striker*. Chandan Arora was a reputed editor at that time. I met him in my Prithvi days when he used to come to meet Makarand Deshpande. He was going to direct a film and he asked me if I'd write it for him. Chandan and I went to Goa to write the film and we came back with a draft. Sagar (Kapoor) got involved in the writing and Pankaj (Saraswat) came with him. The process took time. It took around two years from writing the first draft to the time the film was made.

I assisted Sujit Sen, who had written *Saaransh, Prahaar, Hum Hain Rahi Pyar Ke*. I got to learn a lot about the craft of film writing from him. Then Ashutosh Gowariker called me to write *Khelein Hum Jee Jaan Sey*, and sometime later, I wrote Harshavardhan Kulkarni's *Hunterrr*. And slowly from dialogue, I started writing screenplays as well. After that, people started calling me a bit more regularly for writing work.

Gully Boy won you a Filmfare Award for Best Dialogue. Could you speak a little about the craft of dialogue writing?

There are two to three aspects to dialogue writing. If you are writing for a director who has already envisioned the world of the film, they give you a basic brief. For instance, a director might tell you not to use swear words, not to be crude. Another might want exactly the opposite. Of course, since I am writing it, I will bring in my own flavour. But in this scenario, the world is the director's.

Dialogue writing is unique. If you consider the case of *Gully Boy*, Zoya (Akhtar) and Reema (Kagti) are themselves phenomenal writers. But the *Gully Boy* lingo is not theirs. That's why I got into the scene. They needed a local boy who would get that specific dialect. Their brief to me was to be authentic with the slum dialect but not use swear words because that might have restricted the reach of the film. It was a very clean brief. Then I underwent a sample writing test. After three scenes, I was through and they loved it so much that they gave me a free hand from then on.

I think there are some people whose work has taught me dialogue writing. Anurag (Kashyap) is a great dialogue writer. The way he weaves in the 'philosophical' with the local is superb. Imtiaz Ali, who I was fortunate to work with earlier, Sudhir Mishra, and Sriram

Raghavan, these guys never did 'dialoguebaazi' on paper; they wrote real dialogue, the way people speak. You could say that these were, in a way, my mentors in dialogue writing. Being around people like them and their work influenced me a lot in my early days.

How often have you faced rejections? How did you take them?

Rejections happen every day. One happened even today. I try to understand why it happened though. I try to think if I am on the same page with the person I am working with. What can I do to get on the same page? You must learn from there. Luckily, these days, people listen to me more than before. So, I'd say my rejection rate has decreased. That feels nice. But at the same time, the challenge is bigger when people are trusting you. Today, I am very careful that what I am sending out really works; earlier, I used to send whatever I wrote because I knew the other person was going to come up with feedback and changes anyway.

You have been in the industry since the 1990s. When did you feel you are now settled as a writer?

I think *Tumhari Sulu* was the first time when I felt that my struggle was over. I started getting some calls. And I also started getting the feeling that I can actually enjoy myself here in this industry … that writing is indeed rewarding. But when *Gully Boy* happened, I felt something else. *Gully Boy* was that one film in my life that changed a lot of things for me. Earlier, friends and people in the circle used to call me to write something. After *Gully Boy*, professional studios started contacting me. People's approach towards me changed. I could tell that the person who was talking to me about writing was really serious about the project. Soon after *Gully Boy*, when the lockdown happened, I worked on around seven to eight projects. Interestingly, I think I was busier during the lockdown than I ever was before. For some writers, lockdown was a time when they could be very productive.

You have also co-written a lot with others. How do you go about the process of that? Do you enjoy that more than writing alone?

When *Tumhari Sulu* was being made, Suresh Triveni, the director of the film, called me and said that he had a film approved and had written a draft of the script but there was something he could see lacking in the film. He said he wanted a collaborator. My credit is that of additional screenplay and dialogues. But when you win an award, everyone gets a trophy each and the trophy that I got wasn't smaller than his in size. Whenever you write anything in a film, even if you write one line or one scene, you are part of the writing team and the award will be for everyone to keep.

Though let's say, I am writing something from scratch tomorrow with another writer, if we are starting from zero, it's a different kind of co-writing. Then we discuss the ideas together, write different scenes, and jam on them. I did that recently with Suresh (Triveni) for an upcoming project and we had a lot of fun.

What's your take on OTT as a platform for both established and emerging screenwriters?

OTT has definitely created more opportunities. Not just for writers but also for technicians, light and sound crew, and everyone. People have a lot of work, and the money is good as well, which is great in that way. People are happy because OTT has generally good stories, unlike TV. OTT is close to cinema in that way. But you know, it's not quite cinema. I am afraid that the emphasis on cinema would get lost in all this. I think nothing can replace the impact of a film on people. People still connect with and remember cinema better. Having said that, I hope OTT sustains all the good things it has brought in. And cinema sustains too, holding its own.

For young writers, the opportunities are more in number than they were in the 1990s. For many OTT shows, writers' rooms are created. They could have four, five, or six writers depending on the scale of the show. But not all are of equal experience. A young writer could fit in with a bunch of senior writers or vice versa. This has created tremendous opportunities for talented people. Though I emphasize the word talented. If you are talented, you will find work. Especially as a writer today. If you don't find work for a sustained period of time, maybe you are not talented. The industry is like a magnet and talent is like iron. If there's talent, it will be pulled in.

Along with talent comes temperament. I have seen lots of writers who bring their egos into a project and clash with everyone. Personal issues should be kept back at home when you leave for a day at work as a writer. Because at the end of the day, cinema is a business. And business needs both talent and temperament.

How do you see writing a show differently from writing a film?

I had written this Eros series called *Smoke*. In the transition from cinema writing to show writing, the first thing that struck me was that there's too much to write! You have to go on and on, page after page, it is relentless and time-consuming to write a show. But the good part is that there's much more scope with characters now. You can have now nuanced subplots that a film cannot accommodate. For example, if there's a character in a film you would have shown only in the office, now you can also explore what he does when he goes home or to a party or maybe even to a secret underground meeting of a cult he's a part of. This is a great opportunity for a writer to explore.

Who are your favourite film-makers and what are your favourite films?

That has to be a long list. I'd say I'd start with *Amores Perros* by Alejandro Gonzalez Inarritu, the Mexican director. In fact, his entire body of work is mad and brilliant. Then I'd say Zoya (Akhtar). Not because I worked with her recently on *Gully Boy* but because she has a fantastic eye and a great set of film-making skills. Farhan (Akhtar), for that matter, as well. *Dil Chahta Hai* was a film like no other and it personally gave me the confidence that dialogue can be written this way as well as opposed to staged and performed writing. Then there's Bimal Roy, and Hrishikesh Mukherjee. Hrishikesh Mukherjee is unique. I haven't seen another film-maker like him. Then there's Francis Ford Coppola too, whom I love. And many, many others.

To tell you about the films and film-makers that influenced me at an early age, I'd say, *Cinema Paradiso* by Giuseppe Tornatore, *Life is Beautiful* by Roberto Benigni, *Mother India*, *Dharti Kahe Pukar Ke*, *Gunga Jumna*. Obviously, *The Godfather*. When I started watching Iranian cinema, I kept wondering how could films be written and made this way! Abbas Kiarostami, Majid Majidi, and Mohsen Makhmalbaf helped me look at cinema in a different light. Satyajit Ray, the master, and Guru Dutt Sahib have all influenced me.

Sometimes, you happen to watch a film suddenly out of nowhere and it inspires you. There was a film called *Perfume*, then another called *Biutiful*. Even *Sarfarosh*, for that matter. When it came out, it was quite fresh for a Hindi film. I like a lot of modern Malayalam cinema as well. I love how they sometimes set a film in a single house and tell a story so beautifully. Even some of the Marathi cinema. Like for instance, *Fandry*. I remember I was stunned when I watched that film.

What's your favourite film of all those you have written?

I think *Gully Boy*. That's my most satisfying work so far. But I'd say *Tumhari Sulu*, *Yeh Ballet*, and *Chillar Party* are not far behind either. To be honest, I don't look at any of the projects I have worked on as a mistake. I am lucky that way. But I'd say *Gully Boy* gave me something rather special. Both creatively and career-wise.

Do you have any one national or international film-maker that you wish you'd someday write for?

Alejandro Gonzalez Inarritu. I think the way he understands characters is otherworldly.

Acknowledgements

First and foremost, I have to thank my editor at the *Hindustan Times*, Manjula Narayan, who commissioned the idea for this series without knowing how far it would go or how long it would last. At the time, I couldn't promise her even three pieces, let alone the thirty-three that have featured in this book. Without Manjula, there was no way this book would have happened.

It was my mother, Shailaja Chitre, who gave me the idea to turn this series of interviews into a book.

Thanks to all the people who helped me with the contacts to reach the writers featured in this book. Some of them are writers themselves and some well-wishers. And thanks to all the screenwriters for their time and generosity in agreeing to talk to me at length about their ideas and journeys and opening up to me in ways that form the very heart of this book.

Thank you, Kanishka Gupta, for recommending only one editor to me for this project and he was the right one. You are really good at what you do.

And thank you, the editor, Shantanu Ray Chaudhuri for accepting my book proposal in less than forty-eight hours. It has been quite a journey since then, and I'm hoping we have produced something one-of-a-kind here.

Lastly, a huge thank you to all my readers in advance. Whether you're a student of cinema reading this book as study material, or a film professional reading this to understand the process of screenwriting, or a film enthusiast reading this book for pure joy, I hope it serves your purpose and becomes worth your while.